I0810405

IMAGES
of America

NORTH CAROLINA RHODODENDRON FESTIVAL

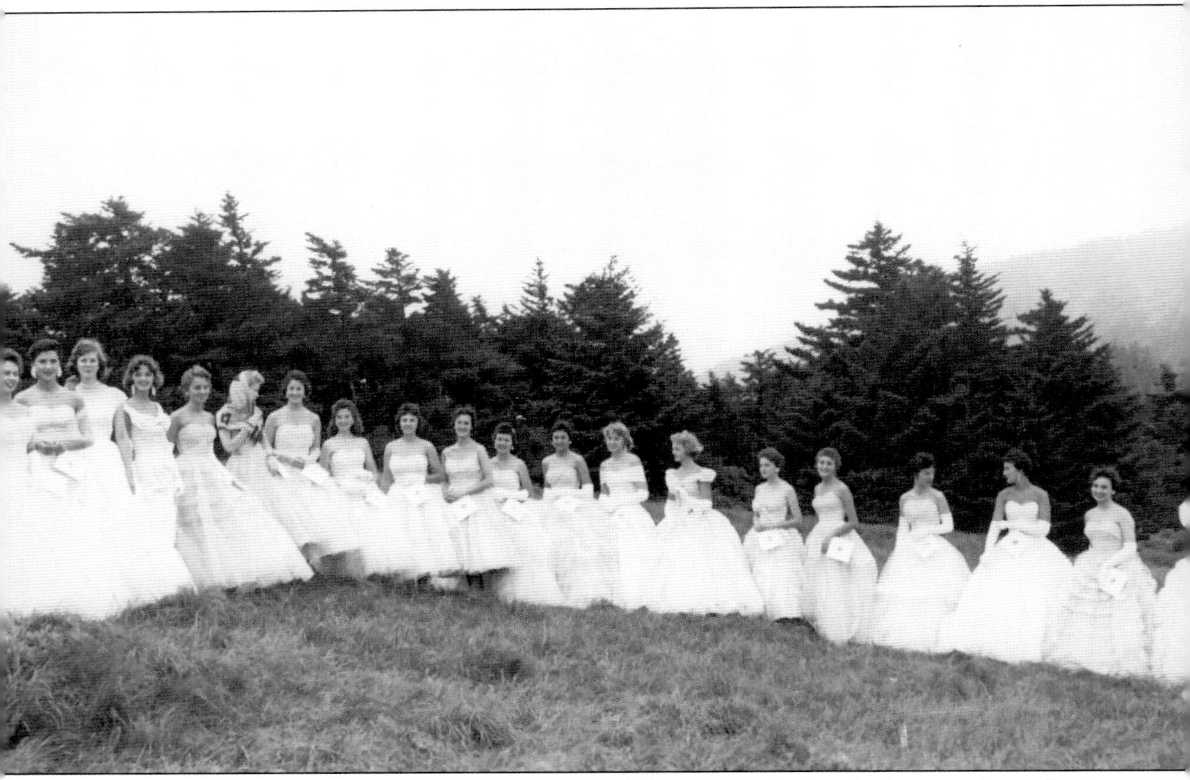

ON THE COVER: In 1958, the North Carolina Rhododendron Festival took place atop beautiful Roan Mountain on a rare sunny day. Amidst 600 acres of naturally blooming Catawba rhododendron, 25 contestants vied for the honor of representing the rhododendron festival for the coming year as the new North Carolina rhododendron queen. At the end of the day, Lolita Buchanan (fifth from left) captured the title. (Courtesy of Lolita Buchanan.)

IMAGES
of America

NORTH CAROLINA RHODODENDRON FESTIVAL

Sharon Webb

ARCADIA
PUBLISHING

ISBN 978-1-4671-2341-9

Published by Arcadia Publishing
Charleston, South Carolina

Printed in the United States of America

Library of Congress Control Number: 2014953871

For all general information, please contact Arcadia Publishing:
Telephone 843-853-2070
Fax 843-853-0044
E-mail sales@arcadiapublishing.com
For customer service and orders:
Toll-Free 1-888-313-2665

Visit us on the Internet at www.arcadiapublishing.com

This work is dedicated to all the faithful, devoted, and passionate volunteers who truly understand the meaning of the phrase "We bleed pink!"

Contents

Acknowledgments

This work could not have been completed or even begun without the input and help so graciously given by a number of former rhododendron queens. Thank you all for sharing your photographs, stories, and remembrances. Former business manager O.D. Calhoun and his wife, Mary, supplied the initial information that was to ultimately be the foundation for this work. Dr. Daniel Barron and June Wilson provided a plethora of photographs and memorabilia dating all the way back to the 1950s, a pure treasure trove of information and memories. Theresa Matthews and Jean Freeman were invaluable sources of knowledge, offering a remarkably insightful vision of the grandeur of an earlier time in the history of the festival. Many thanks to Terry Campbell, coordinator of the annual Rhododendron Run, for providing pictures and information about the event. A special and heartfelt thanks is due Bob Hensley, who always came through when questions could not be answered, when information was maddeningly elusive, when subjects in photographs could not be identified and most importantly, when a serious pep talk was in order. Thank you all for enabling me to undertake this project and encouraging me through to its fruition.

INTRODUCTION

The North Carolina Rhododendron Festival is one of many festivals celebrated across the state each year. During the third week of June, thousands flock to Bakersville, a tiny, quaint town located in the heart of the southern Appalachian Mountains. In recent years, Bakersville has become a mecca for a plethora of artists and craftspeople, lured by the proximity of the world-renowned Penland School of Crafts. But Bakersville's greatest claim to fame is that of being the gateway to Roan Mountain and home to the North Carolina Rhododendron Festival; a celebration of the annual blooming of the world's largest naturally blooming Catawba rhododendron gardens, atop beautiful Roan Mountain. Now in its 69th year, the North Carolina Rhododendron Festival is considered to be among the most elite festivals in the Southeast, and the title of North Carolina rhododendron queen is one of the most coveted titles in the nation.

Since 1946, the annual event has brought thousands of visitors who come from far and wide to view one of nature's most astounding displays to be seen anywhere. The festival is centered around Roan Mountain and the world-famous Rhododendron Gardens. The Roan, as it is respectfully referred to by the mountain people, is one of the highest peaks east of the Mississippi River. At an elevation of 6,286 feet, it boasts over 600 acres of grassy meadows bordered with evergreens and dotted with thousands of rhododendrons. In 1836, the famous naturalist and botanist Dr. Elisha Mitchell, for whom Mount Mitchell is named, wrote the following: "It is the most beautiful of all the high mountains. The top of the Roan may be described as a vast meadow without a tree to obstruct this prospect, where a person may gallop his horse for a mile or two with North Carolina at his feet on one side and Tennessee on the other, and a green ocean of mountains rising in tremendous billows immediately around him."

The famous French botanist André Michaux is credited with discovering and naming the shrub Rhododendron Catawbiense (Catawba rhododendron) in an 1803 publication. Asa Gray, a pioneer in the study of botany, also visited Roan Mountain in the 1700s and early 1800s.

Over the years, several varieties of plants and wildlife identified on the Roan have been determined to be indigenous to only a few other locations in the world, including the Scottish Highlands and a remote range of mountains in northern Canada.

The Roan is a place where mosquitoes are non-existent, blackberry bushes have no thorns, there are no snakes, and visitors can find naturally-occurring waterfalls and springs that offer a pure, sweet water that cannot be surpassed.

The uniqueness of Roan Mountain and its incredible Rhododendron Gardens is certainly cause for celebration. And the North Carolina Rhododendron Festival is a celebration like no other.

One

In the Beginning
The Grandeur of the 1950s

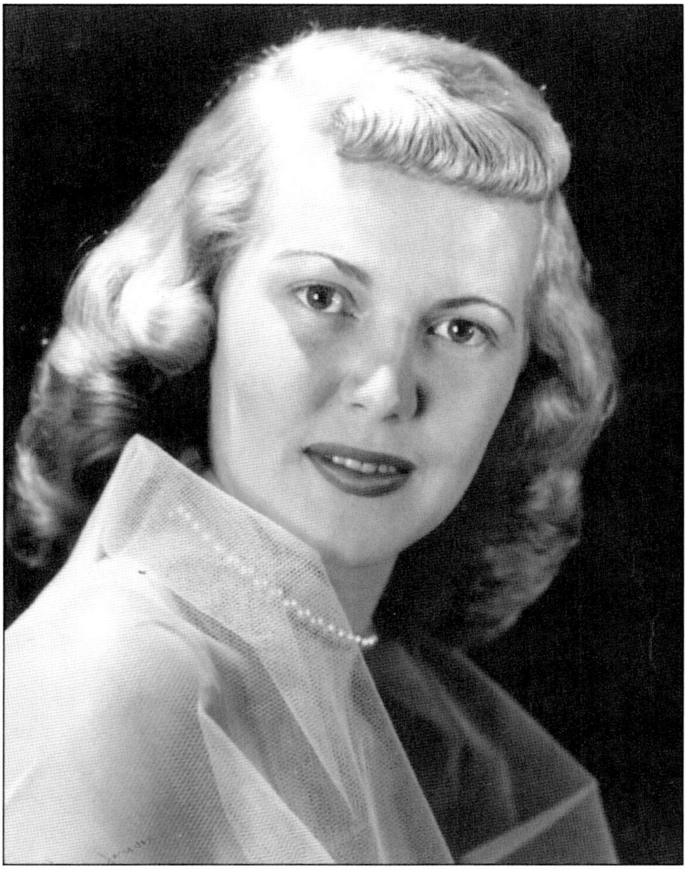

The first rhododendron festival, in 1946, was a joint effort between the Citizen's Club of Roan Mountain, Tennessee, and the Bakersville Lions Club. At that time, the Roan was accessible only by a rough and winding one-way road. For a number of years after new roads were built, the states continued with the tradition of holding a combined festival, with each state crowning its own queen. In 1952, Zula Kate Smith of Burnsville became North Carolina's first rhododendron queen. (Courtesy of the Rhododendron Festival Committee Collection.)

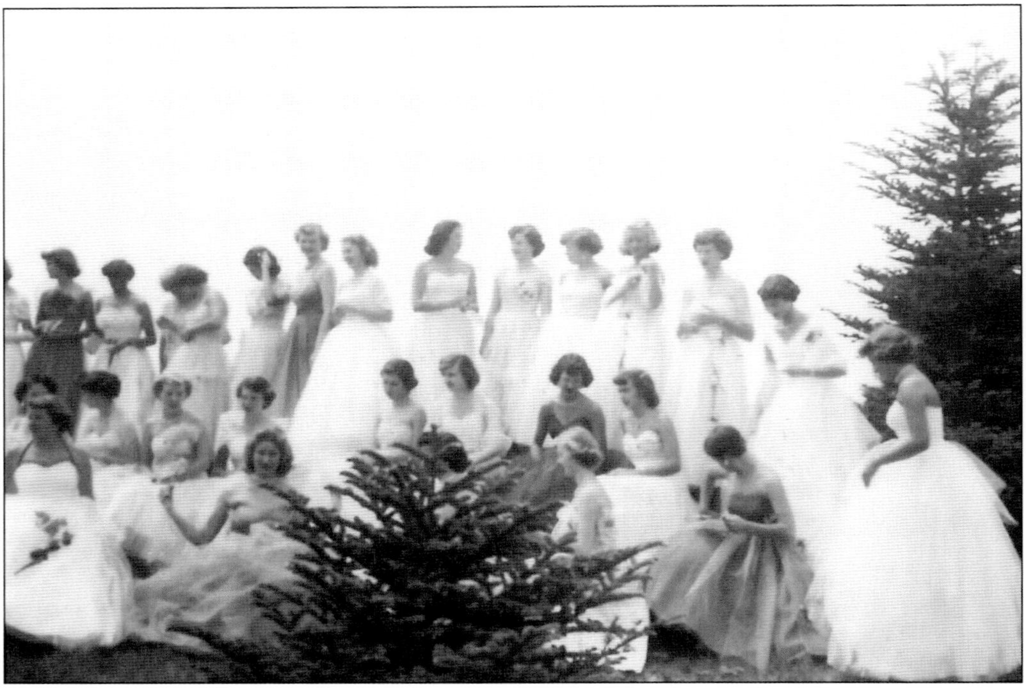

This photograph of the contestants vying for the title of North Carolina rhododendron queen was taken atop Roan Mountain by Zula Kate Smith's mother in June 1952. The contestants gathered in the damp grass for a portrait despite the inclement weather. (Courtesy of Jean Freeman.)

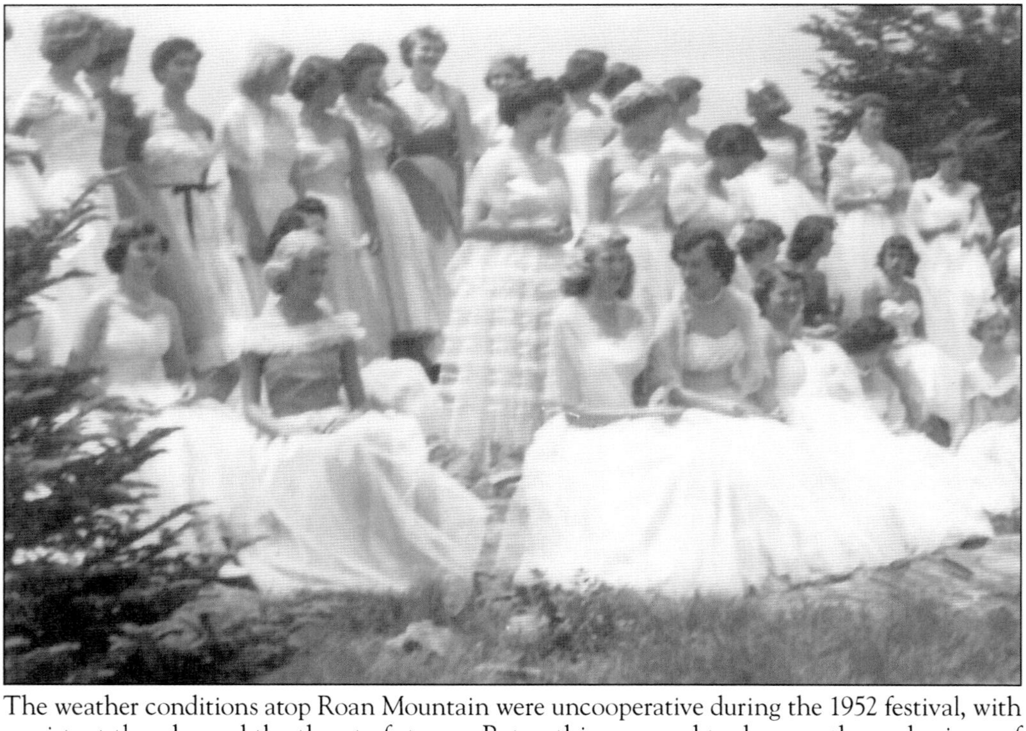

The weather conditions atop Roan Mountain were uncooperative during the 1952 festival, with persistent thunder and the threat of storms. But nothing seemed to dampen the enthusiasm of the crowd or the excitement of the hopeful contestants. (Courtesy of Jean Freeman.)

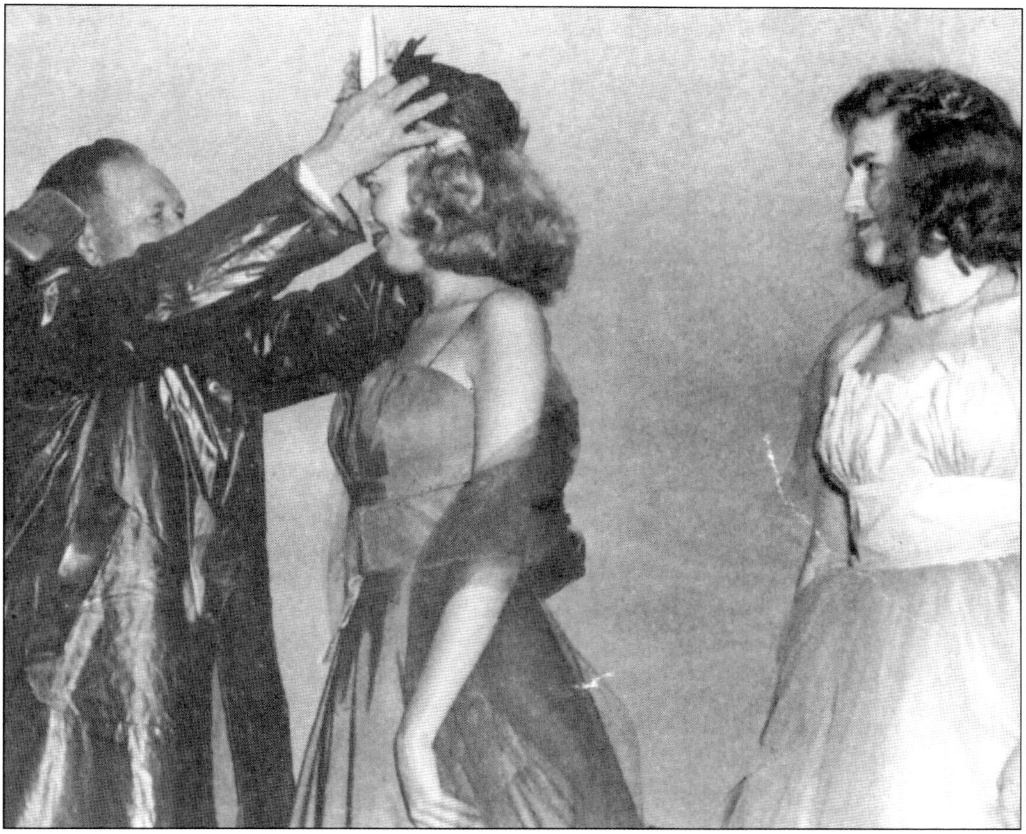

The original crown was fashioned from actual rhododendron leaves, with a rhododendron blossom in front. Kate Smith, North Carolina's first rhododendron queen, was crowned by Belmont Winters, the postmaster from Elk Park, Tennessee, as Wilma Shepherd, the retiring rhododendron queen, looked on. (Courtesy of Jean Freeman.)

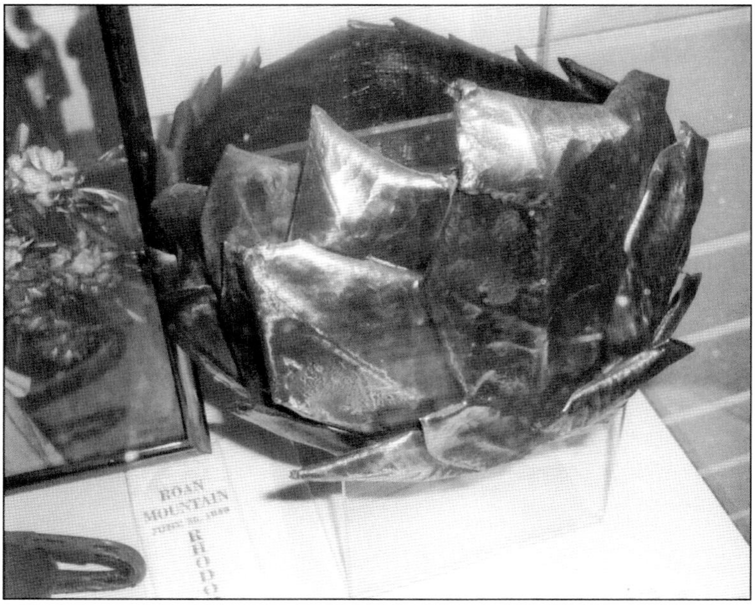

A bronzed replica of the original crown is on display at the visitors' center near Roan Mountain State Park, on the Tennessee side of the Roan. (Photograph by the author.)

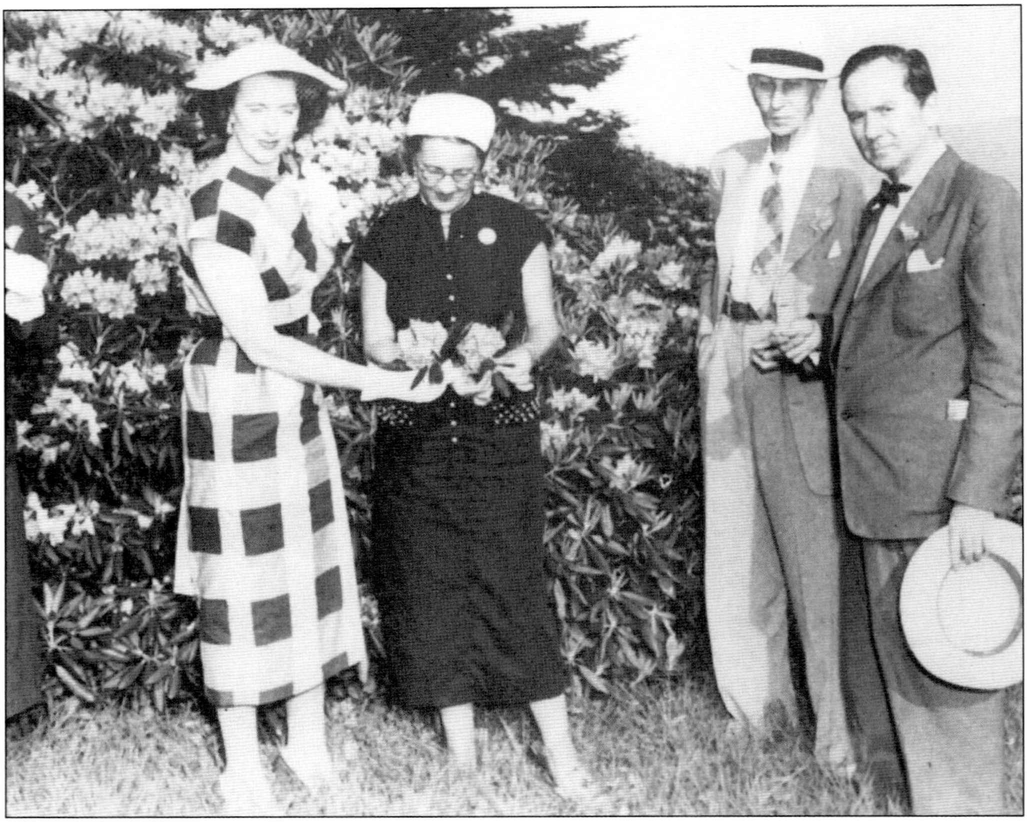

In the early years, the rhododendron festival was often a very political event. In 1952, R.C. Kefauver (second from right), father of Tennessee senator Estes Kefauver, attended the festivities along with Senator Kefauver's wife, Nancy (on left). Estes Kefauver served in the Senate from 1949 until his death in 1963. He was the Democratic Party's choice for Adlai Stevenson's running mate during the 1956 presidential election. Tennessee governor Gordon Browning (below, center) also attended. (Both, courtesy of Jean Freeman.)

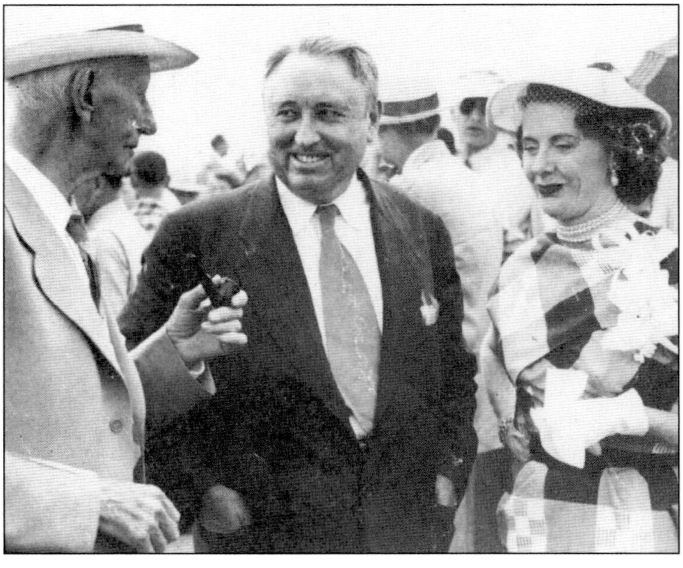

Among the judges for the 1952 pageant was David Marshall Williams, best known by the moniker "Carbine" Williams. He was the inventor of the world-famous M1 carbine automatic rifle used in World War II. Williams served time in prison after he was held responsible for the death of a federal officer during a raid on his moonshine still. It was during his incarceration, while working in the prison's tool shop, that he designed the gas system for his famous rifle. After his release in 1929, Williams worked with Winchester Firearms on the development of the M1 carbine. (Courtesy of Jean Freeman.)

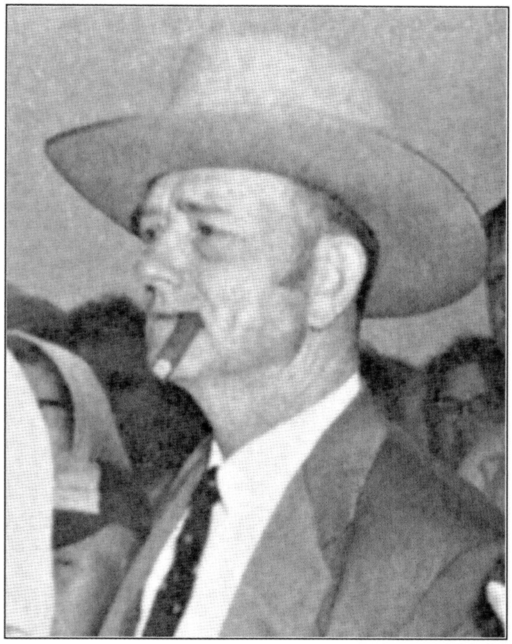

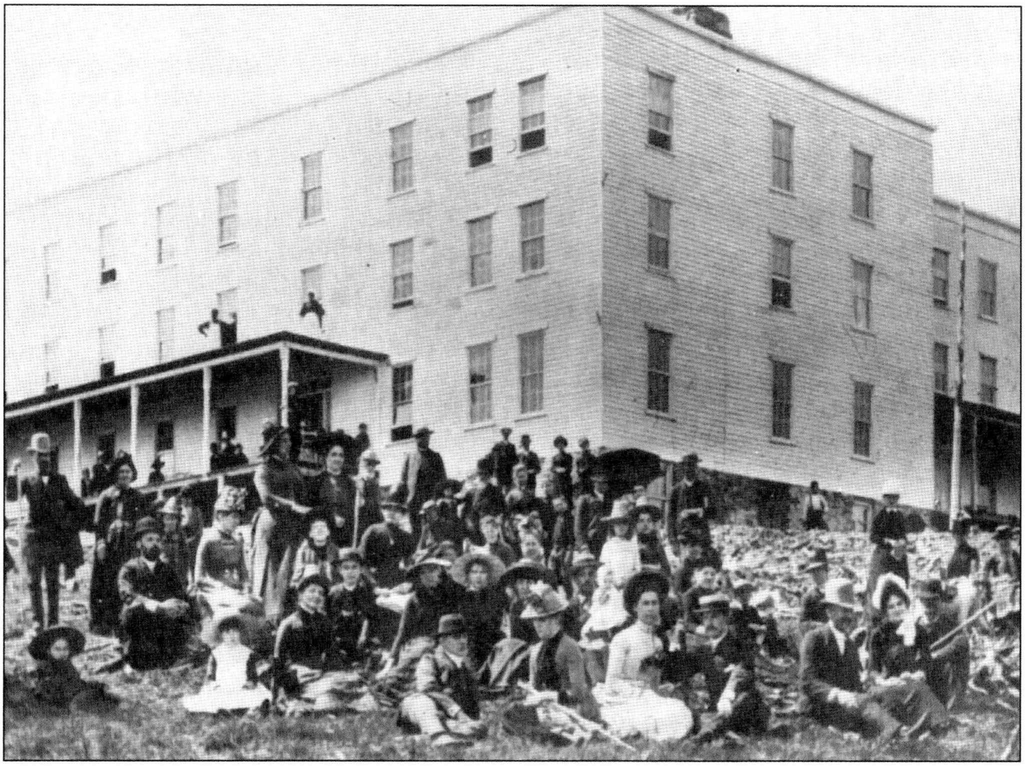

The Cloudland Hotel, built in 1884 by Civil War Union general John Wilder, was a luxury resort that sat atop Roan Mountain, straddling the North Carolina-Tennessee line. Sometime after 1910, the resort closed and was dismantled. The site of the old hotel overlooks the platform that was once used for crowning the rhododendron queen. (Courtesy of the Rhododendron Festival Collection.)

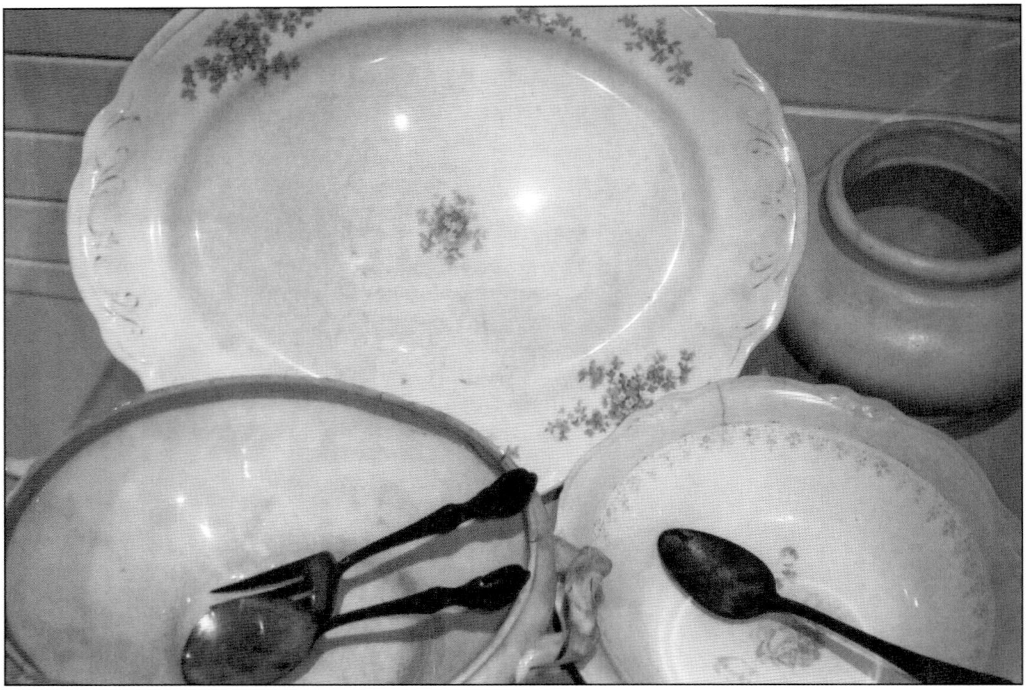

Artifacts from the old Cloudland Hotel are on display at the visitors' center near the town of Roan Mountain, Tennessee. Pictured here is a bed recovered from the site, as well as dishes and kitchen implements. (Both, photograph by the author.)

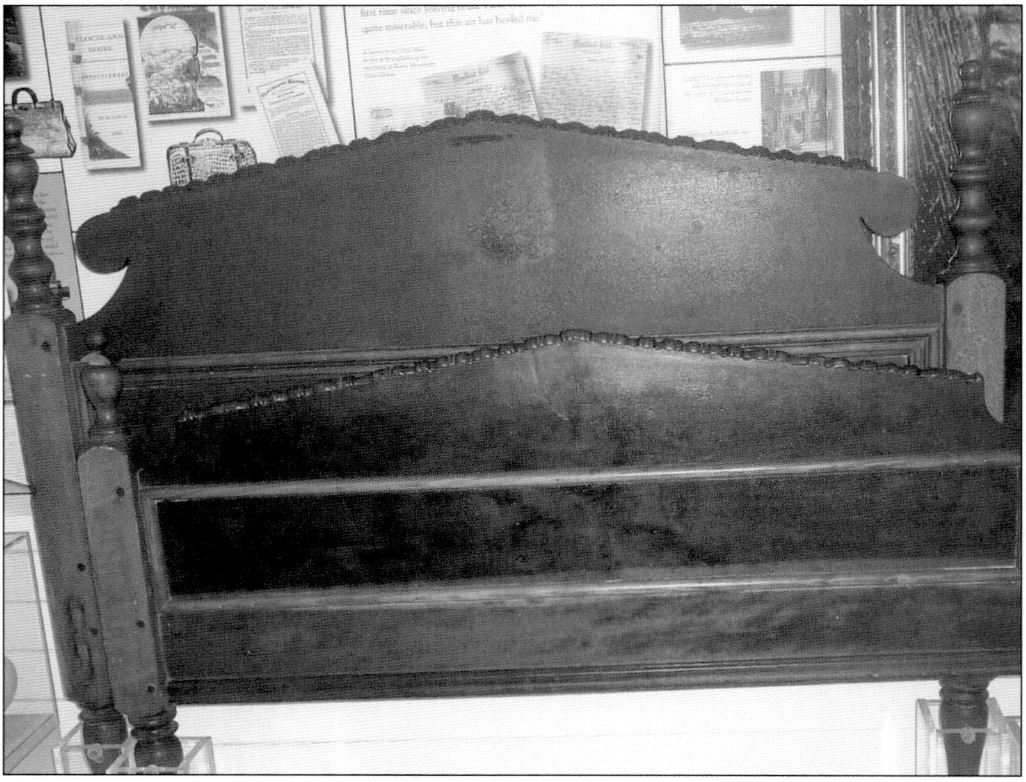

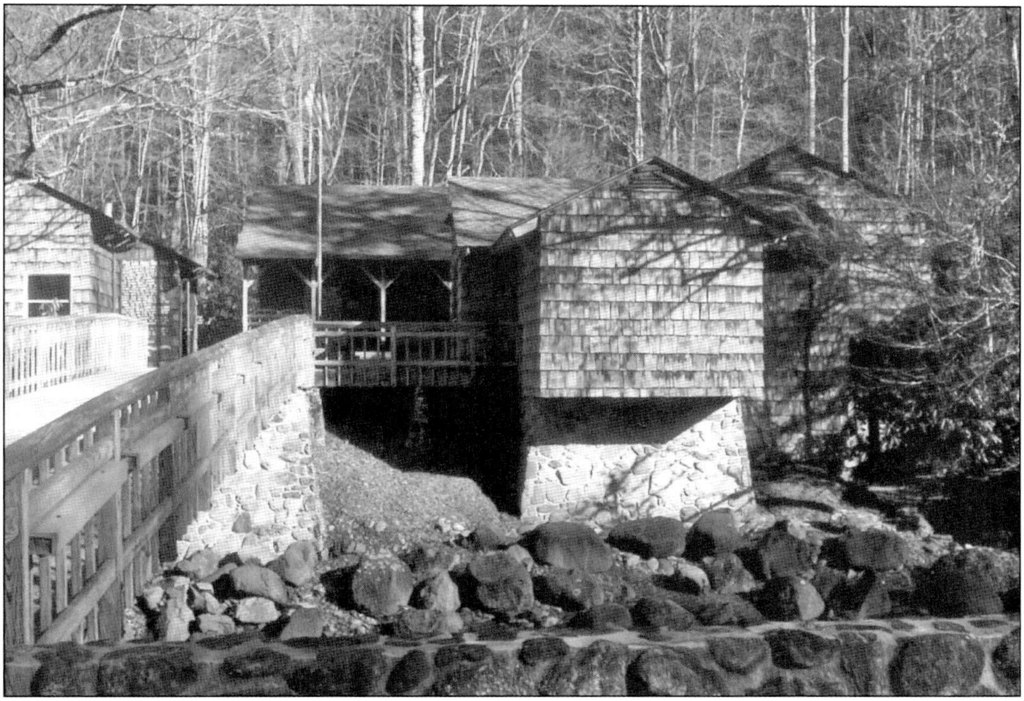

The visitors' center near Roan Mountain State Park features a plaque commemorating a Tennessee hero. The visitors' center has a small museum addressing the flora and fauna of the area, as well as its history. Located at the base of Roan Mountain between Roan Mountain State Park and the town of Roan Mountain, Tennessee, the center also features an old mill and wagon wheel. The Peg Leg Ore Mine can be found on site, and it is just a short walk along a trail. (Both, photograph by the author.)

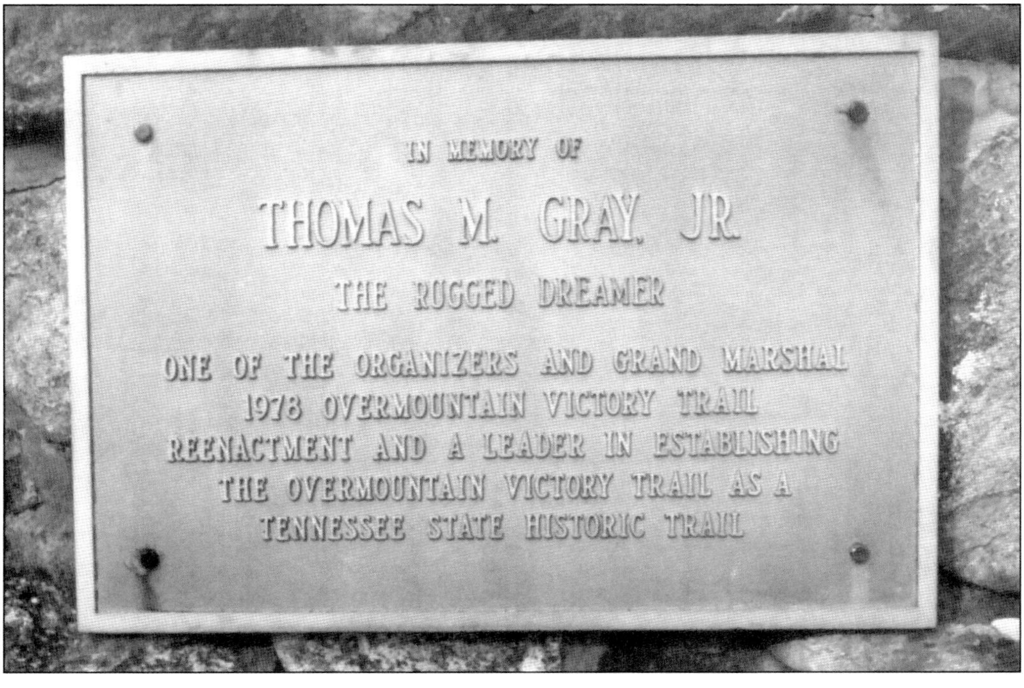

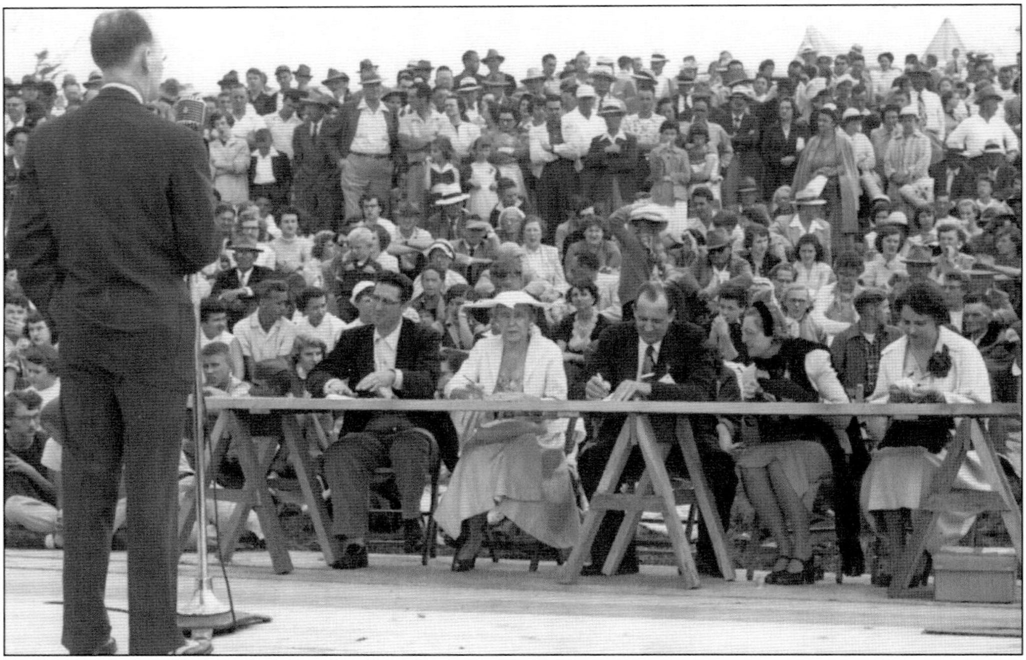

Times have certainly changed. In 1954, the pageant judges scored the contestants while seated at a table constructed of rough planks supported by sawhorses. At the end of the competition, Vivian Wilson of Bakersville would be selected the new North Carolina rhododendron queen. (Courtesy of the Wilson Collection.)

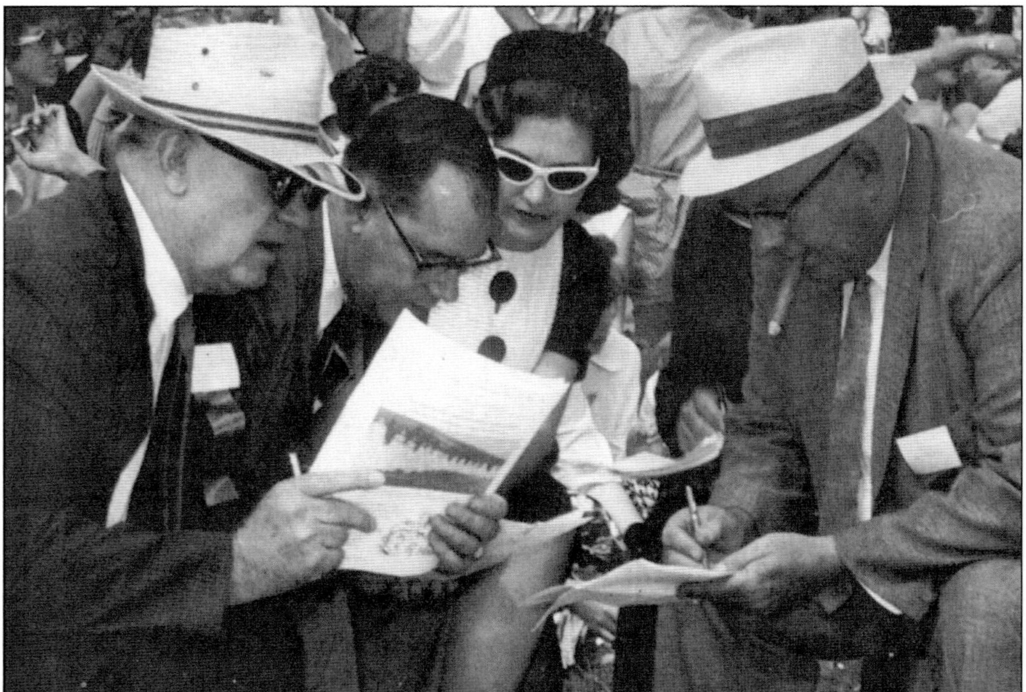

The judges of the 1961 pageant confer before choosing a winner. (Courtesy of the North Carolina Rhododendron Festival.)

Until the early 1970s, the crowning ceremony for the new rhododendron queen took place atop Roan Mountain on the Saturday afternoon of the festival. But, after years of inclement weather, the decision was made to move the crowning to Bowman School's auditorium, where the pageant is still held today. June Wilson, a longtime resident of Bakersville who served with her husband, Ed, as festival business manager for a number of years, recalls a year when the temperatures were so low that the contestants were shivering in their thin, chiffon gowns, prompting local residents to return to town in order to gather wraps for the young women. Mary Vann Hughes, the 1955 queen, poses here in her pageant finery. (Both, courtesy of the Barron Collection.)

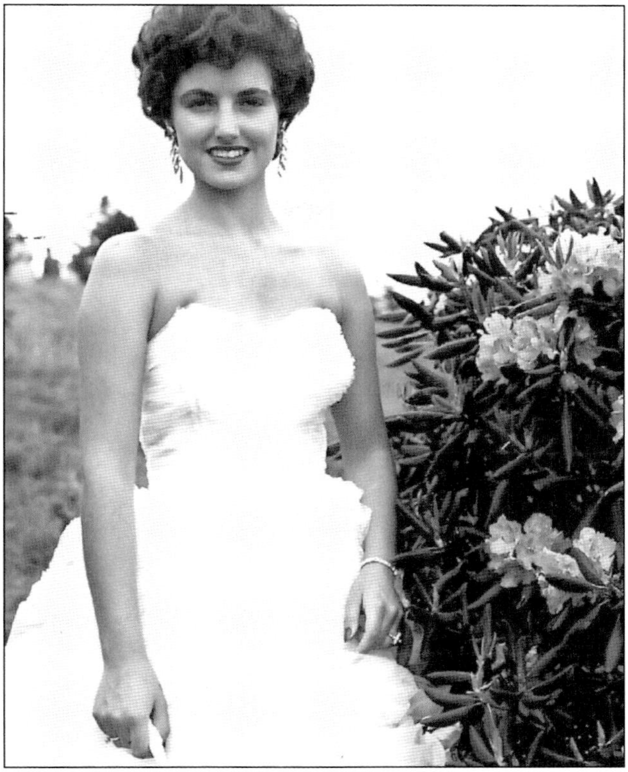

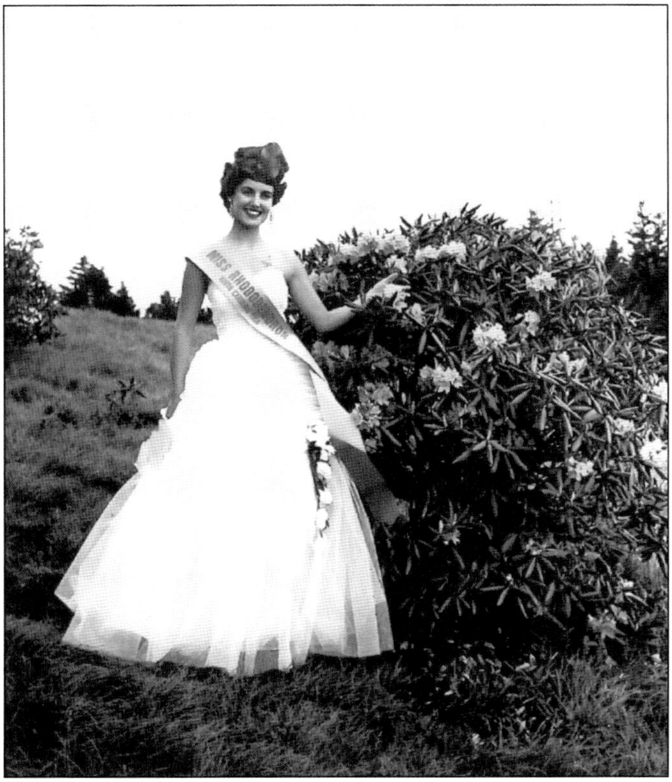

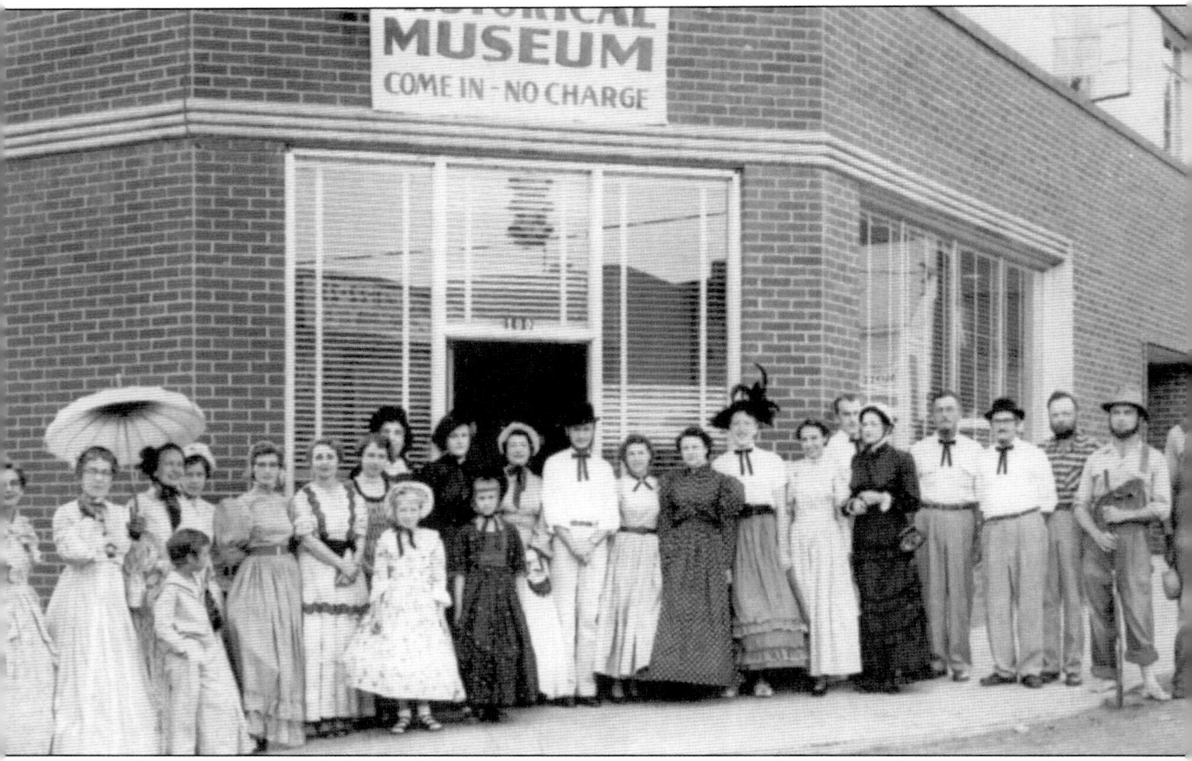

In 1956, the North Carolina Rhododendron Festival coincided with Bakersville's centennial celebration. Local residents dressed in period costume to commemorate the occasion. A play, *A Place of Some Mark*, was also performed for the festival crowd. The same production would be performed once again during the rhododendron festival in 1961. It was billed as "dramatized sketches of the history of Bakersville, presented by Bakersville Volunteer Firemen and Auxiliary, written by the people of Bakersville." (Courtesy of the North Carolina Rhododendron Festival.)

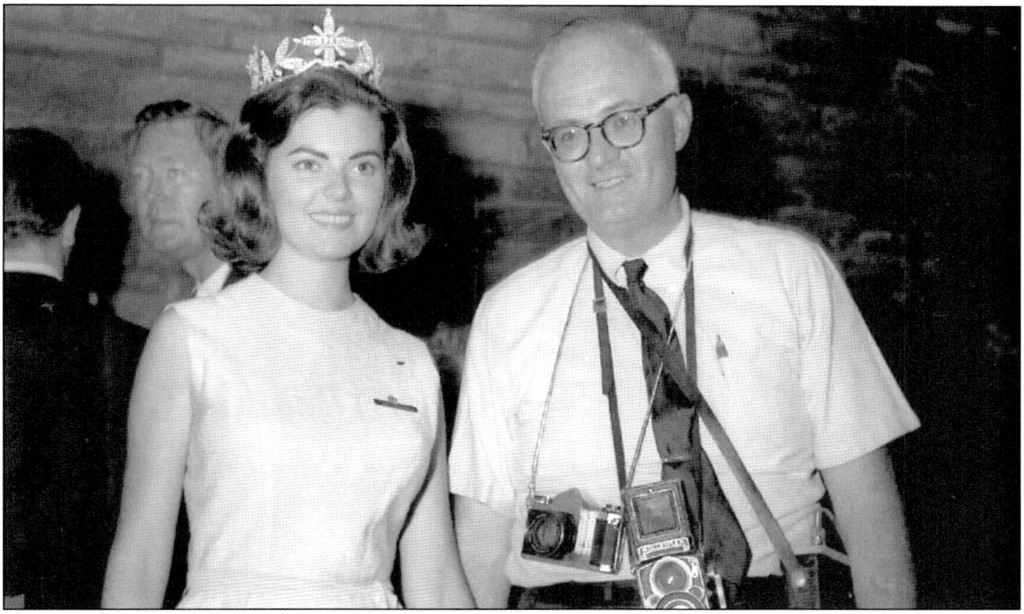

In 1957, Hugh Morton served for the first time as master of ceremonies for the rhododendron festival pageant. A renowned photographer and nature conservationist, Morton served as official photographer for the festival in the 1960s. Morton was quite instrumental in the development of Grandfather Mountain. It was often said of Morton that he captured many a fine photograph but seldom posed for the camera himself. He is pictured above in a rare candid shot with 1967 queen Linda Blair. (Courtesy of the Barron Collection.)

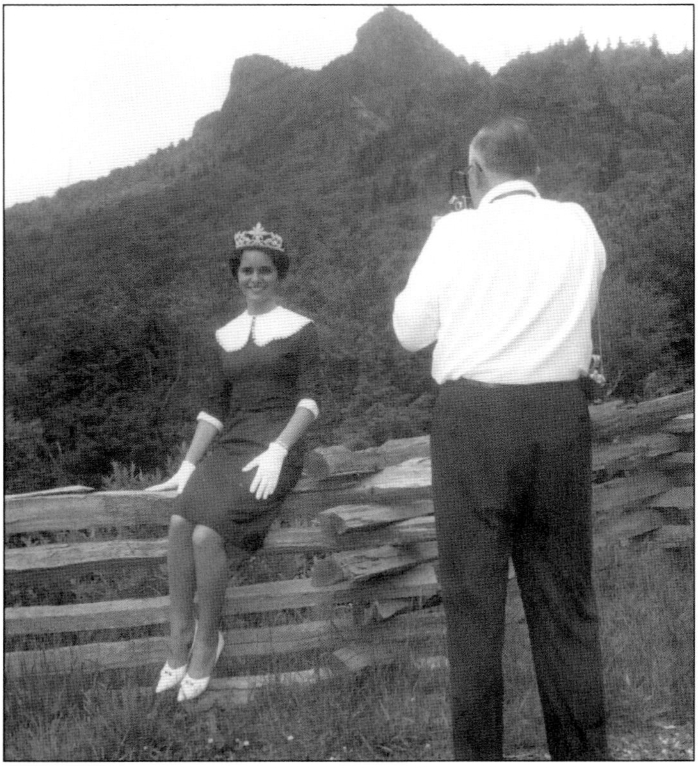

Morton died in June 2006 at the age of 85. Photographer Jack Reynolds also served as official photographer and a member of the Rhododendron Advisory Committee for a period of time. He was a radio executive and served as president of Carolina Press Photographers' Association. Reynolds was a writer and correspondent for AP, and his photographs of western North Carolina were seen all over the country. In 1963, Reynolds captured this shot of Hugh Morton in the act of photographing Betty Rae Lawhon, the 1963 queen. (Courtesy of Betty Lawhon Deviney.)

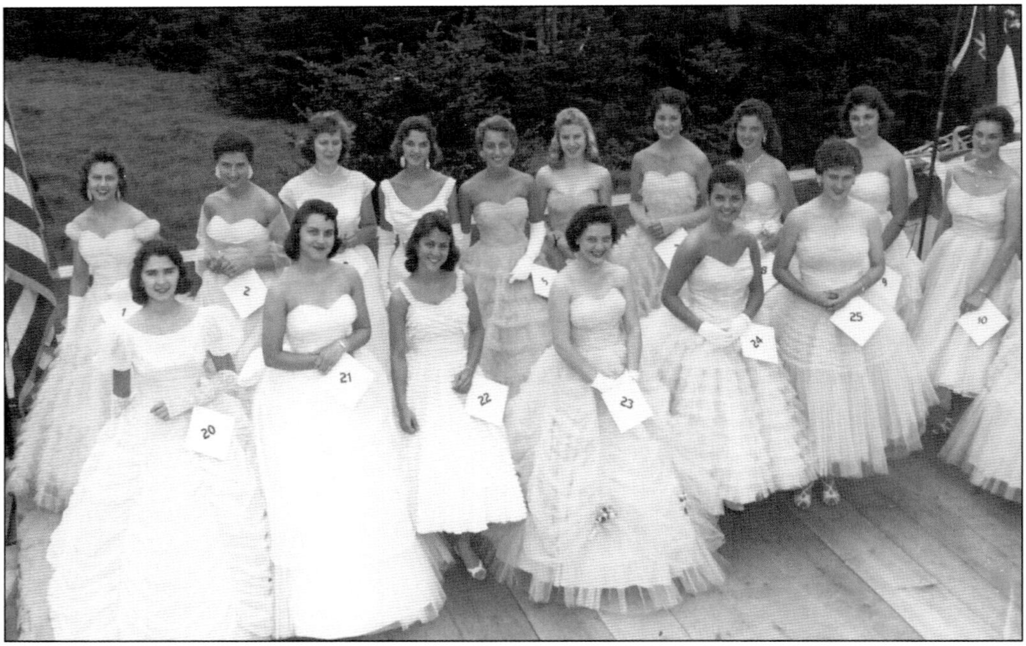

In 1958, Lolita Buchanan (pictured above, fifth from left in the second row), from the neighboring town of Spruce Pine captured the title of North Carolina rhododendron queen, competing in a field of 25 contestants. She is also pictured below on the right with two other lovely contestants. Lolita returned in 2014 to serve as a pageant judge and to celebrate 55 years since her crowning. (Both, courtesy of Lolita Buchanan.)

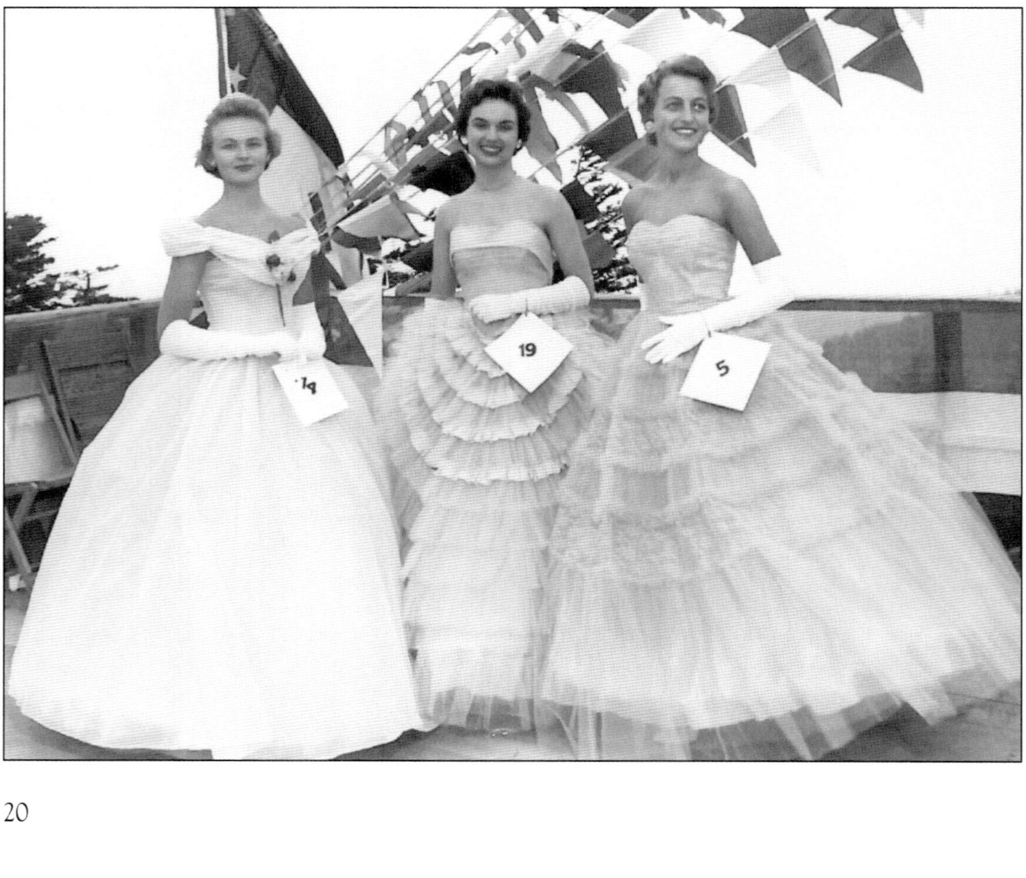

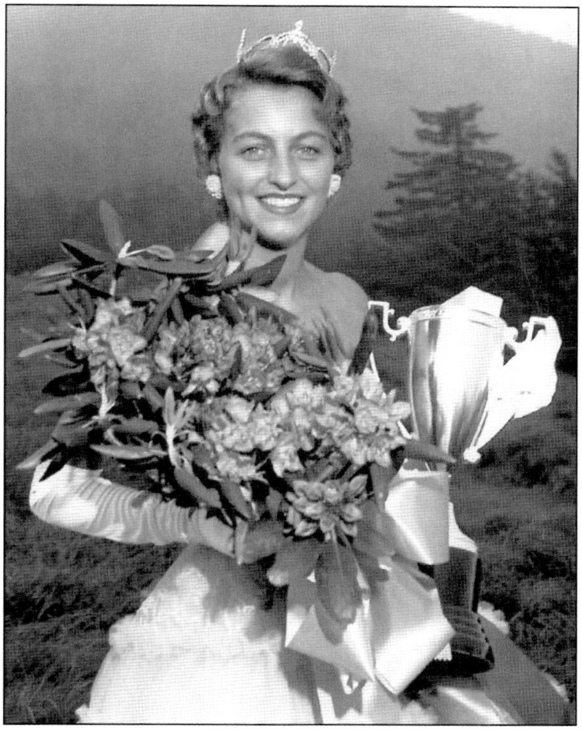

John Jones from the *Asheville Citizen-Times* was on hand to offer his congratulations to the newly crowned North Carolina rhododendron queen, Lolita Buchanan. For many years, a *Times* representative was on hand to cover the festival and pageant and present the gift of a wristwatch to the new queen. (Both, courtesy of Lolita Buchanan.)

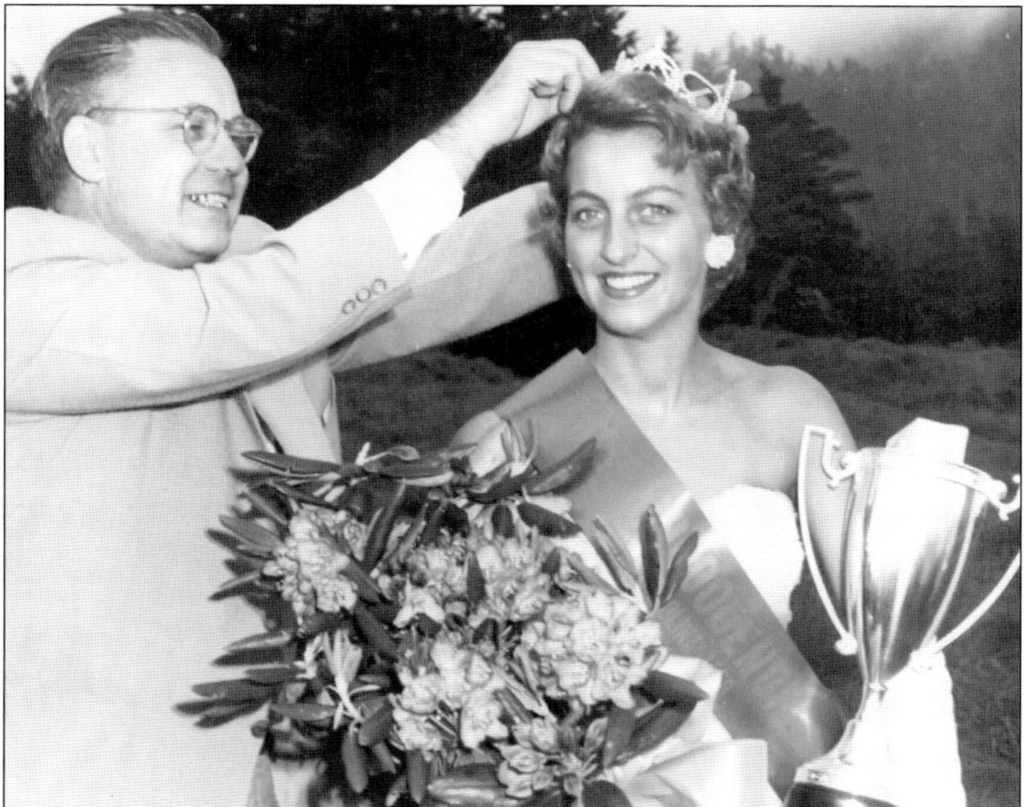

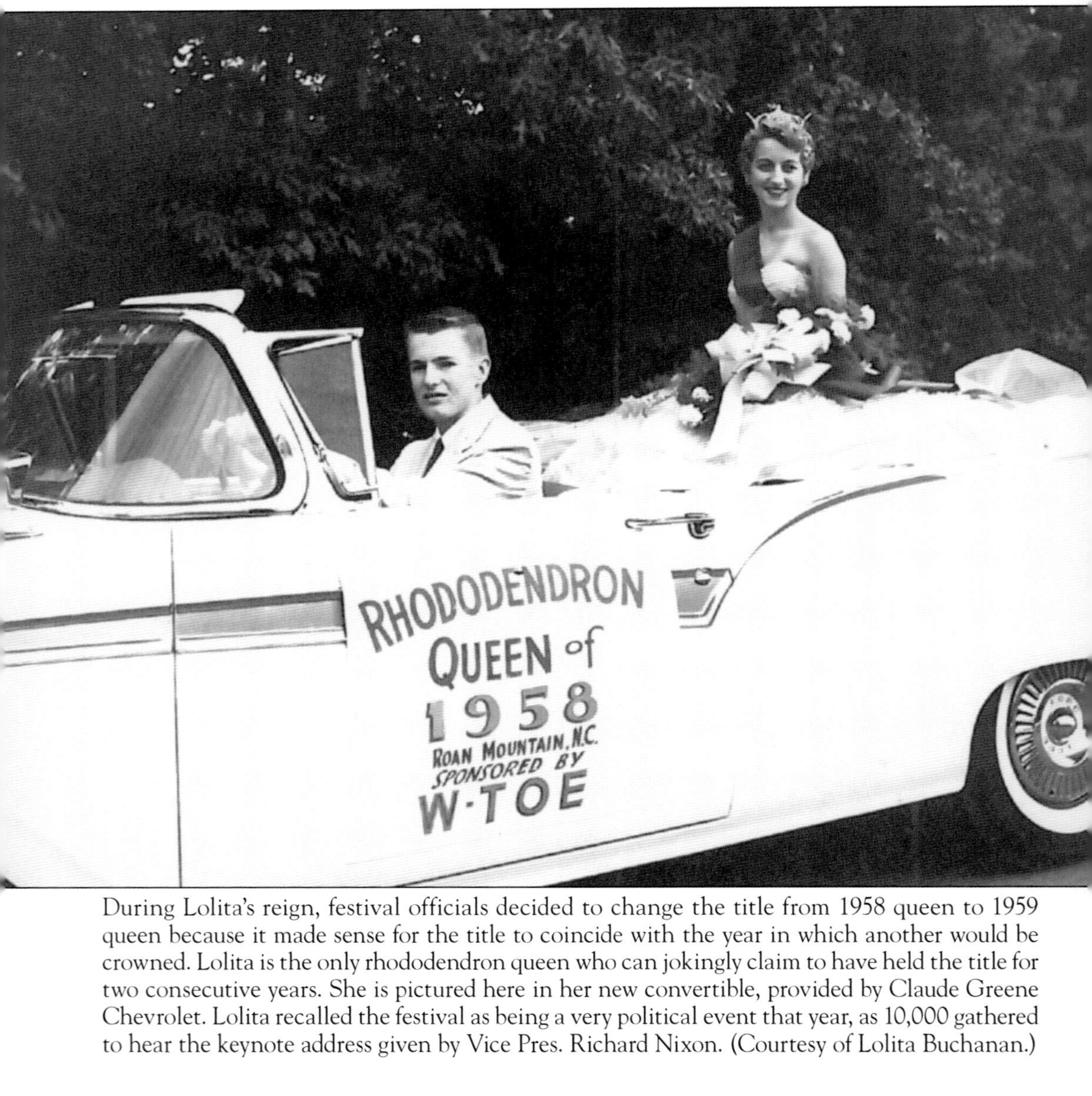

During Lolita's reign, festival officials decided to change the title from 1958 queen to 1959 queen because it made sense for the title to coincide with the year in which another would be crowned. Lolita is the only rhododendron queen who can jokingly claim to have held the title for two consecutive years. She is pictured here in her new convertible, provided by Claude Greene Chevrolet. Lolita recalled the festival as being a very political event that year, as 10,000 gathered to hear the keynote address given by Vice Pres. Richard Nixon. (Courtesy of Lolita Buchanan.)

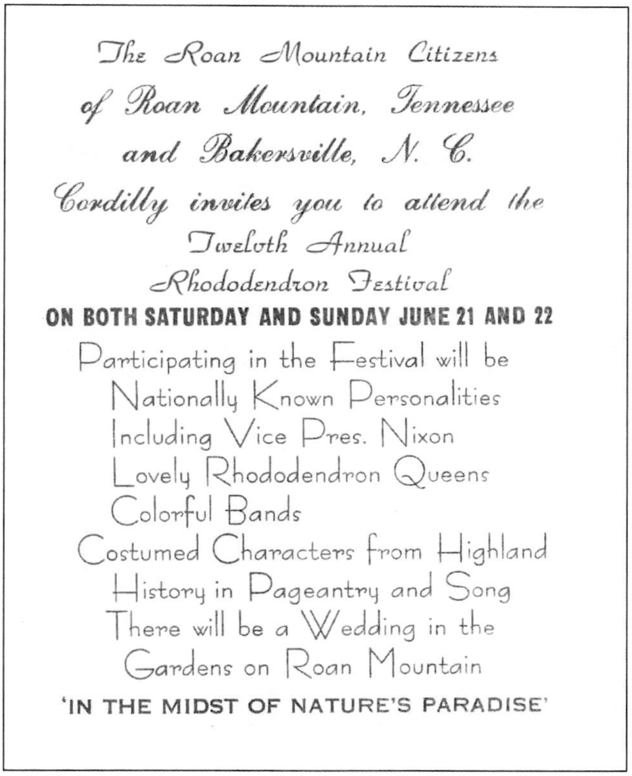

The Roan Mountain Citizens
of Roan Mountain, Tennessee
and Bakersville, N. C.
Cordilly invites you to attend the
Twelfth Annual
Rhododendron Festival
ON BOTH SATURDAY AND SUNDAY JUNE 21 AND 22
Participating in the Festival will be
Nationally Known Personalities
Including Vice Pres. Nixon
Lovely Rhododendron Queens
Colorful Bands
Costumed Characters from Highland
History in Pageantry and Song
There will be a Wedding in the
Gardens on Roan Mountain
'IN THE MIDST OF NATURE'S PARADISE'

When an event's keynote speaker is the vice president of the United States, an engraved invitation seems quite apropos. This invitation was sent to local dignitaries and festival officials as well as visiting pageant and festival representatives across the state of North Carolina. (Courtesy of the Wilson Collection.)

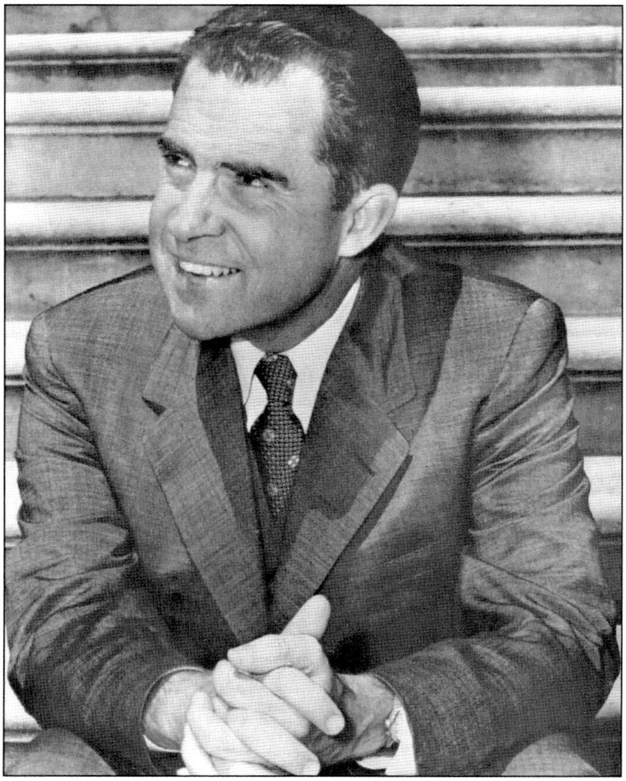

This photograph of Richard Nixon appeared in the 1958 rhododendron festival program book. The vice president arrived by motorcade to Roan Mountain for the festival. The trip included several stops along the way: a ground-breaking ceremony for Grace Hartley Memorial Hospital in Banner Elk and visits to Bakersville, Spruce Pine, Linville, and Blowing Rock, where they were guests at a reception given by Mr. and Mrs. J.E. Broyhill. (Courtesy of the North Carolina Rhododendron Festival.)

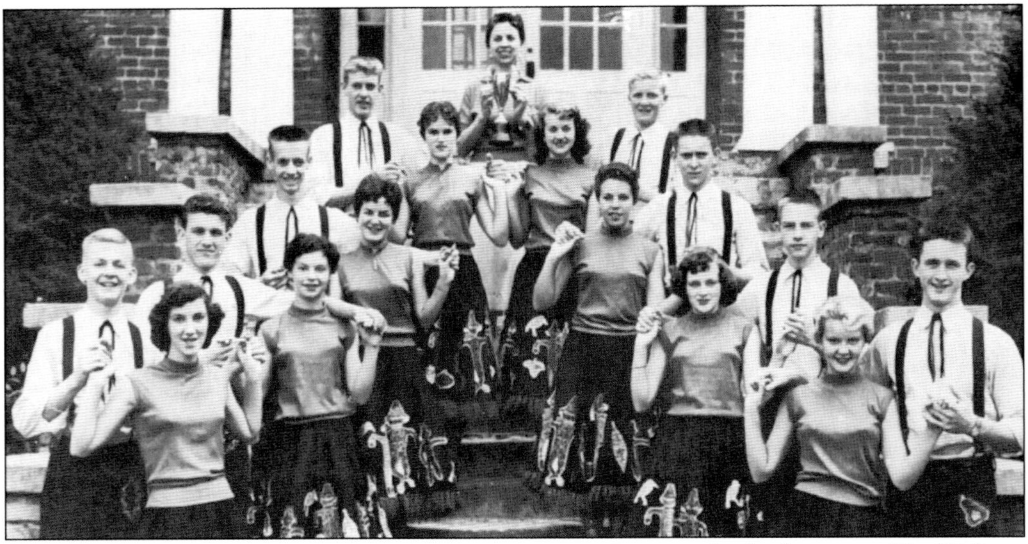

Beginning in the 1950s, the famous Cranberry Square Dance Team, under the direction of Kay Wilkins, performed on Roan Mountain during the rhododendron festival. The performance venue was an outdoor stage that was used for special entertainment and the crowning ceremony of the new North Carolina rhododendron queen. (Courtesy of the North Carolina Rhododendron Festival.)

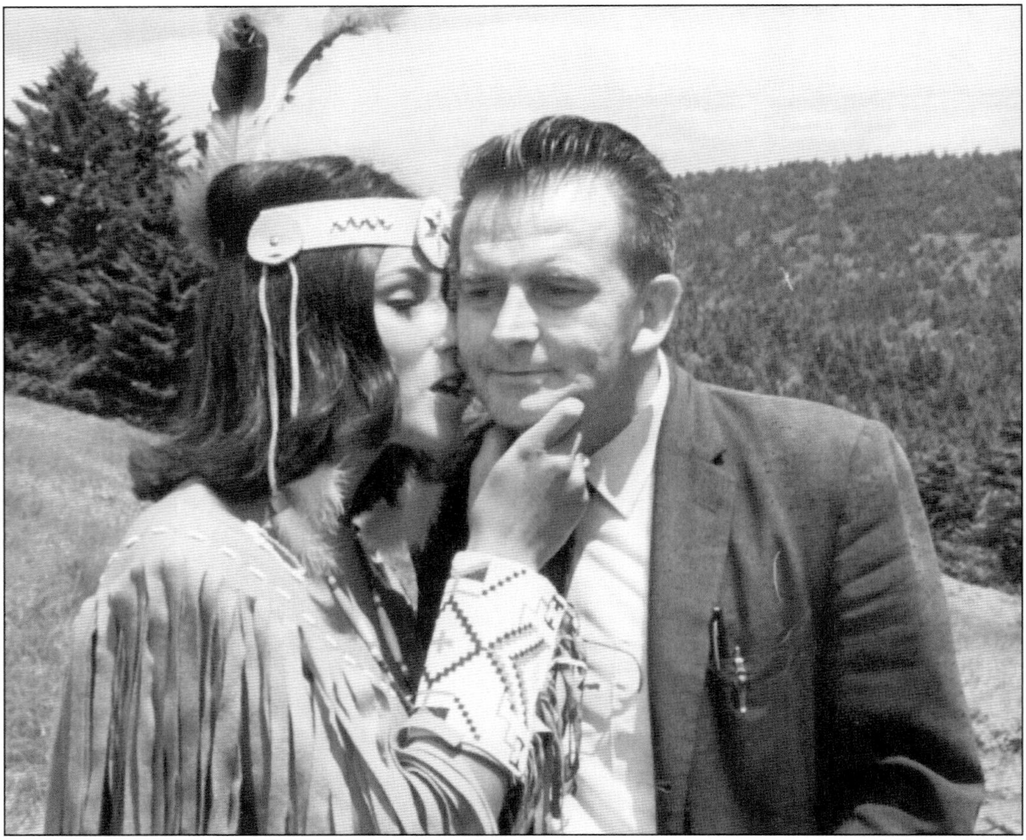

Also part of the entertainment agenda were presentations and plays billed as "History in Pageantry and Song." (Courtesy of the Barron Collection.)

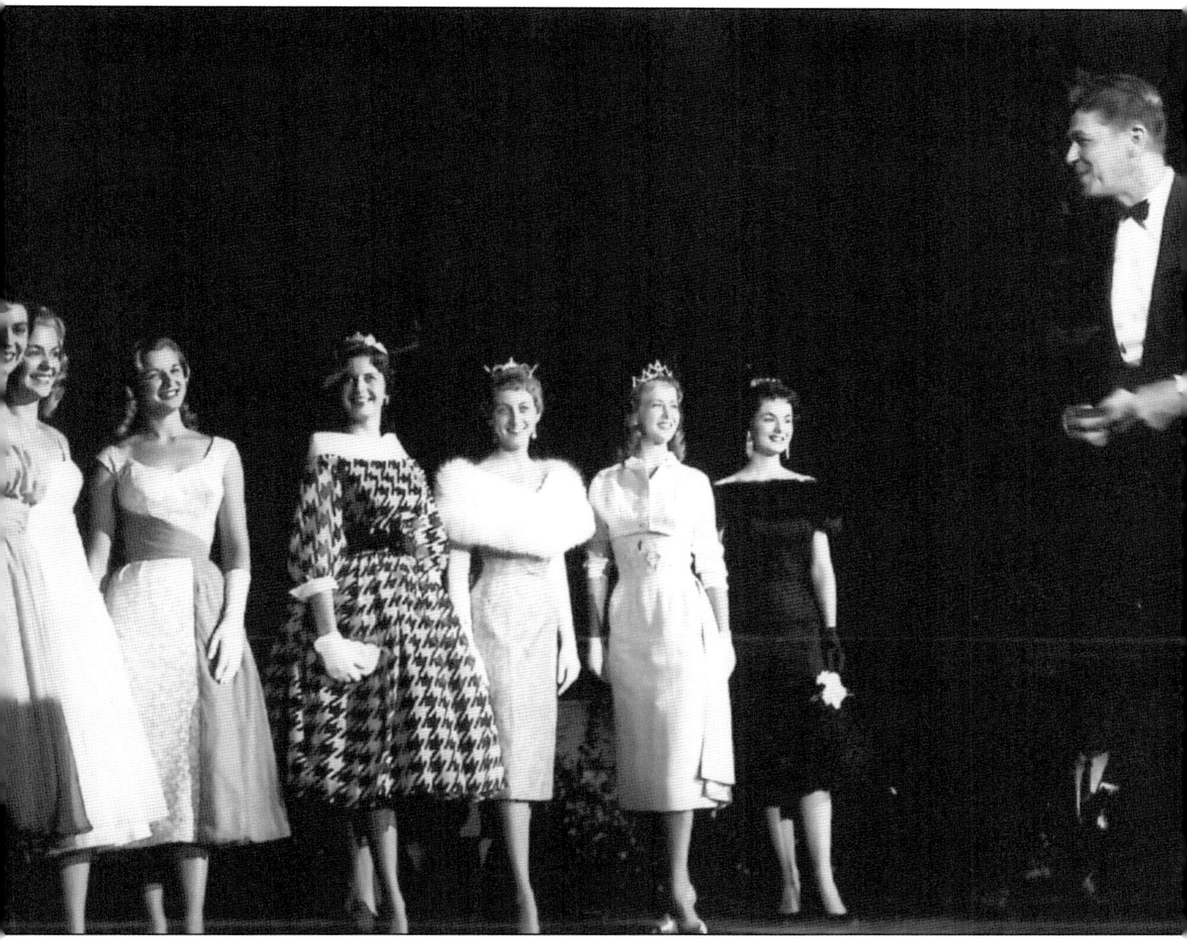

During an appearance at the azalea festival in Wilmington, North Carolina, in the spring of 1959, Lolita Buchanan had the opportunity to meet actor and future president Ronald Reagan, who had been selected king of the azalea festival. Actress Debra Paget, who appeared in Elvis Presley's debut film, *Love Me Tender*, as well as Cecil B. DeMille's monumental production of the *Ten Commandments*, was azalea queen. The Air Force's Blue Angel precision fliers were also guests. Lolita (third from right) is pictured here on stage with Reagan. (Courtesy of Lolita Buchanan.)

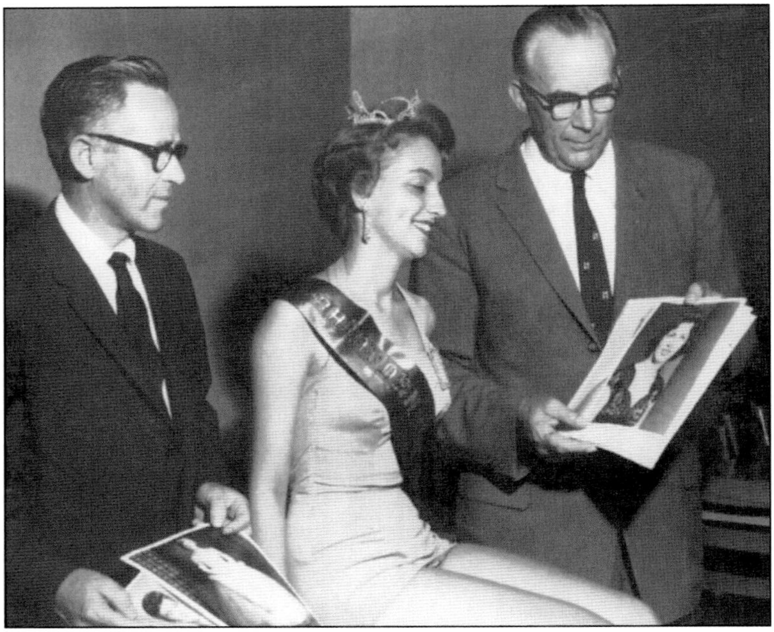

Prior to the 1959 festival and pageant, retiring queen Lolita Buchanan, along with festival official and Lion's Club member Fred Brummitt and business manager O.D. Calhoun had the opportunity to review photographs of contestants competing for the title of 1960 North Carolina rhododendron queen. (Courtesy of Lolita Buchanan.)

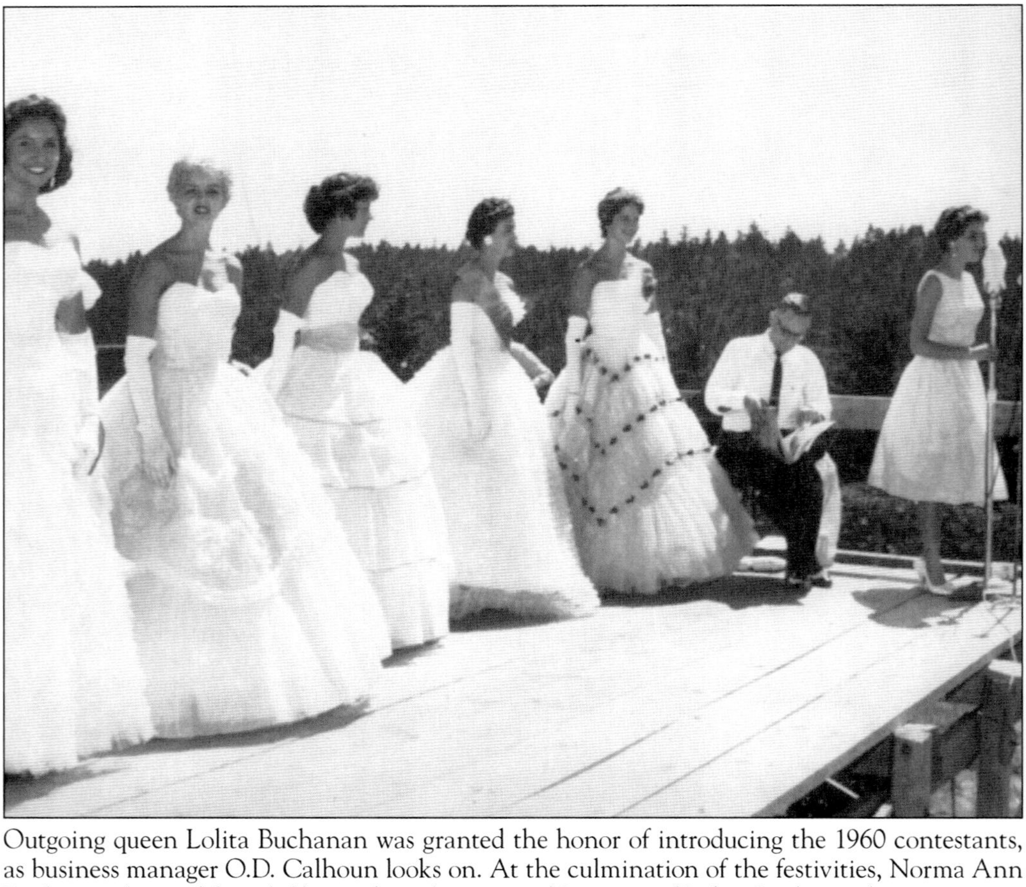

Outgoing queen Lolita Buchanan was granted the honor of introducing the 1960 contestants, as business manager O.D. Calhoun looks on. At the culmination of the festivities, Norma Ann Buchanan (second from left) was the title winner. (Courtesy of Lolita Buchanan.)

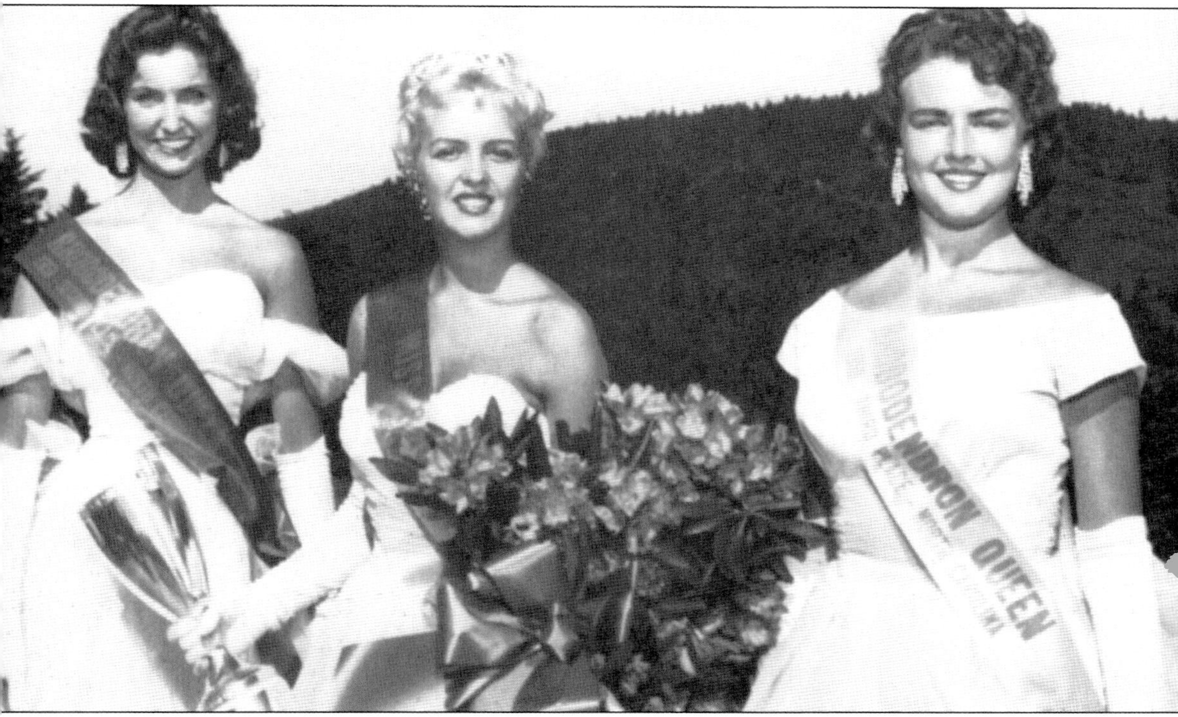

Norma Ann Buchanan (center) is pictured with two other contestants. (Courtesy of the North Carolina Rhododendron Festival.)

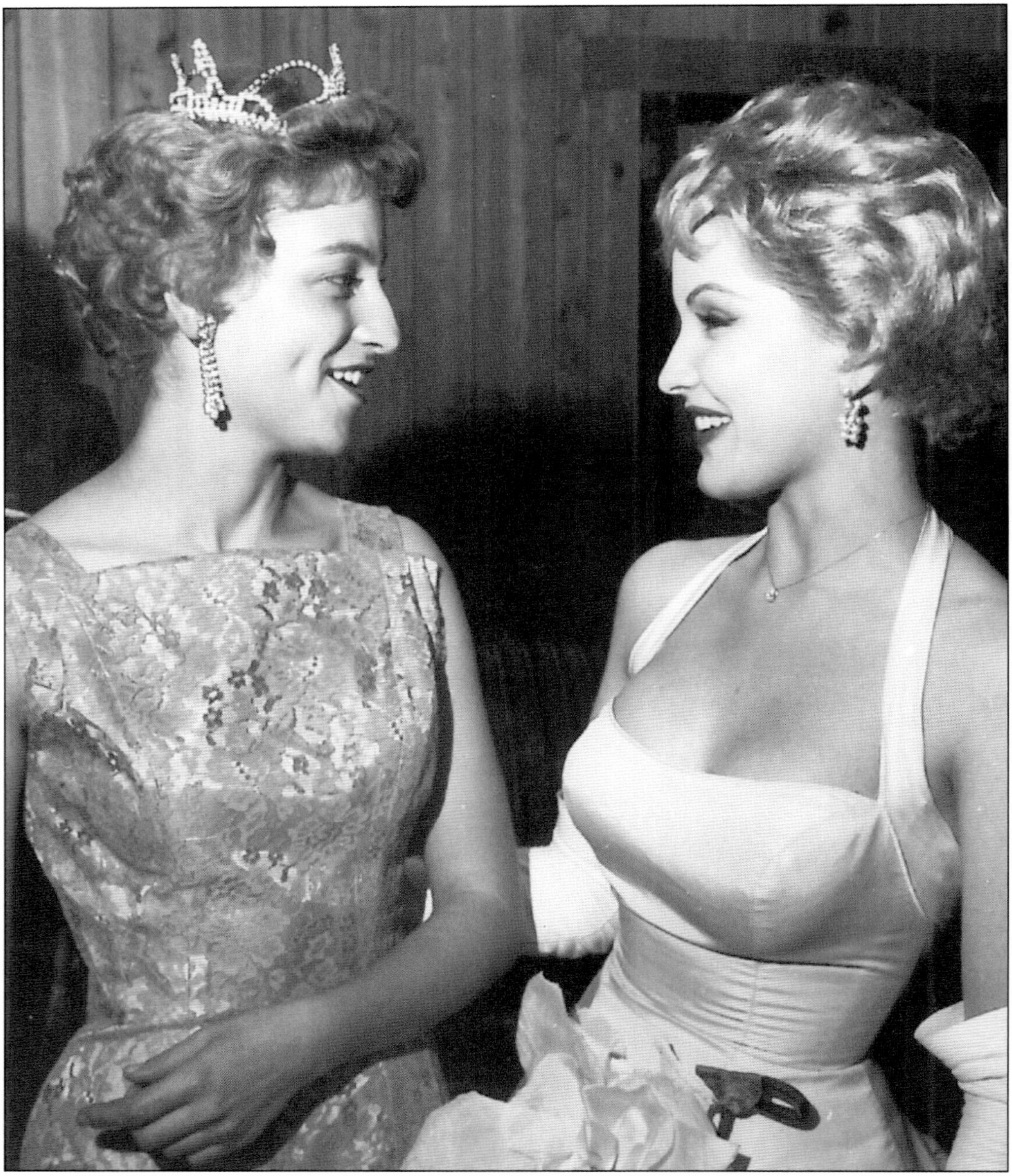

Lolita Buchanan congratulated her successor, Norma Ann Buchanan, on winning the title of North Carolina rhododendron queen. Norma Ann was a resident of neighboring Avery County. After relinquishing the title of North Carolina rhododendron queen, Norma Ann went on to win several more pageants. (Courtesy of Lolita Buchanan.)

Two

The Glory Days

1960s Reign

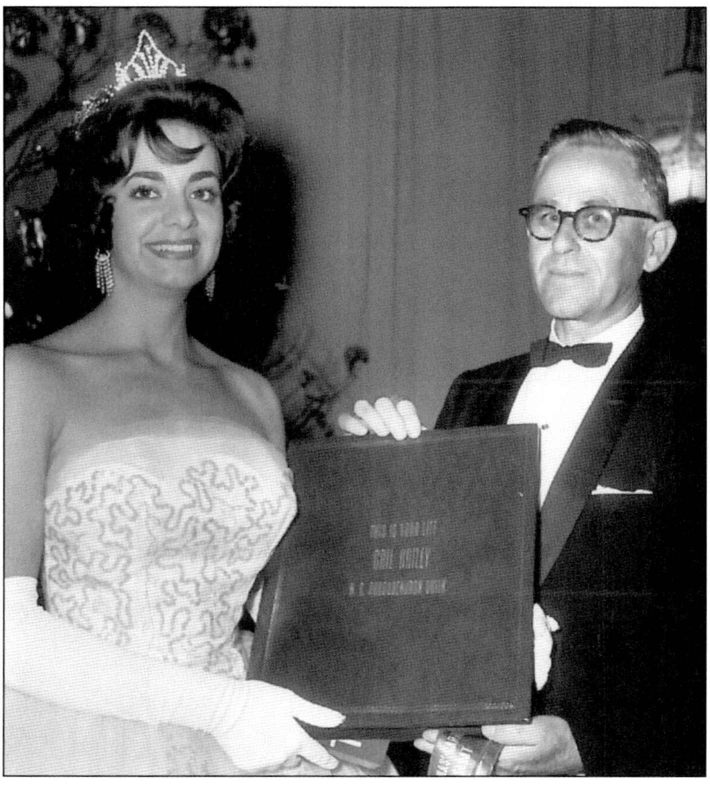

The 1960s marked the beginning of a new and prestigious era for the North Carolina Rhododendron Festival. The rhododendron queen was now a traveler, touring the country. The 1960s queens traveled internationally as well, promoting North Carolina on five continents. Gail Bailey was the first of the decade to wear the crown. Still in high school, she managed to meet the demands of a busy schedule while completing her graduation requirements. She is pictured here with business manager O.D. Calhoun, receiving an achievement award. (Courtesy of the Barron Collection.)

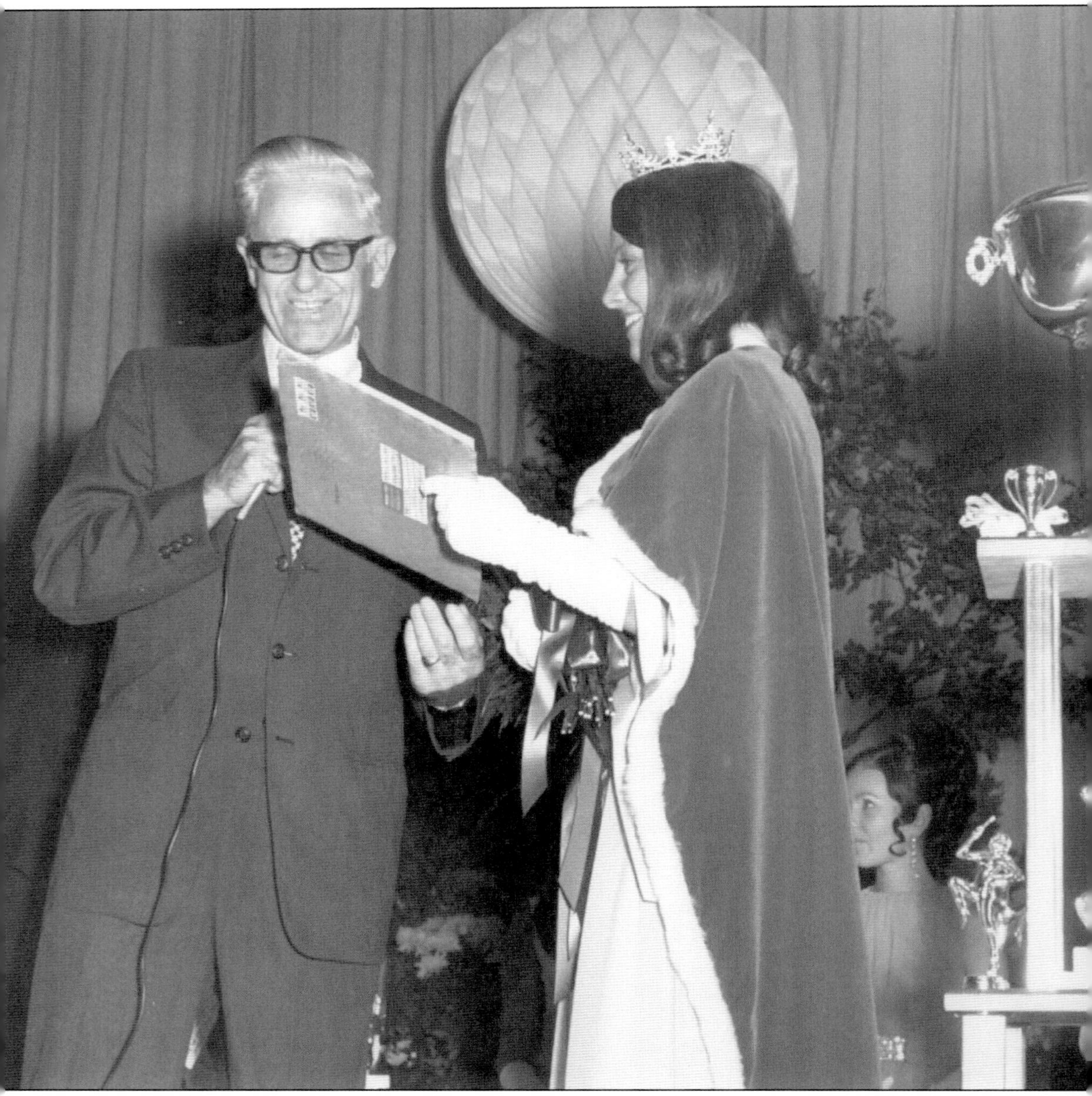

O.D. Calhoun served as business manager for the rhododendron festival for 18 years. He was responsible for applying for and securing a state charter, officially recognizing the North Carolina Rhododendron Festival as a state festival. Calhoun was a personal friend of Walt Disney, who made it possible for the rhododendron queen to appear in the Rose Bowl parade. (Courtesy of Mary Calhoun.)

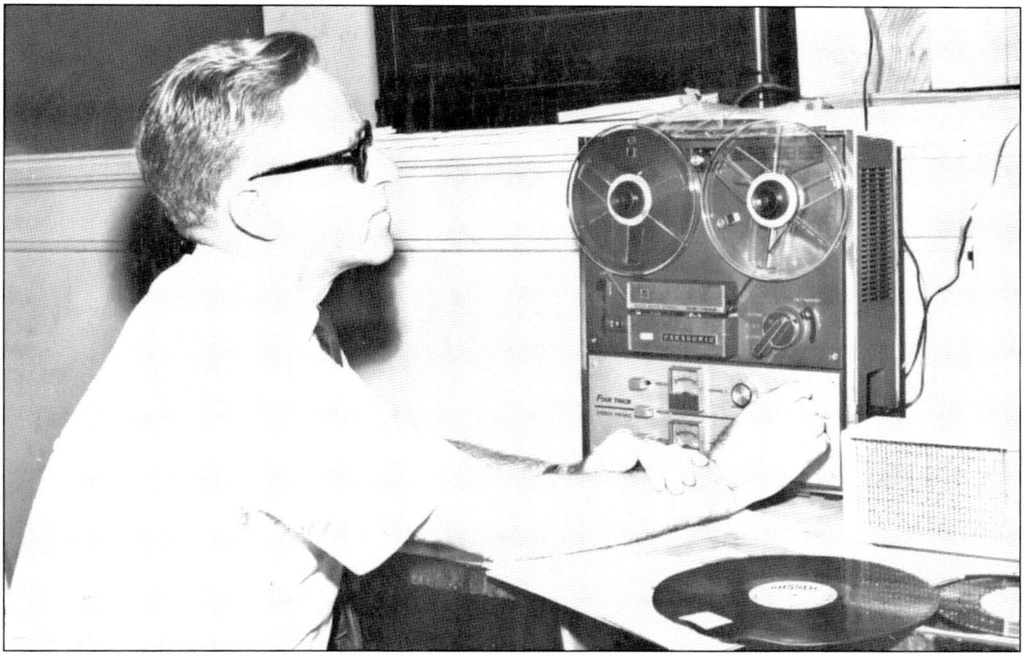

Calhoun was the originator of the *Carolina Barn Dance*, which broadcast on more than 500 stations in 47 states. He was also an original partner in the radio station WTOE, as well as a marketing executive and promoter of such entertainment venues as Tweetsie Railroad and the Land of Oz. (Both, courtesy of Mary Calhoun.)

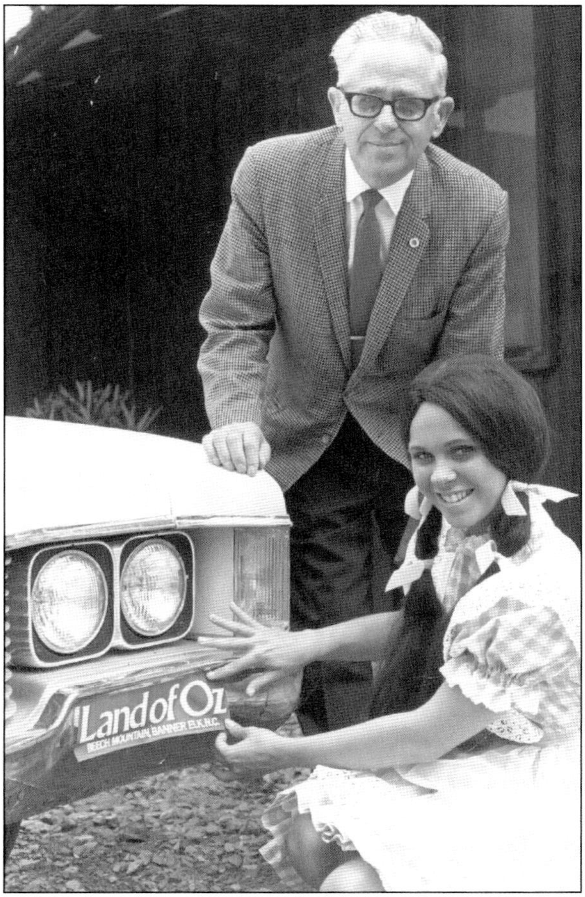

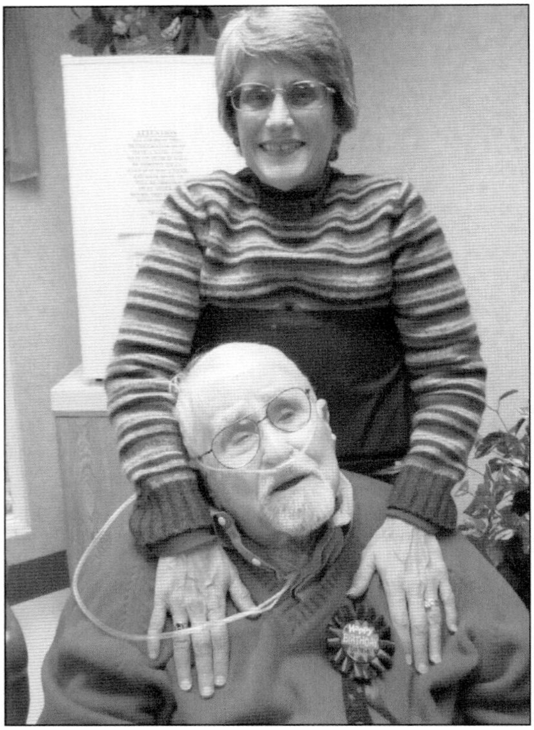

In 2004, Calhoun was presented with North Carolina's highest civilian honor: induction into the Order of the Long Leaf Pine, an achievement he shares with Maya Angelou, Charles Kuralt, and Billy Graham. Calhoun is pictured at left with his wife, Mary, celebrating his 104th birthday in January 2014 and below in 1996 at a reception that took place during the rhododendron festival's 50th anniversary celebration. Pictured below from left to right are (first row) Brenda Bost Trott, O.D. Calhoun, and Lolita Buchanan Peeler; (second row) Nyla Banner Greene, Gail Robertson Walker, Mary Calhoun, Judy Bryant Umminger, Sara Triplett Caldwell, and the first North Carolina rhododendron queen, Kate Smith Welch. (Courtesy of Mary Calhoun.)

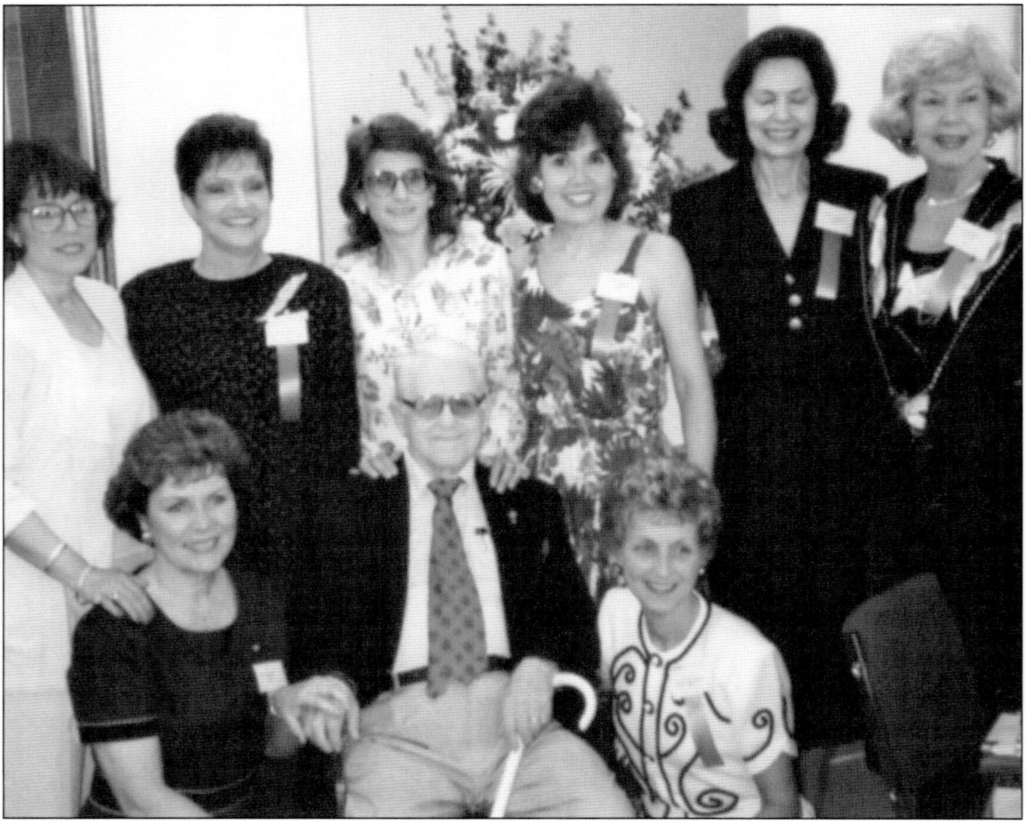

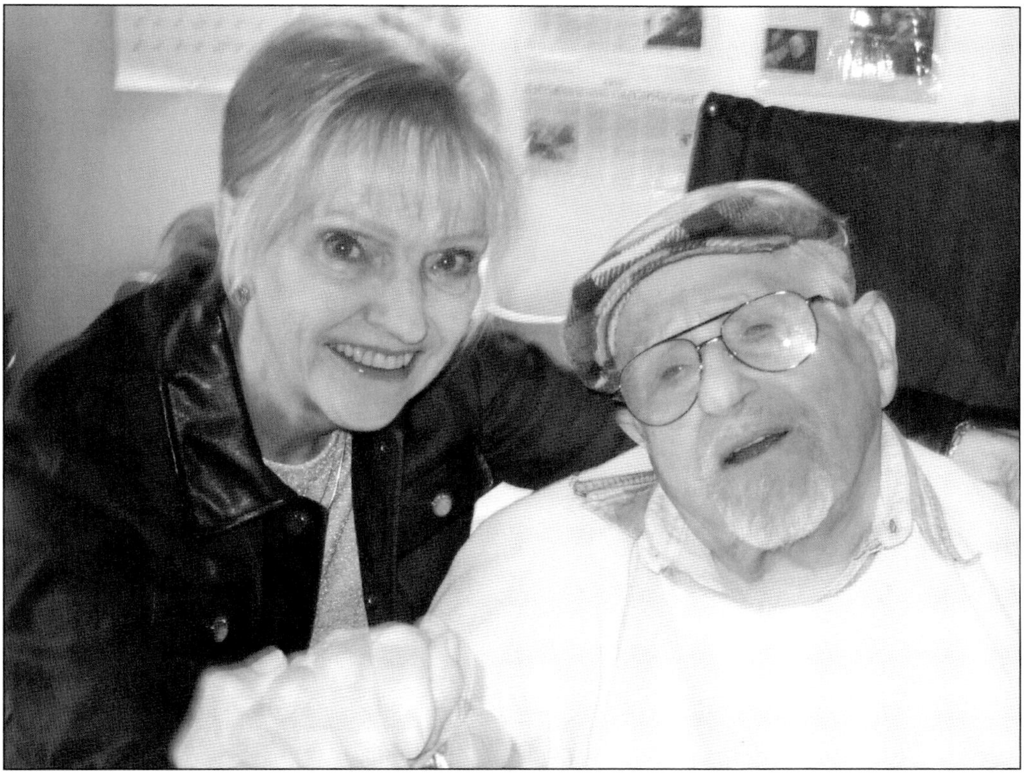

Gail Robertson Walker, the 1962 North Carolina rhododendron queen, visited with Calhoun in October 2014. Gail has many fond memories of the time she spent with Calhoun and his late wife, Ruth, during her year's reign. A few years ago, Walker returned to Bakersville to attend the North Carolina Rhododendron Festival pageant, where she paid tribute to Calhoun by singing a song in his honor. (Courtesy of Mary Calhoun.)

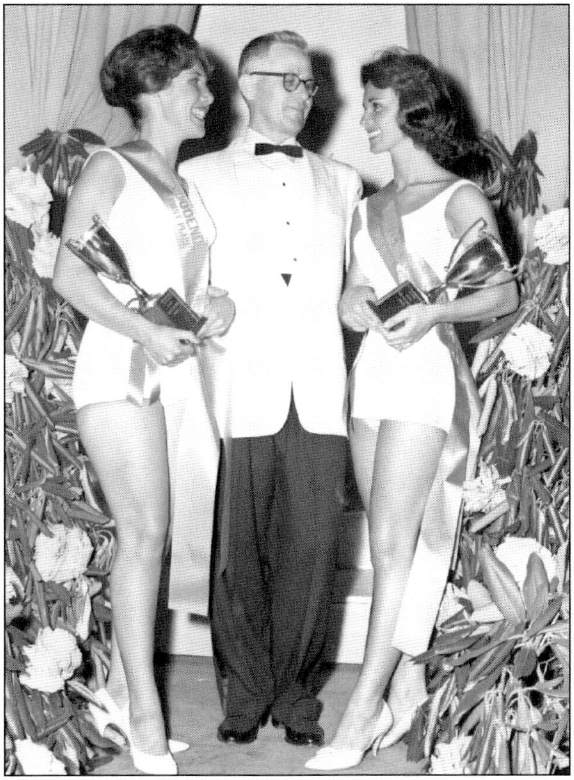

Calhoun served as business manager for the 1963 North Carolina rhododendron queen, Betty Rae Lawhon. In addition to winning the title, she also won the swimsuit award. The talent award winner for the pageant was Donna Summers (pictured above on left with O.D. Calhoun and Betty Lawhon). Betty shared the story of how she and Donna became friends during the pageant. That friendship is still intact today, after 52 years. (Courtesy of Betty Lawhon Deviney.)

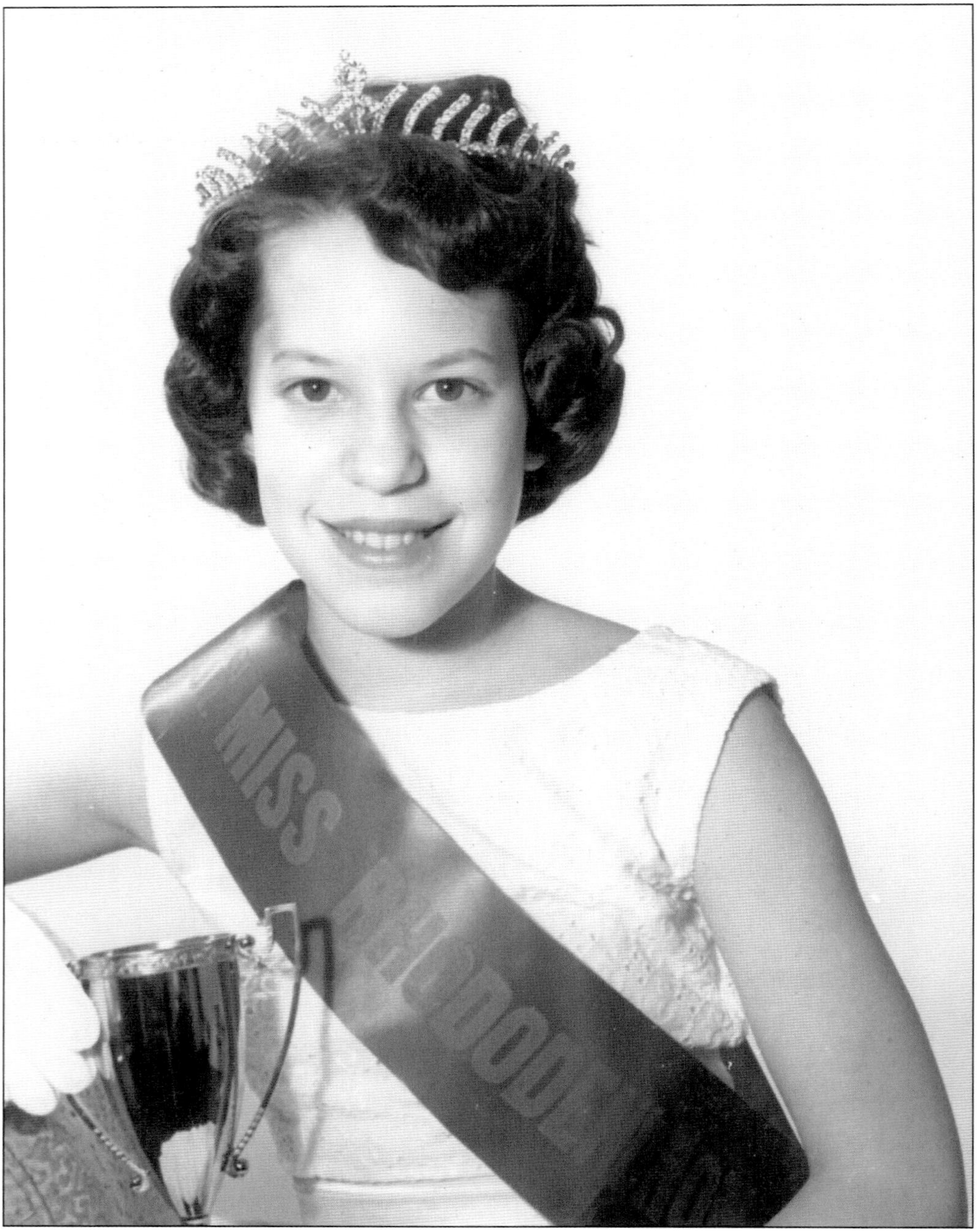

Prompted by the urging of business manager O.D. Calhoun, the first junior pageant was held in 1961, with Nyla Kay Banner winning the title. Banner shared her memory of that first junior pageant: "Being the first Jr. Rhododendron Queen was so exciting for me. On stage, near the end of the pageant, the judges asked all the contestants the same question: 'Why do you want to be Junior Rhododendron Queen?' Amid answers such as, 'It would be a wonderful experience' . . . I blurted out, 'To prove to my daddy it's not a bunch of foolishness, because he wouldn't even come!' The audience roared! The rest is history and a magical year followed. Long story short, always be yourself." (Courtesy of the North Carolina Rhododendron Festival.)

Since that first junior pageant, lasting relationships between the rhododendron queen and her junior counterpart have been formed. The 1969 North Carolina junior rhododendron queen, Lynn Neighbors, is pictured here, standing beside queen Brenda Heath's official car. (Courtesy of the Barron Collection.)

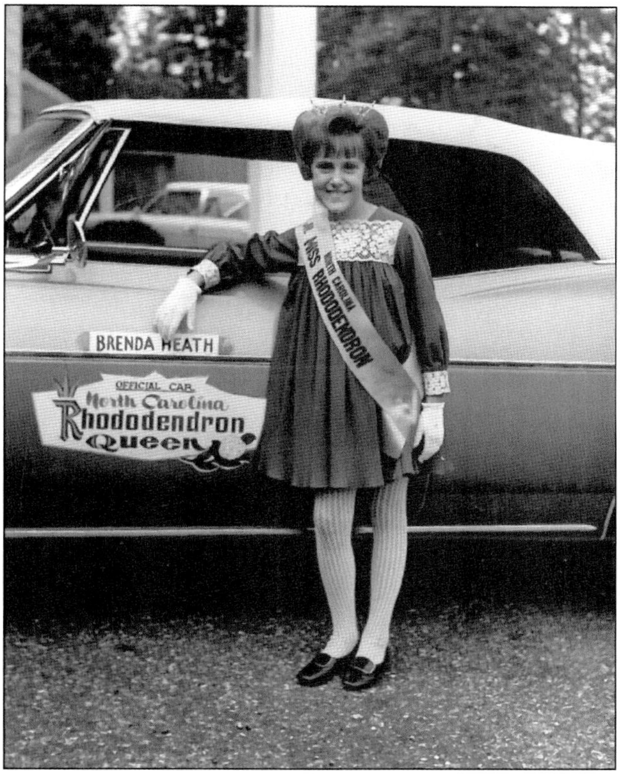

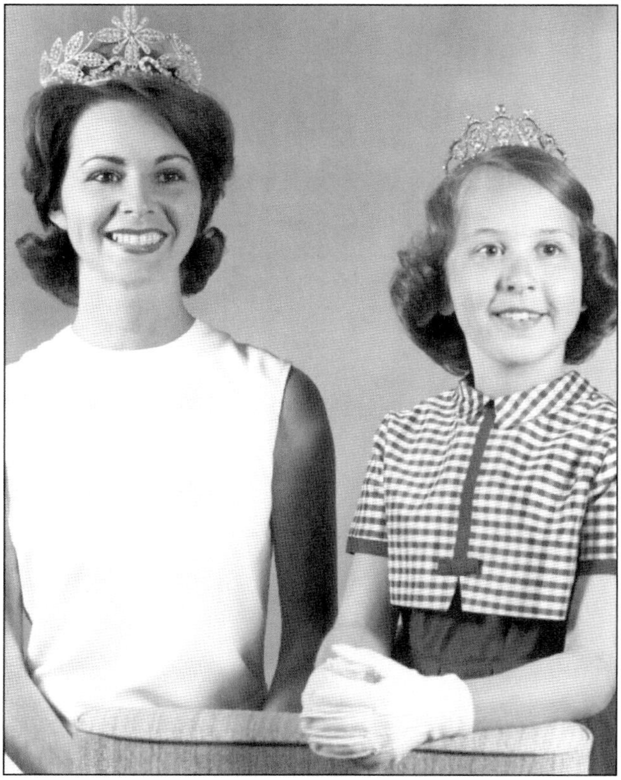

Betty Rae Lawhon (left) and Mary Gwen Graham represented Bakersville and the rhododendron festival as the 1963 queens. Graham was a Bakersville native. (Courtesy of Betty Lawhon Deviney.)

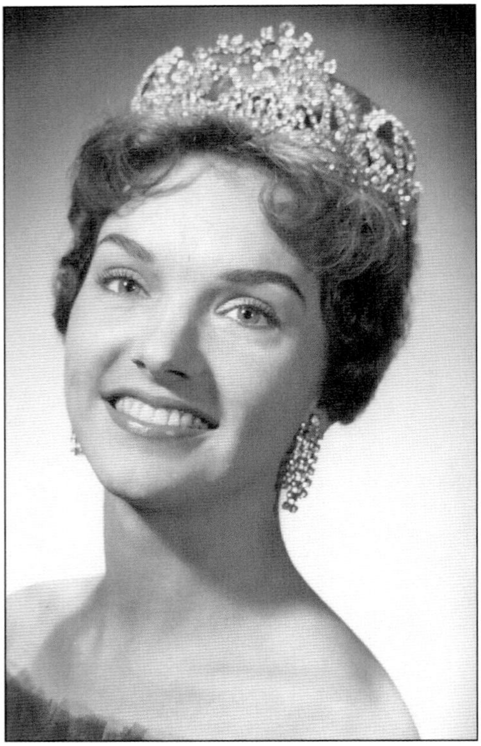

Gail Robertson, the 1962 North Carolina rhododendron queen, had the distinction of being the first to have a junior queen. While a full-time student at Western Carolina University, she still managed to set new personal appearance records. Robertson recalls that during particularly demanding times, when she was making appearances every weekend and missing many of her Friday classes, her fellow students were very supportive. They took notes and kept her abreast of her classes. (Courtesy of the North Carolina Rhododendron Festival.)

In October 1961, Gail made an appearance at the North Carolina Trade Fair in Charlotte, where she had the honor of meeting members of the Brazilian Military Mission. (Courtesy of the North Carolina Rhododendron Festival.)

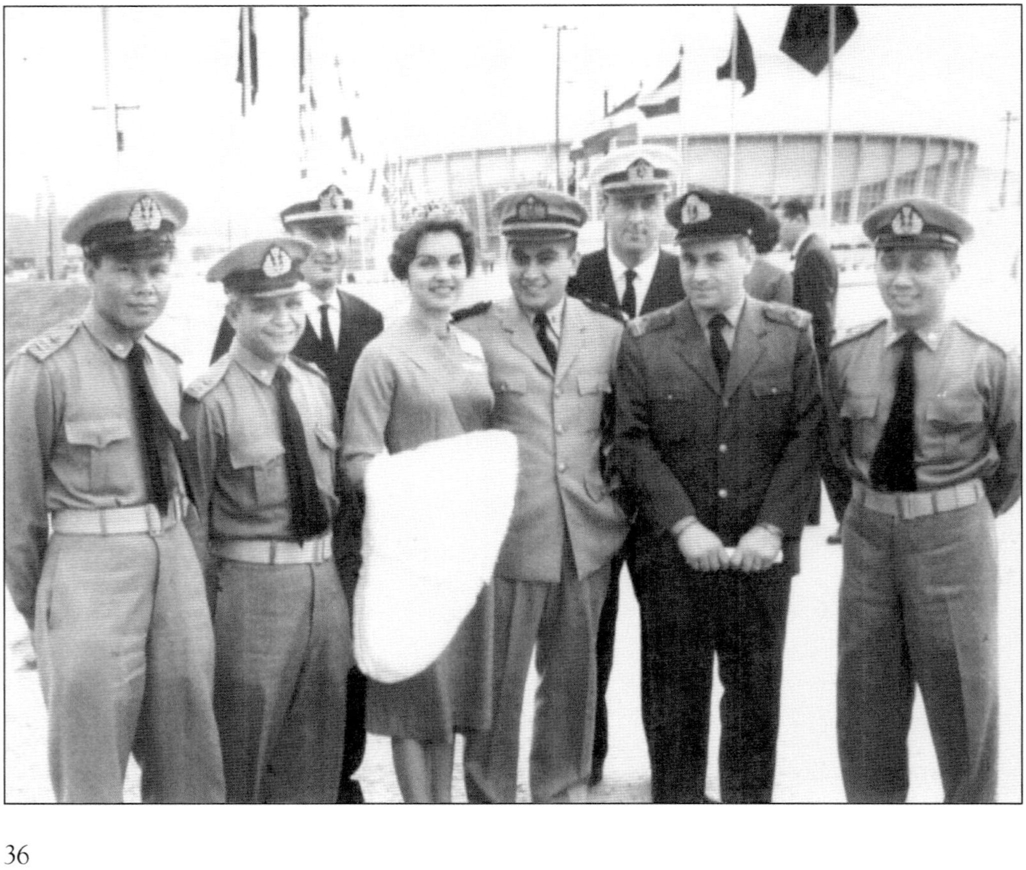

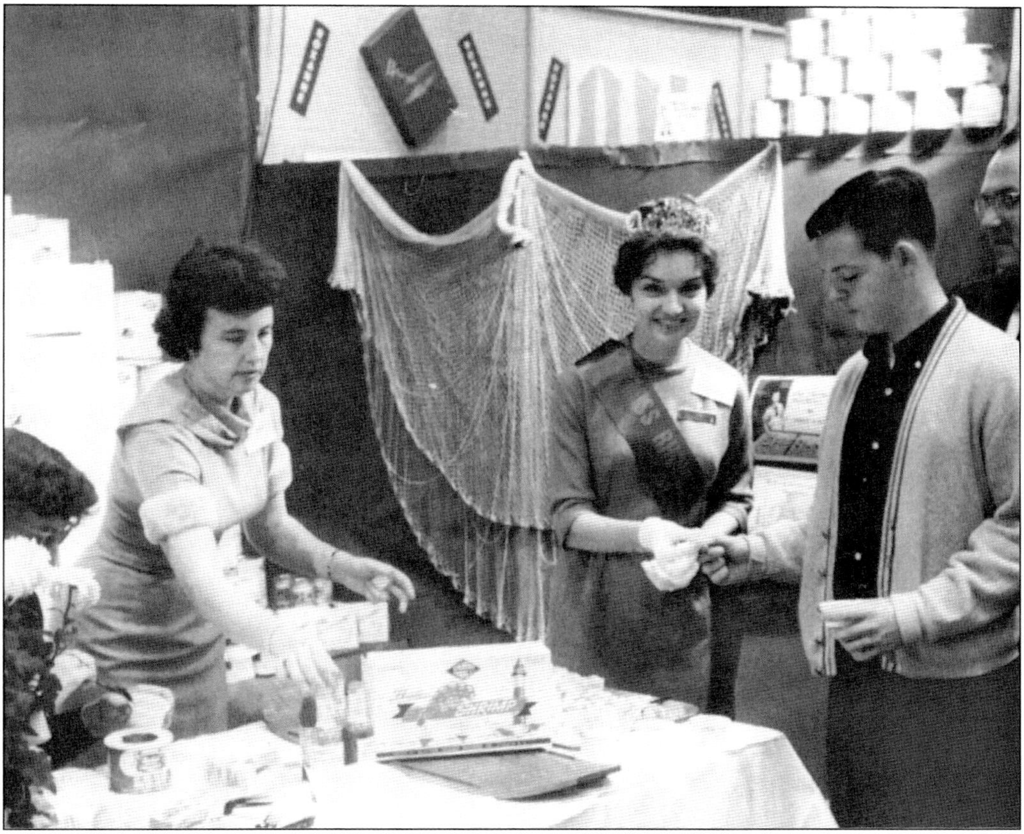

During her travel representing North Carolina as Miss Variety Vacationland, Gail Robertson visited the North Carolina Fisheries in New Bern. (Courtesy of the North Carolina Rhododendron Festival.)

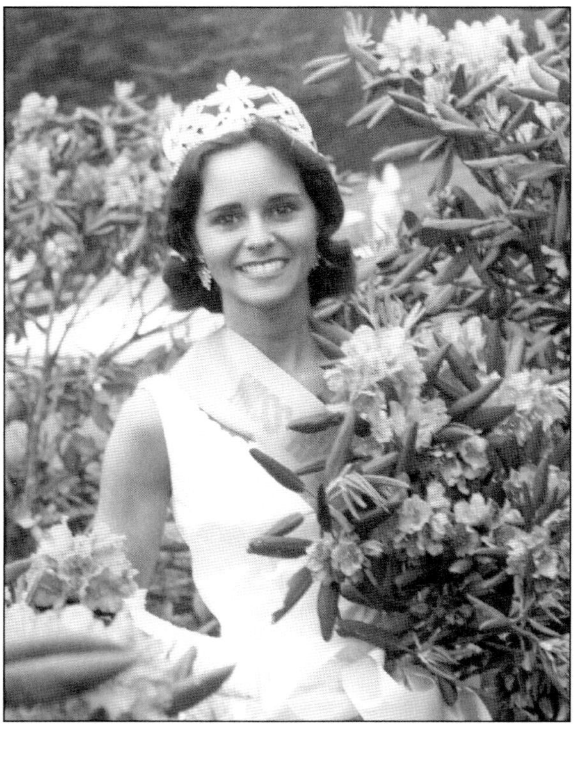

Betty Rae Lawhon, the first full-time North Carolina rhododendron queen, captured the 1963 title from a field of more than 25 contestants. This photograph was taken in the Rhododendron Gardens atop Roan Mountain, a beautiful depiction of the Catawba rhododendron in full bloom. (Courtesy of Betty Lawhon Deviney.)

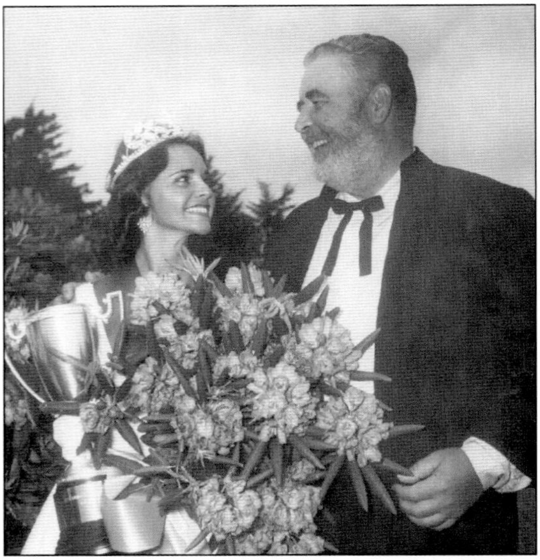

One of the first to congratulate the 1963 rhododendron queen was Charles Elledge, lead actor from the outdoor drama *Horn in the West*. Lawhon has some very fond memories of her year as rhododendron queen. She recalls being at the 10th anniversary of the mile-high swinging bridge on Grandfather Mountain. Hugh Morton invited her to hold a three-tiered cake with him as part of the celebration. (Courtesy of Betty Lawhon Deviney.)

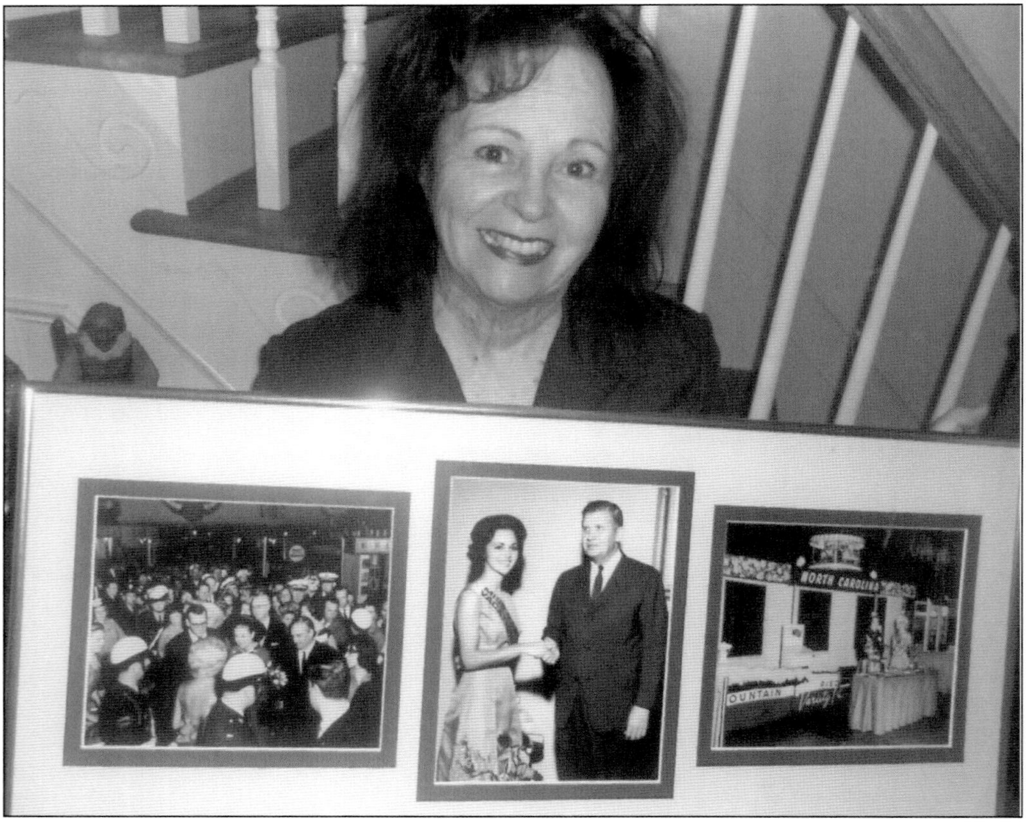

While representing North Carolina as Miss Variety Vacationland, Lawhon had the opportunity to meet both Bob Hope and Princess Grace and Prince Rainier of Monaco. She personally presented the princess with a gift from North Carolina governor Terry Sanford. Lawhon is pictured here proudly holding a framed display depicting some of her fondest memories of her year as rhododendron queen, including the presentation to Princess Grace and a meeting with Governor Sanford. (Courtesy of Betty Lawhon Deviney.)

Betty Lawhon was the first full-time North Carolina rhododendron queen, which means she voluntarily took a year's sabbatical from her studies in order to meet an ever-growing appearance schedule. She also served a dual role, taking on the job of traveling across the country representing the Travel Council of North Carolina as Miss Variety Vacationland. She is pictured here touring an orthopedic hospital for children and with North Carolina governor Terry Sanford and dignitaries. (Both, courtesy of Betty Lawhon Deviney.)

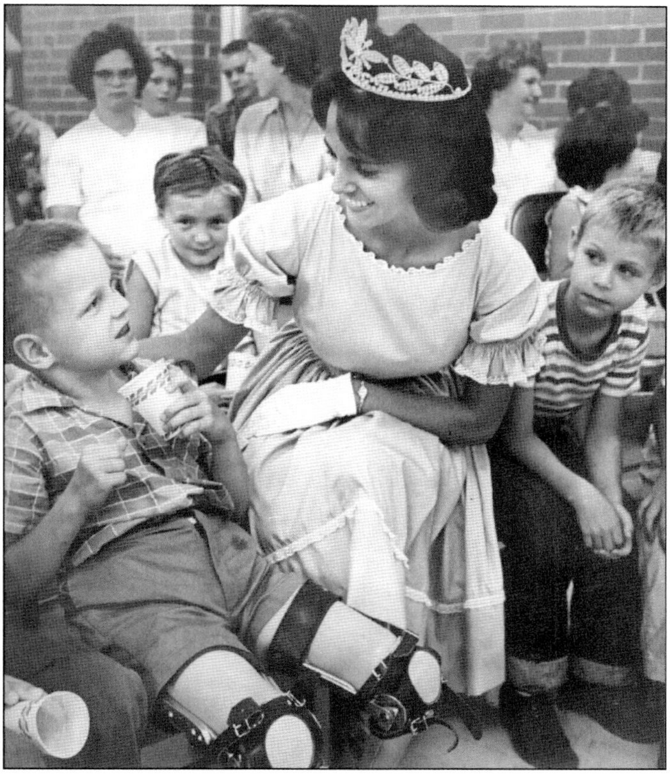

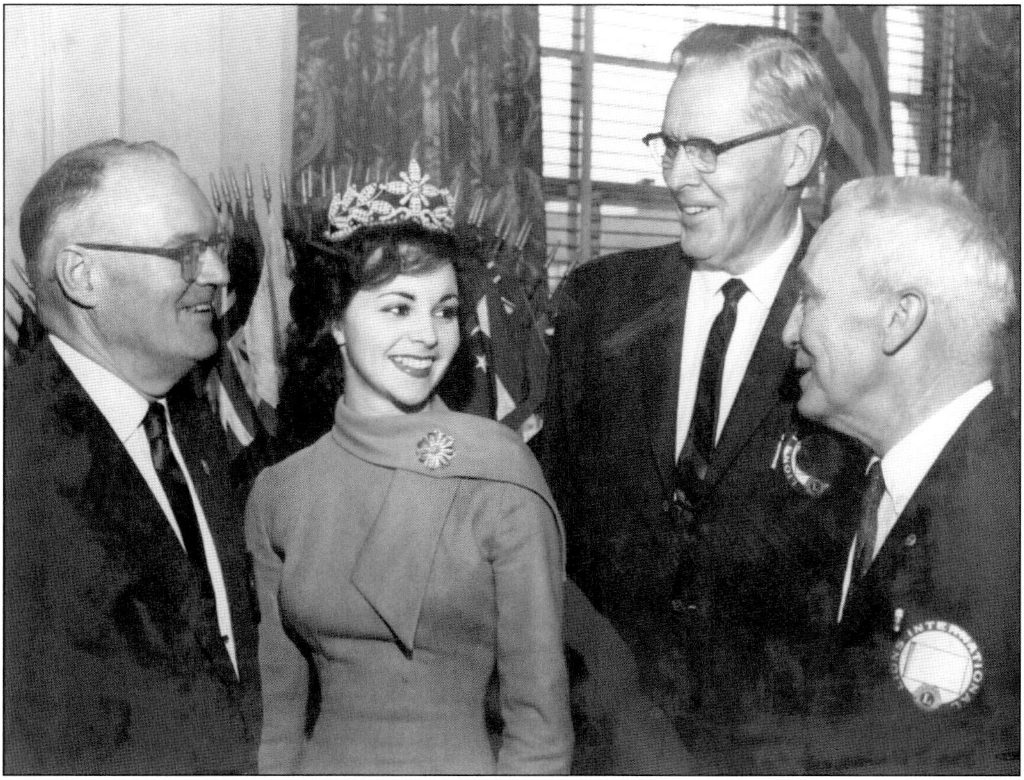

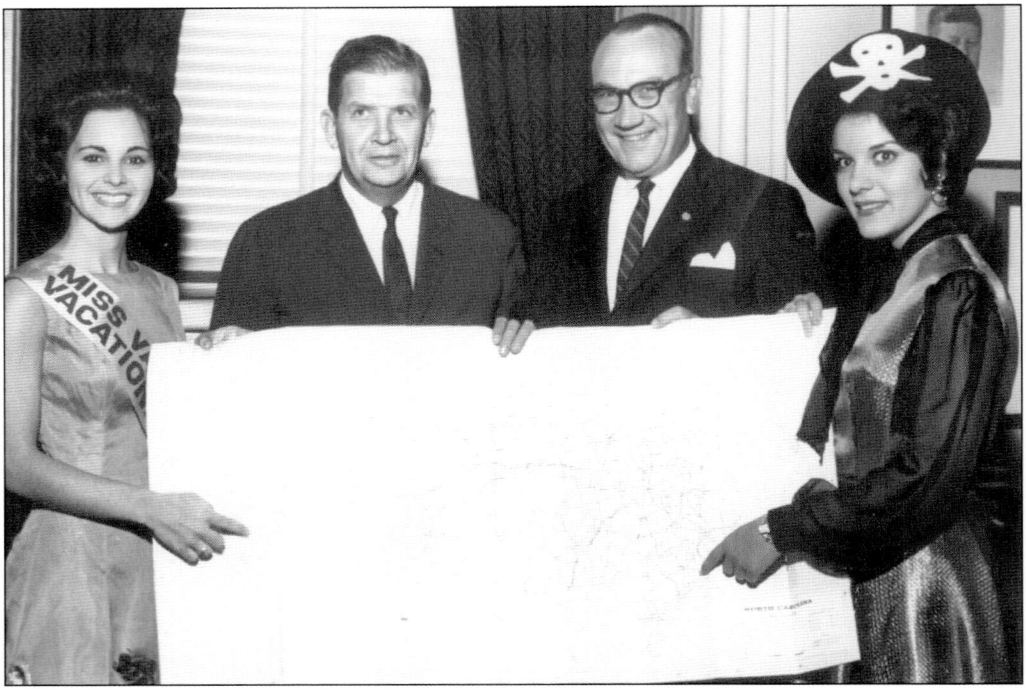

Betty Lawhon (above, left), serving in the role of Miss Variety Vacationland, met with Lions International representatives. She is also pictured below in a reflective moment atop Grandfather Mountain. (Both, courtesy of Betty Lawhon Deviney.)

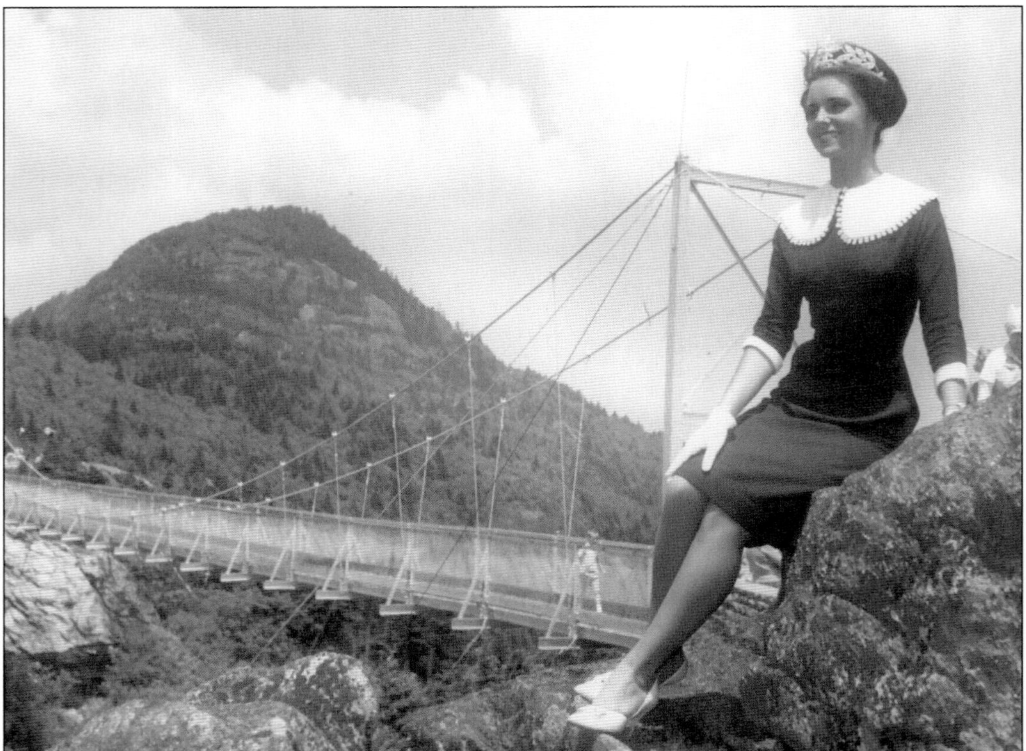

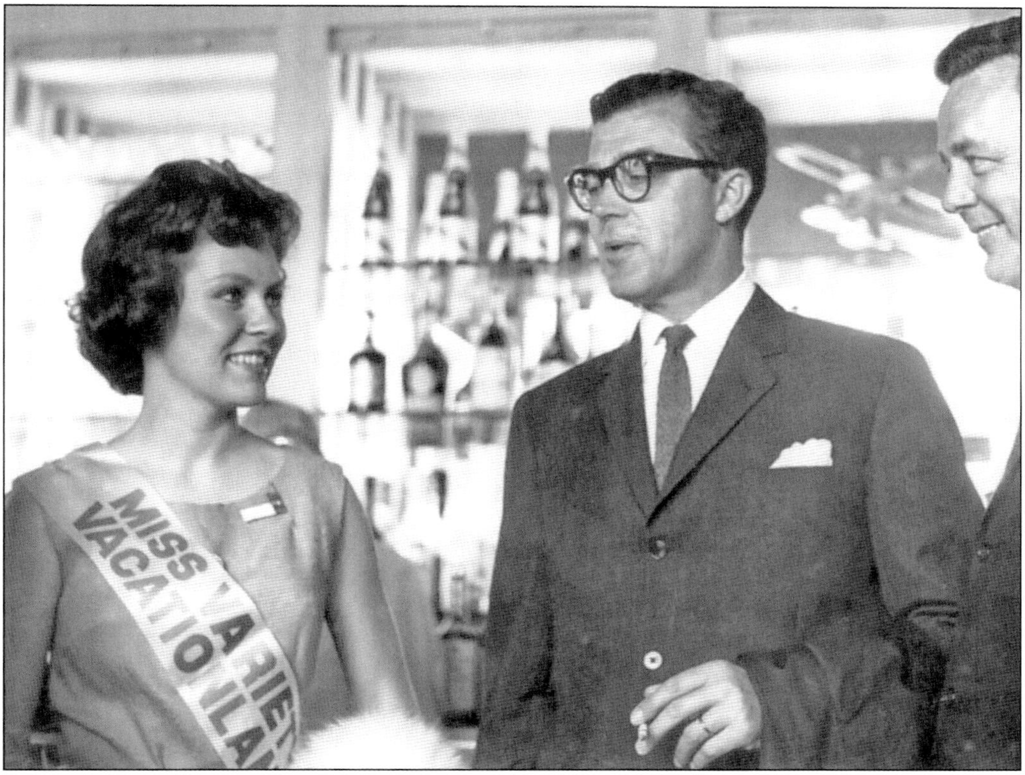

During her reign, the 1964 queen, Brenda Bost, also served as Miss Variety Vacationland, traveling coast to coast and making more than 180 appearances. She was one of several North Carolina rhododendron queens to participate in the Tournament of Roses parade in Pasadena, California. Bost is pictured above in her spokesperson capacity at the 1964 New York World's Fair and below at the 1964 Spring Flower Show in Charlotte. (Both, courtesy of Brenda Bost Trott.)

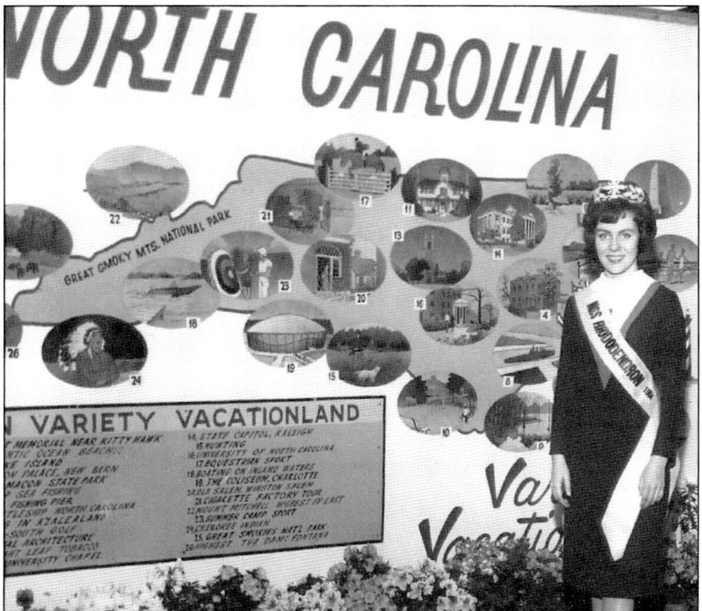

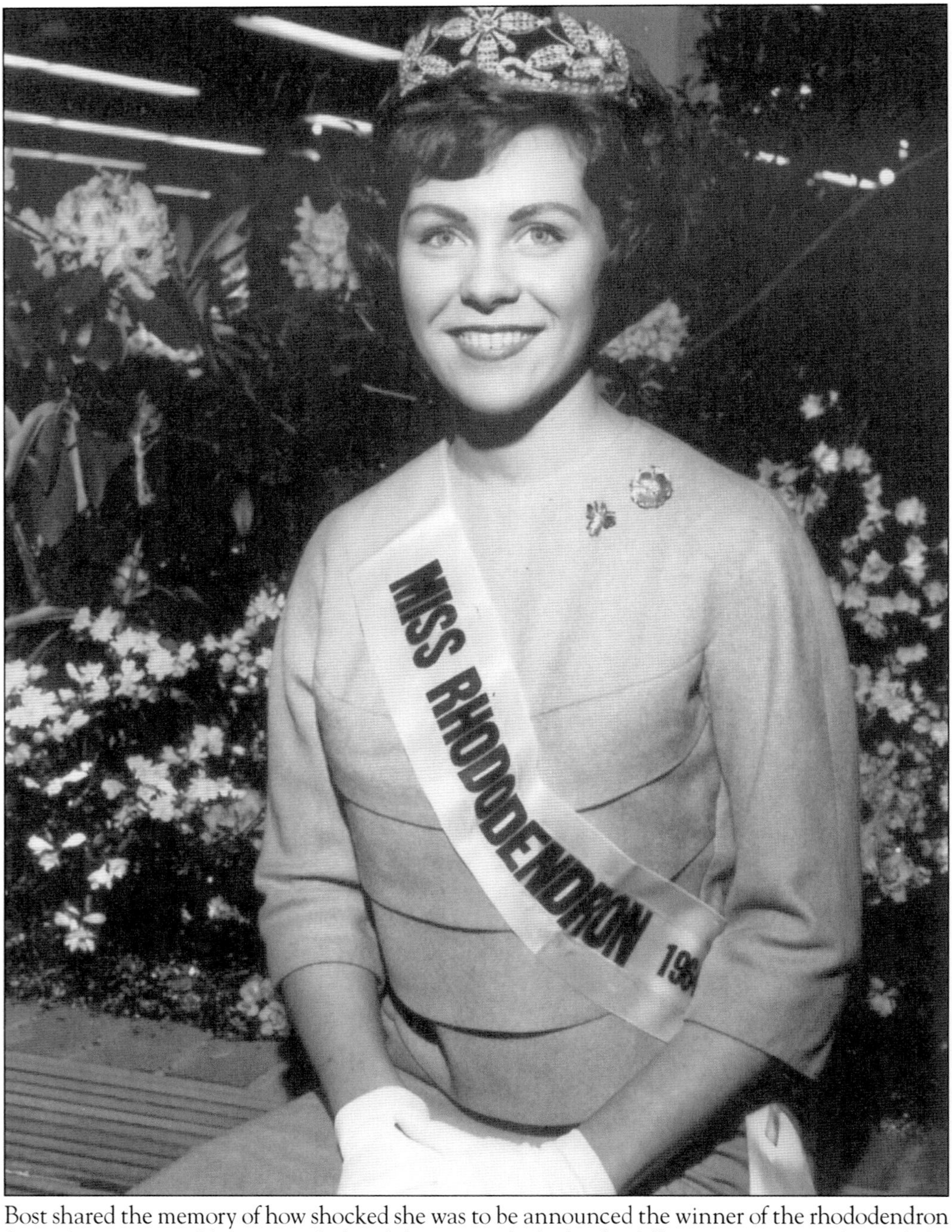

Bost shared the memory of how shocked she was to be announced the winner of the rhododendron festival pageant and how overwhelmed she was with doubt the following morning. She said she actually considered conceding to the first runner-up, fearing that she would not be able to adequately fulfill the role of rhododendron queen. But O.D. Calhoun convinced her that she was perfect for the job, and the ensuing year proved to be one of the most magical and unforgettable of her life. Brenda returned in 2014 to serve as pageant judge on the 50th anniversary of her crowning. (Courtesy of the North Carolina Rhododendron Festival.)

Three

PRIDE IN TRADITION

THE 1960S CONTINUE

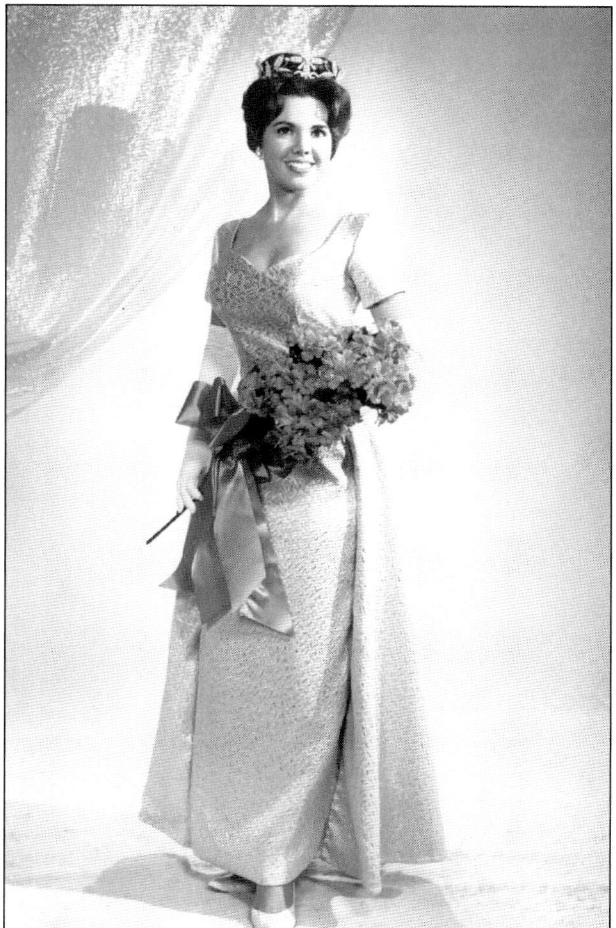

From 1965 until the end of the decade, North Carolina rhododendron queens continued to travel extensively. Judith "Judy" Bryant, the 1965 queen, traveled over 100,000 miles, visiting Italy, Greece, Egypt, Israel, and Syria. Bryant recalls that on the day of her crowning atop beautiful Roan Mountain, she had gone to one side of the tent that served as a dressing room and was reading a prayer that she had tucked into her shoe, when her name was announced as the new North Carolina rhododendron queen. (Courtesy of the North Carolina Rhododendron Festival.)

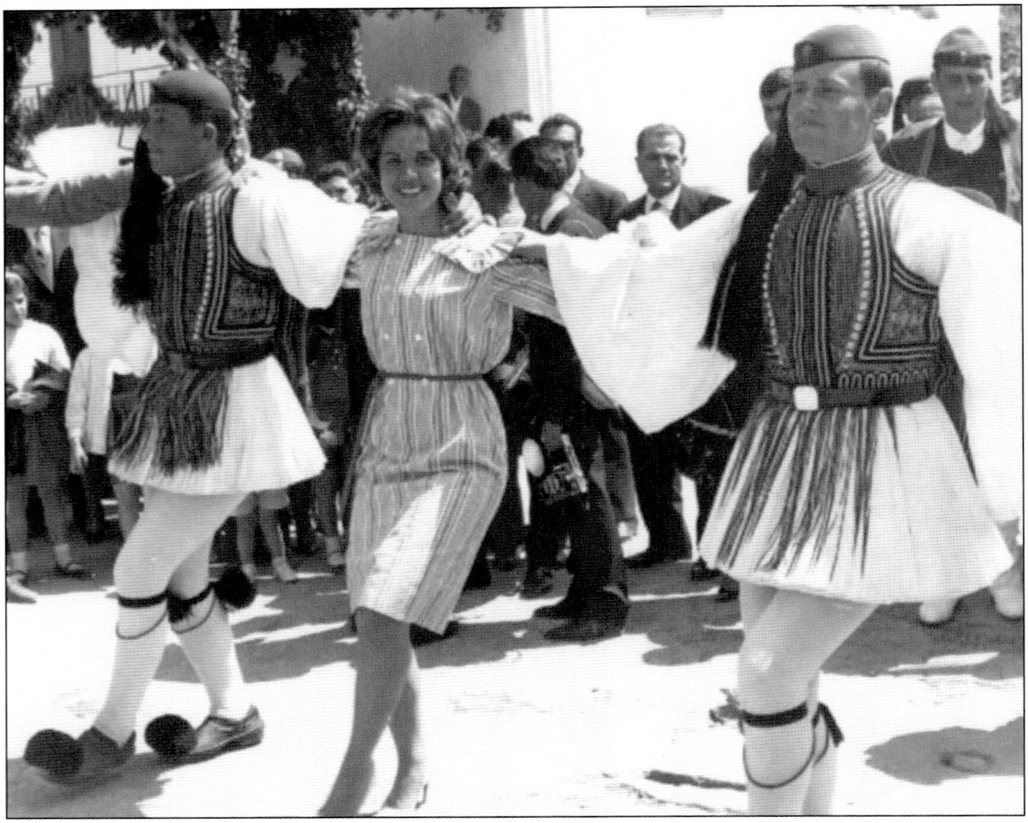

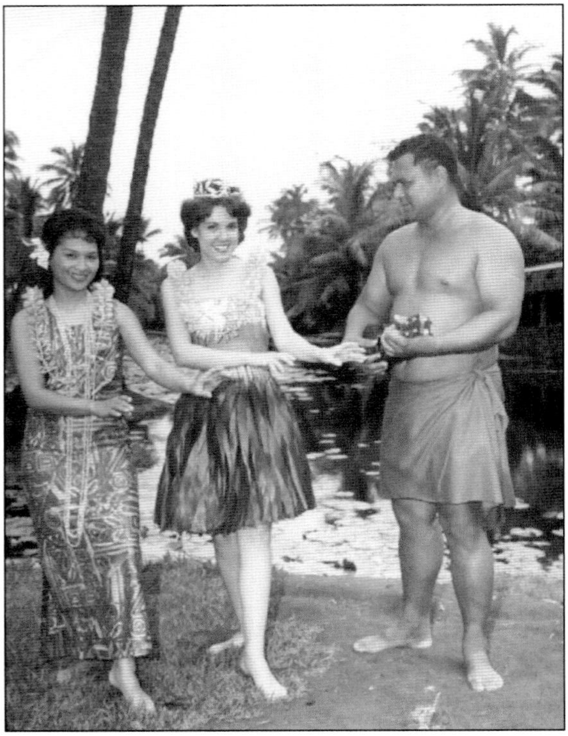

Judith Bryant's favorite memories of her year as rhododendron queen include dancing for the king and queen of Greece in Athens and touring the Hawaiian Islands with the president of the International Lions Club. (Both, courtesy of Judy Bryant Umminger.)

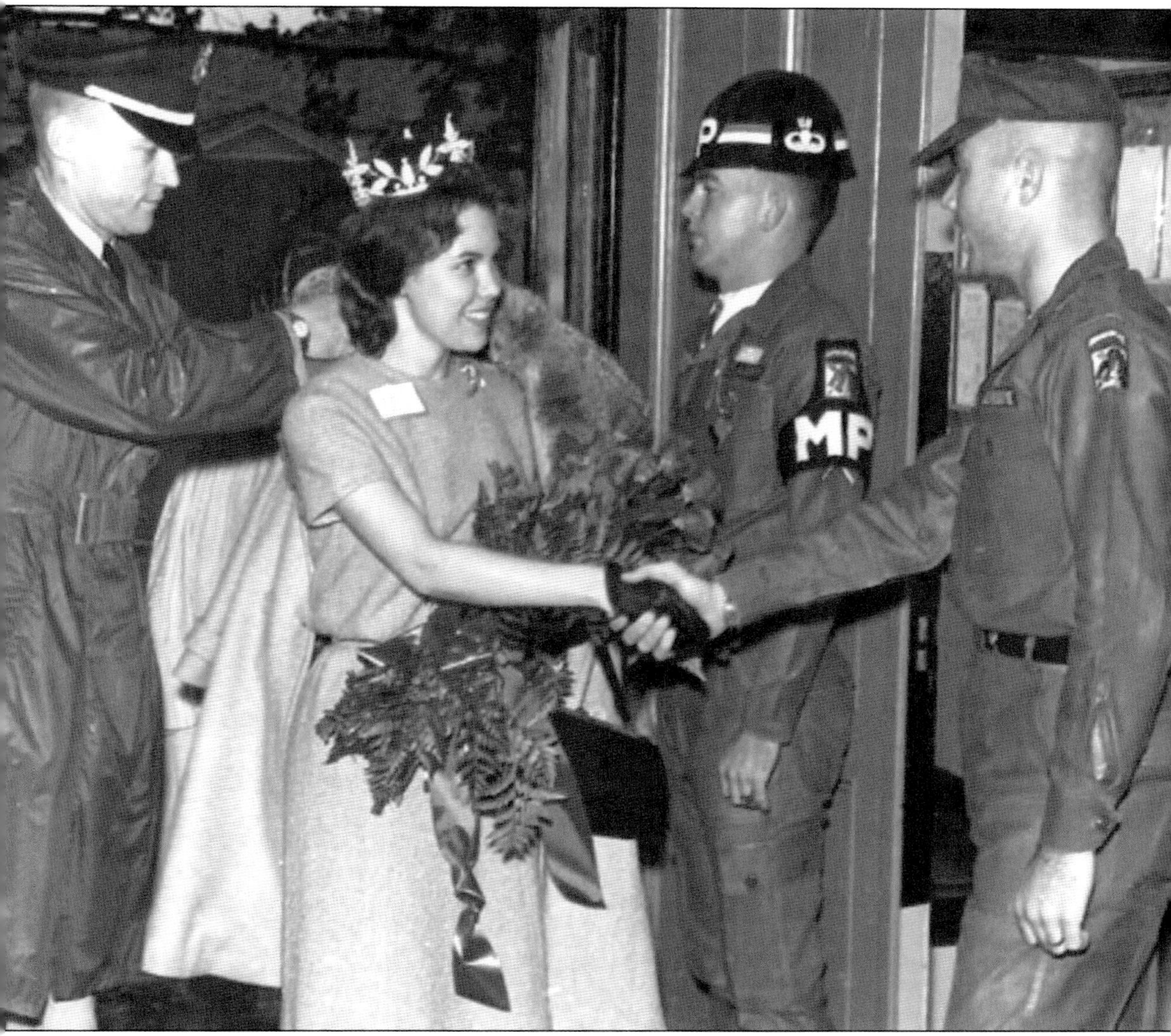

During her reign, Bryant had the privilege of visiting Fort Bragg. She is shown here being officially greeted by members of the military. Judy also led an Easter pilgrimage to the Holy Land and had an audience with the Pope in Vatican City. She danced on the *Lawrence Welk Show* and helped to announce the delayed transmission of the Tournament of Roses Parade on Hawaiian television. Judy received the Founder's Award from the American Heart Association for outstanding performance as the Triangle Research queen of hearts and did commercials promoting the Heart Association on television with Burl Ives. (Courtesy of Judith Bryant Umminger.)

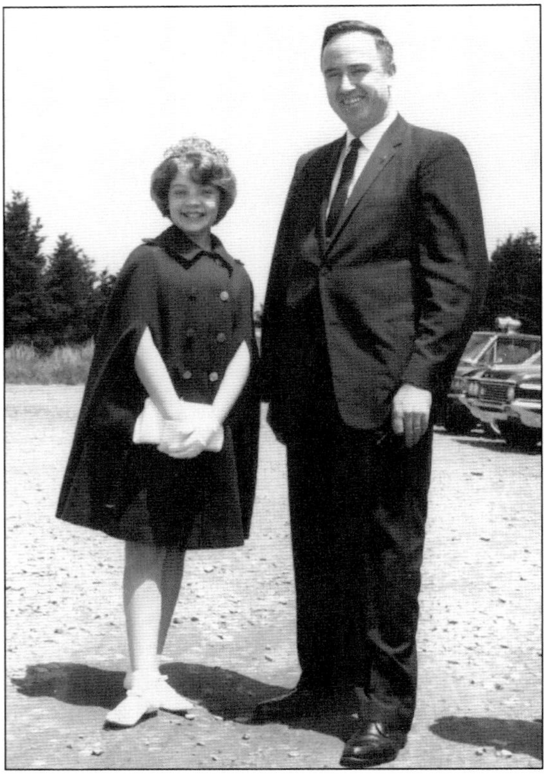

During the 1960s, the junior queens also began to take a more active role in promoting the festival. The 1966 junior queen, Sheryl Miller, poses with North Carolina lieutenant governor Bob Scott. He was also on hand to escort an ecstatic Jean Rhodes after she was announced the winner of the 1966 pageant, along with Harold Little (left), representative of the Miss Mecklenburg pageant. Scott went on to be elected governor in 1968. (Both, courtesy of the Barron Collection.)

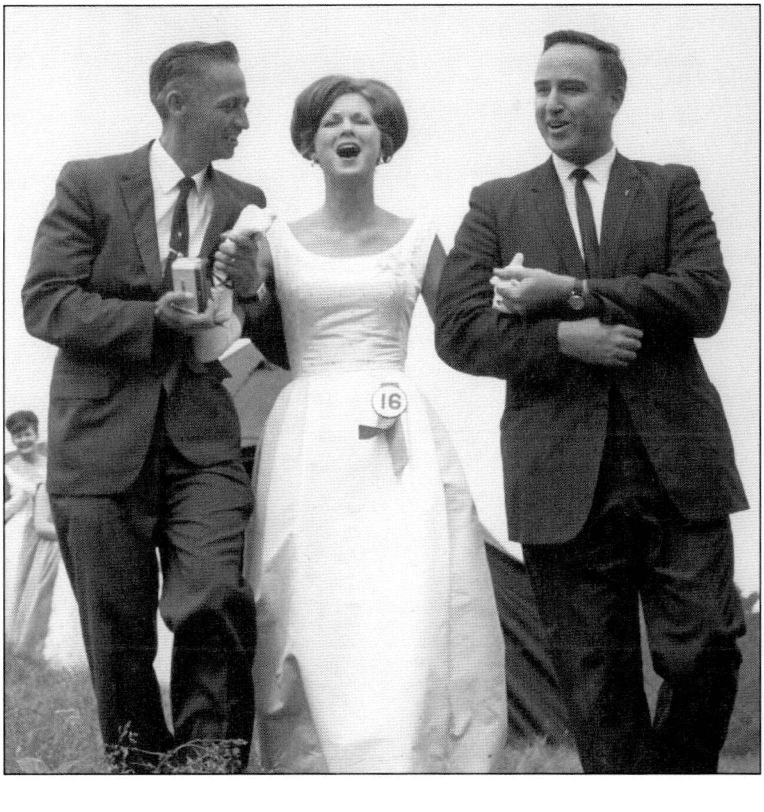

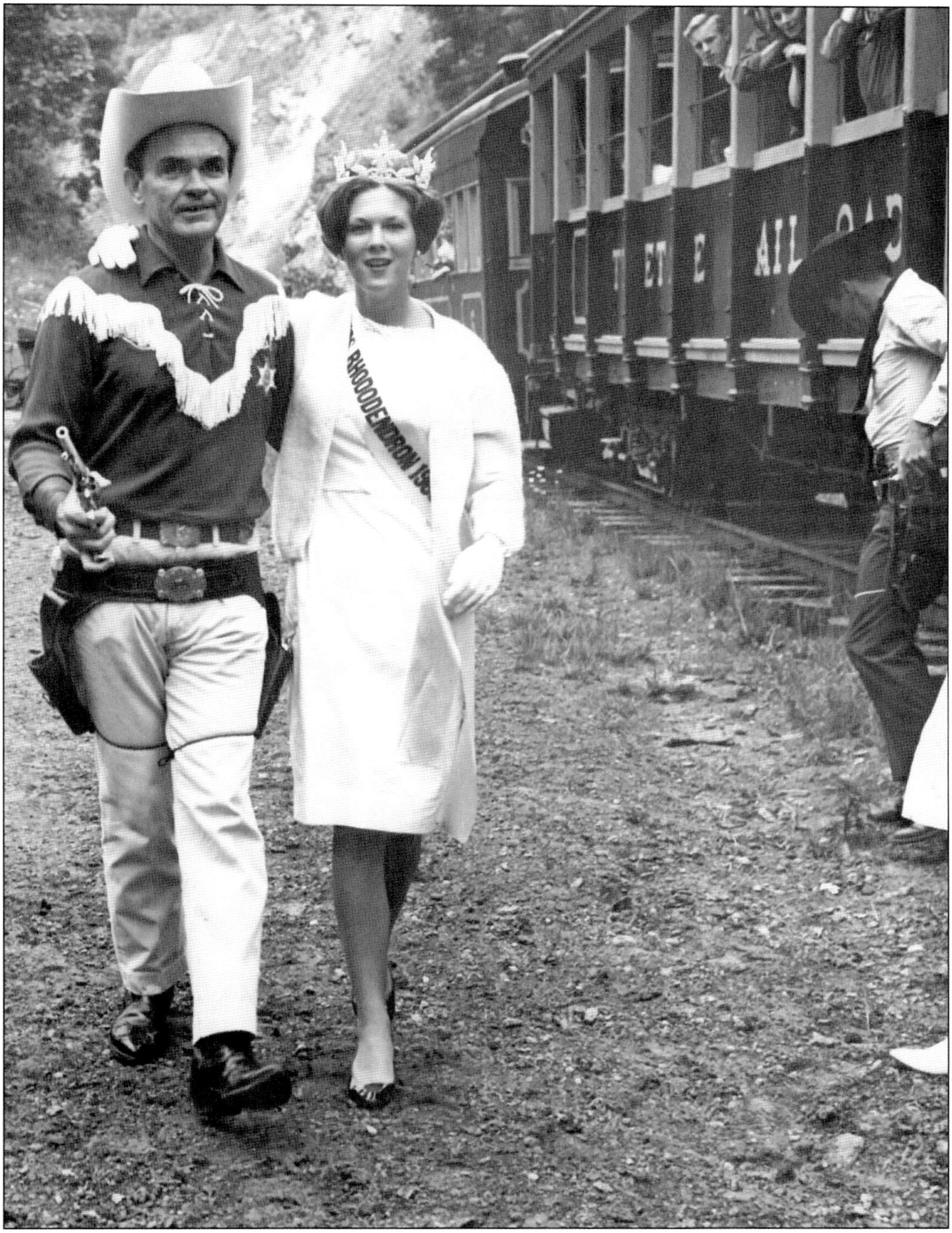

For many years, the newly crowned rhododendron queens made one of their first official appearances at Tweetsie Railroad in Blowing Rock, followed by a tour of Grandfather Mountain. Fred Kirby, a well-known radio and television personality was always on hand at Tweetsie to offer a personal greeting. Jean Rhodes, the 1966 North Carolina rhododendron queen, got friendly with him after he rescued her from an attempted raid by Tweetsie Indians. (Courtesy of the Barron Collection.)

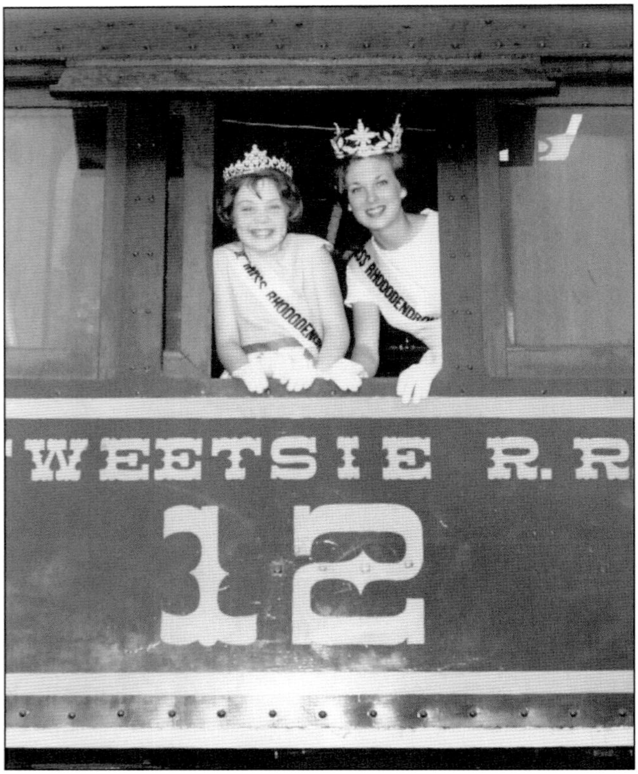

Jean Rhodes and Sheryl Miller enjoyed a ride on the Tweetsie train, even though, just a few years earlier, Betty Lawhon and Mary Gwen Graham were captured by one of the Tweetsie Indians. (Left, courtesy of the North Carolina Rhododendron Festival Collection; below, courtesy of Betty Lawhon Deviney.)

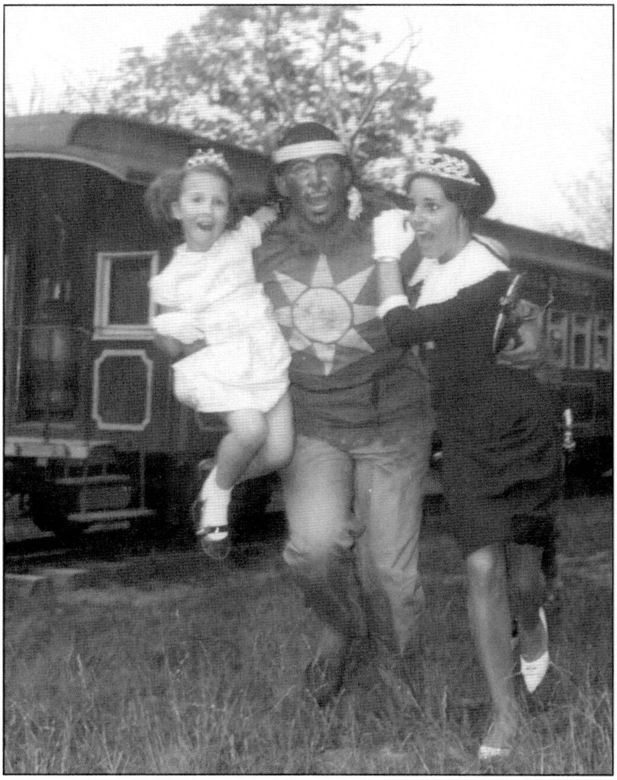

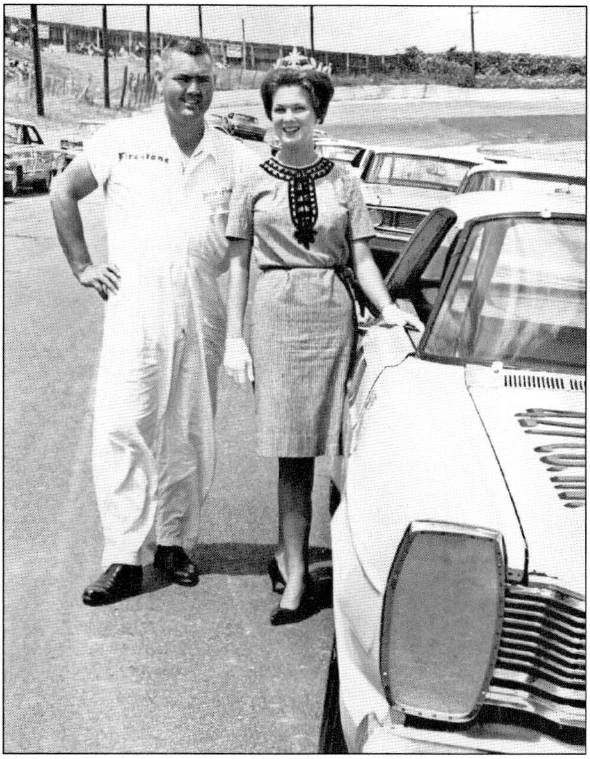

Jean Rhodes, the 1966 queen, had a very busy appearance schedule during her reign. While traveling across the state, representing North Carolina as both North Carolina rhododendron queen and Miss Variety Vacationland, she had the opportunity to meet race car drivers Junior Johnson (right) and Ned Jarrett (below). (Both, courtesy of the Barron Collection.)

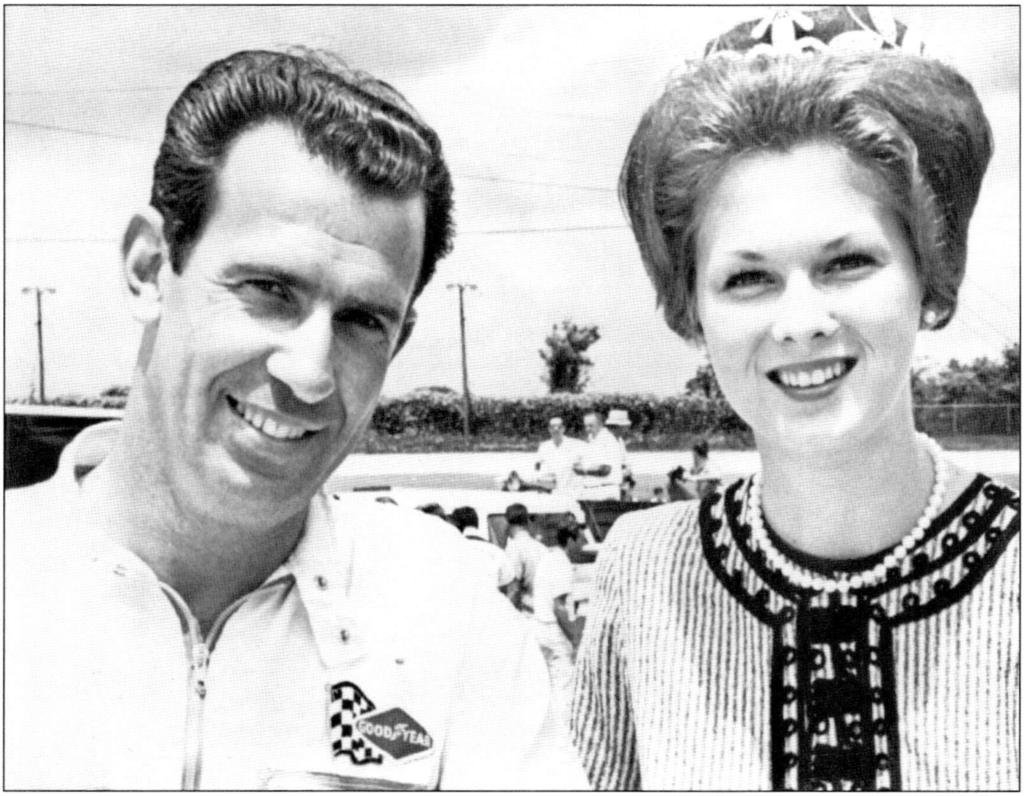

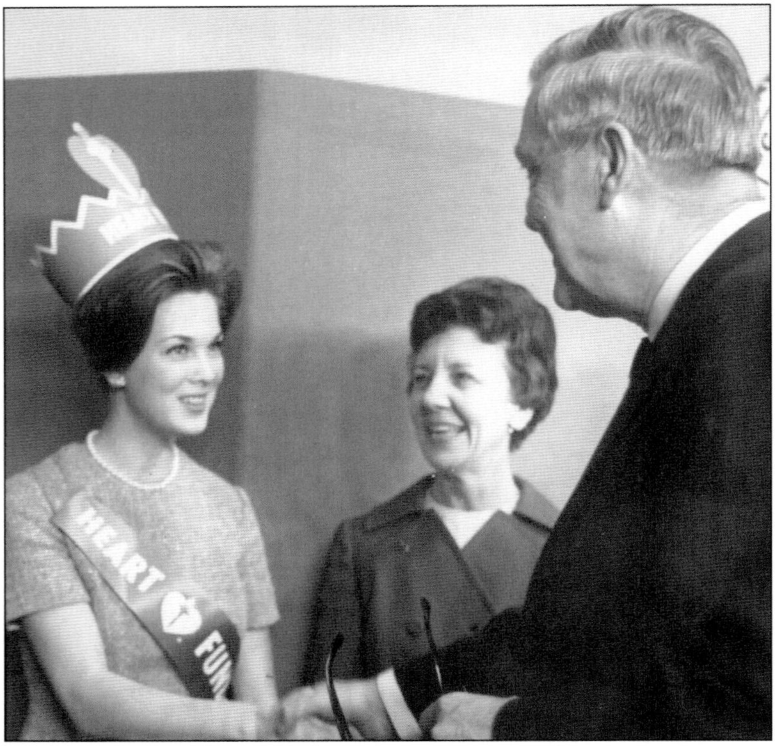

During her year's reign, Jean Rhodes was a spokesperson for the North Carolina Heart Association. She was honored at the charity's dance, held at the University of North Carolina at Chapel Hill, and was also an honored guest at the annual North Carolina Heart Association meeting. She had the opportunity to meet with Gov. Dan Moore and his wife, Jeanelle. (Both, courtesy of the Barron Collection.)

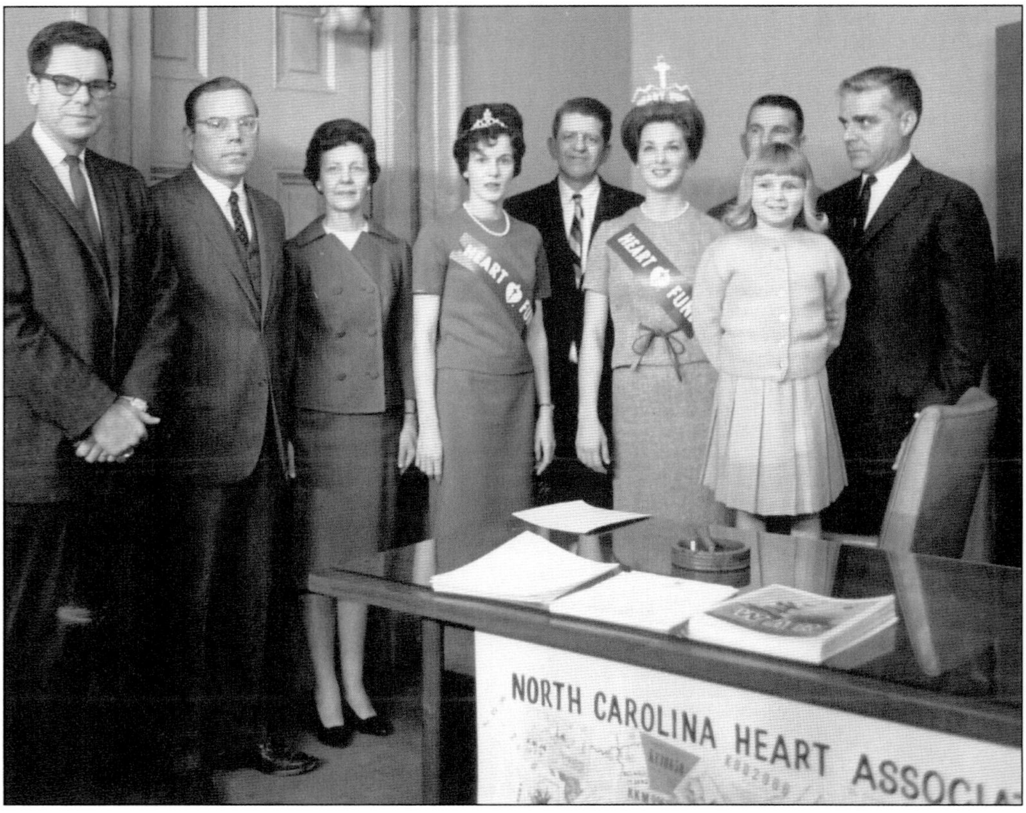

Rhodes was also a featured guest during a promotional taping at the television studios of WSJS, interviewed during the broadcast by promotional director Reese Felts. Felts had served as a pageant judge for the rhododendron festival, helping to select Rhodes as queen. (Courtesy of the Barron Collection.)

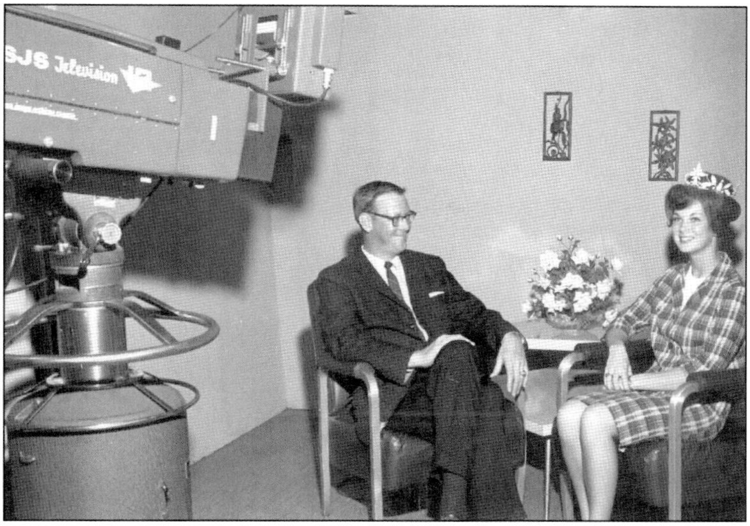

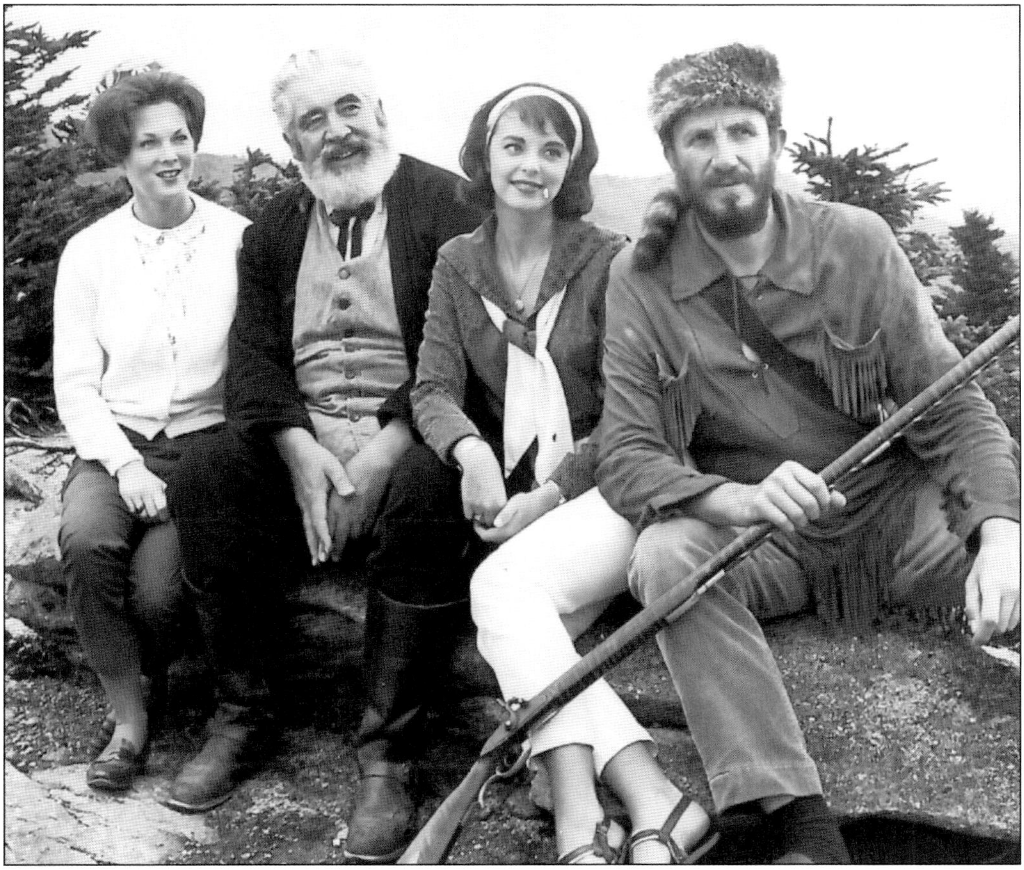

Jean Rhodes made an official appearance in Boone, North Carolina, during a presentation of the outdoor drama *Horn in the West*. She is pictured here with the play's actors, including Charles Elledge in the role of Reverend Sims. (Courtesy of the Barron Collection.)

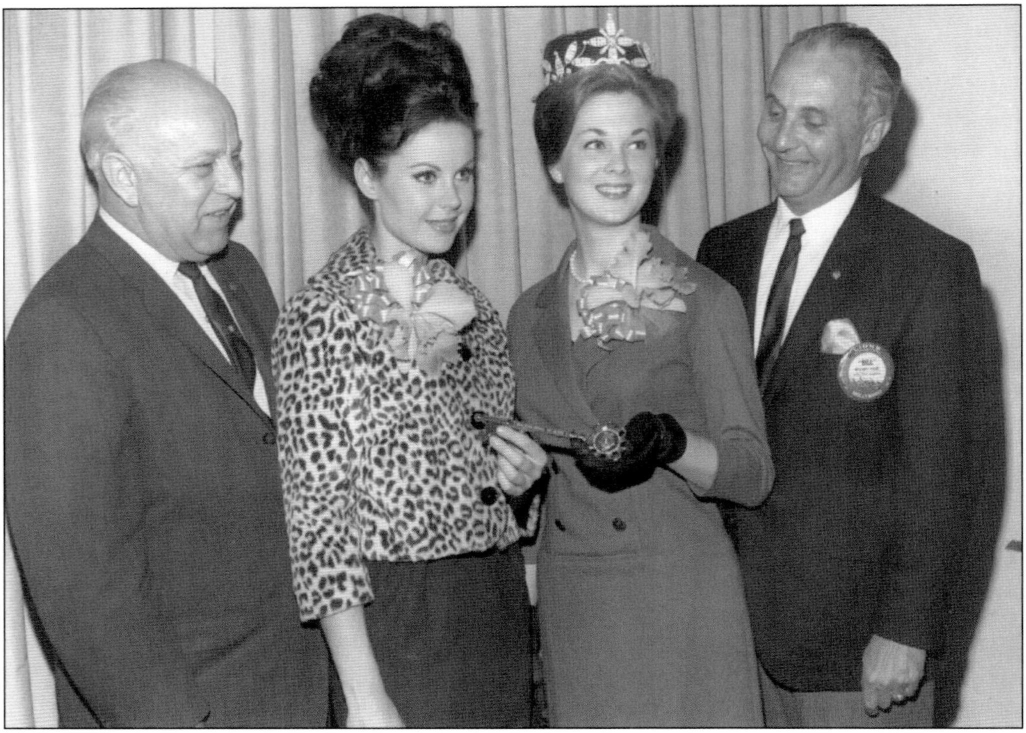

As an ambassador for North Carolina and a representative of the Bakersville Lions Club, 1966 queen Jean Rhodes had the opportunity to travel to California, where she was presented with a key to Hollywood and honored by members of the Hollywood Lions Club. (Courtesy of the Barron Collection.)

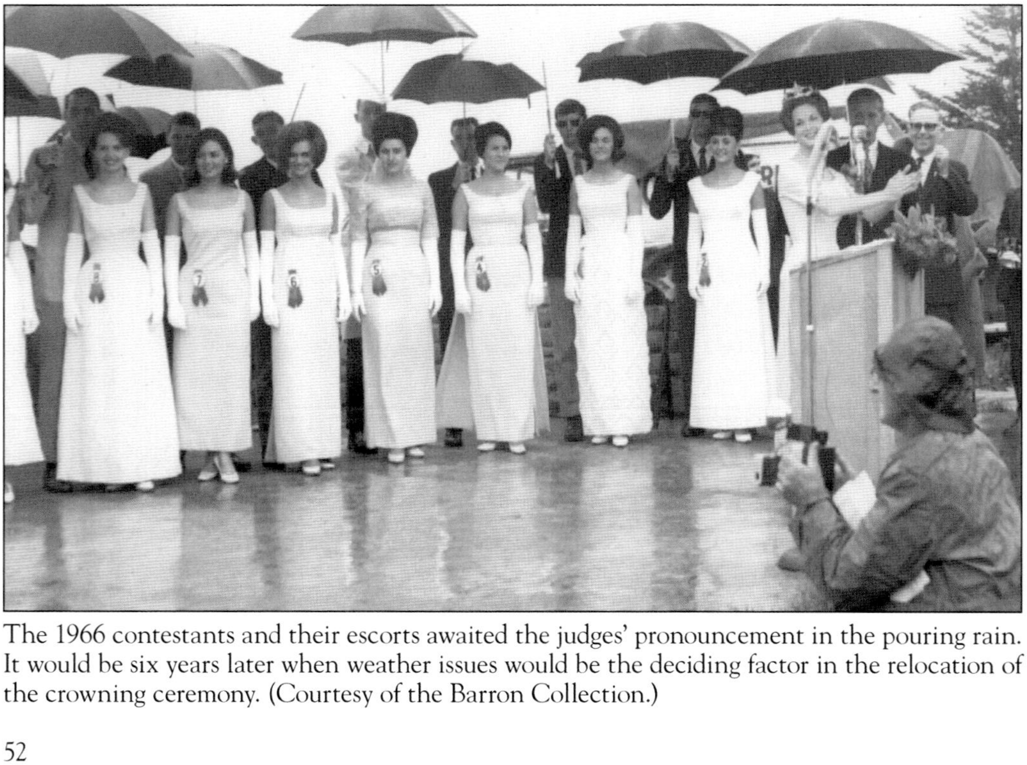

The 1966 contestants and their escorts awaited the judges' pronouncement in the pouring rain. It would be six years later when weather issues would be the deciding factor in the relocation of the crowning ceremony. (Courtesy of the Barron Collection.)

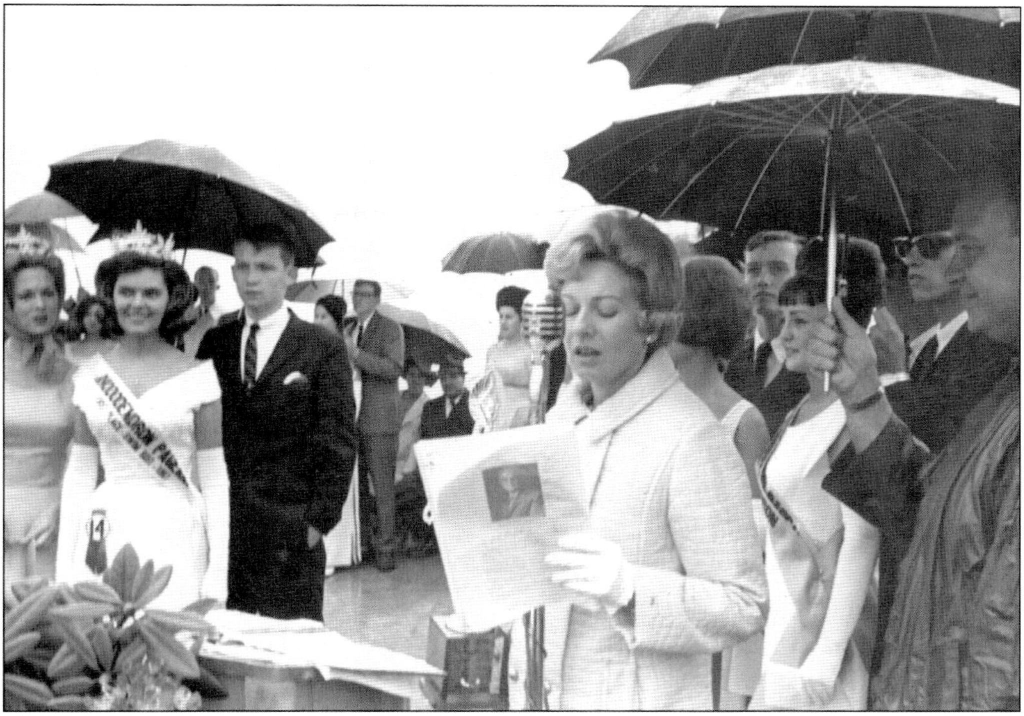

In 1966, the crowning of the new rhododendron queen took place atop beautiful Roan Mountain during extremely inclement weather. Louise Broyhill, a former Miss North Carolina and wife of Congressman Broyhill, presented Linda Blair, the newly crowned 1967 queen, with her scholarship while outgoing queen, Jean Rhodes, looked on. (Courtesy of the Barron Collection.)

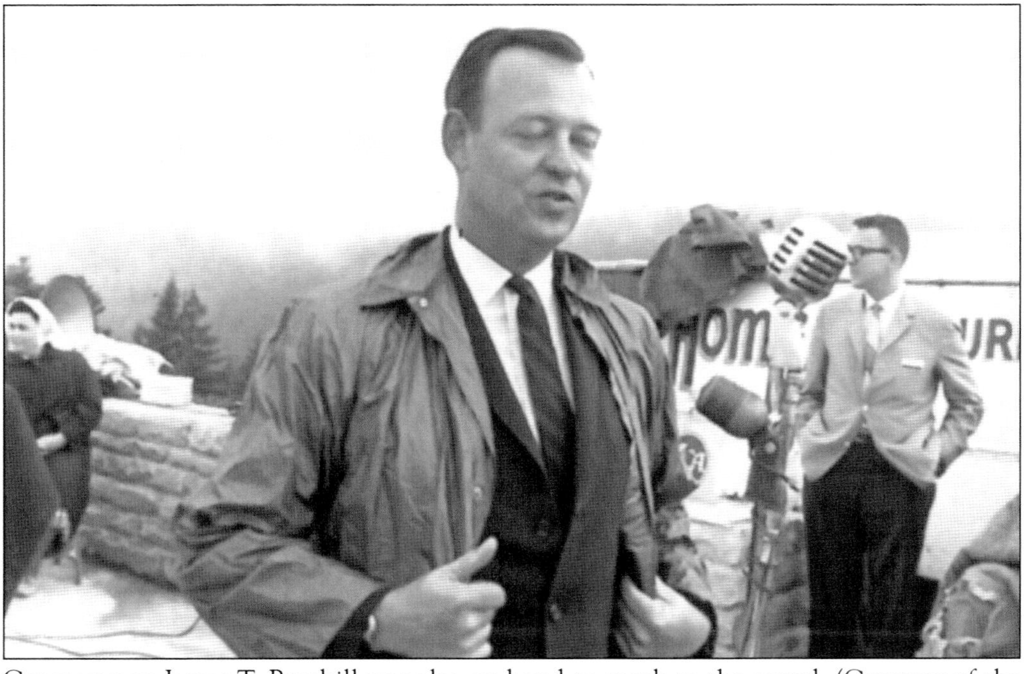

Congressman James T. Broyhill was also on hand to speak to the crowd. (Courtesy of the Barron Collection.)

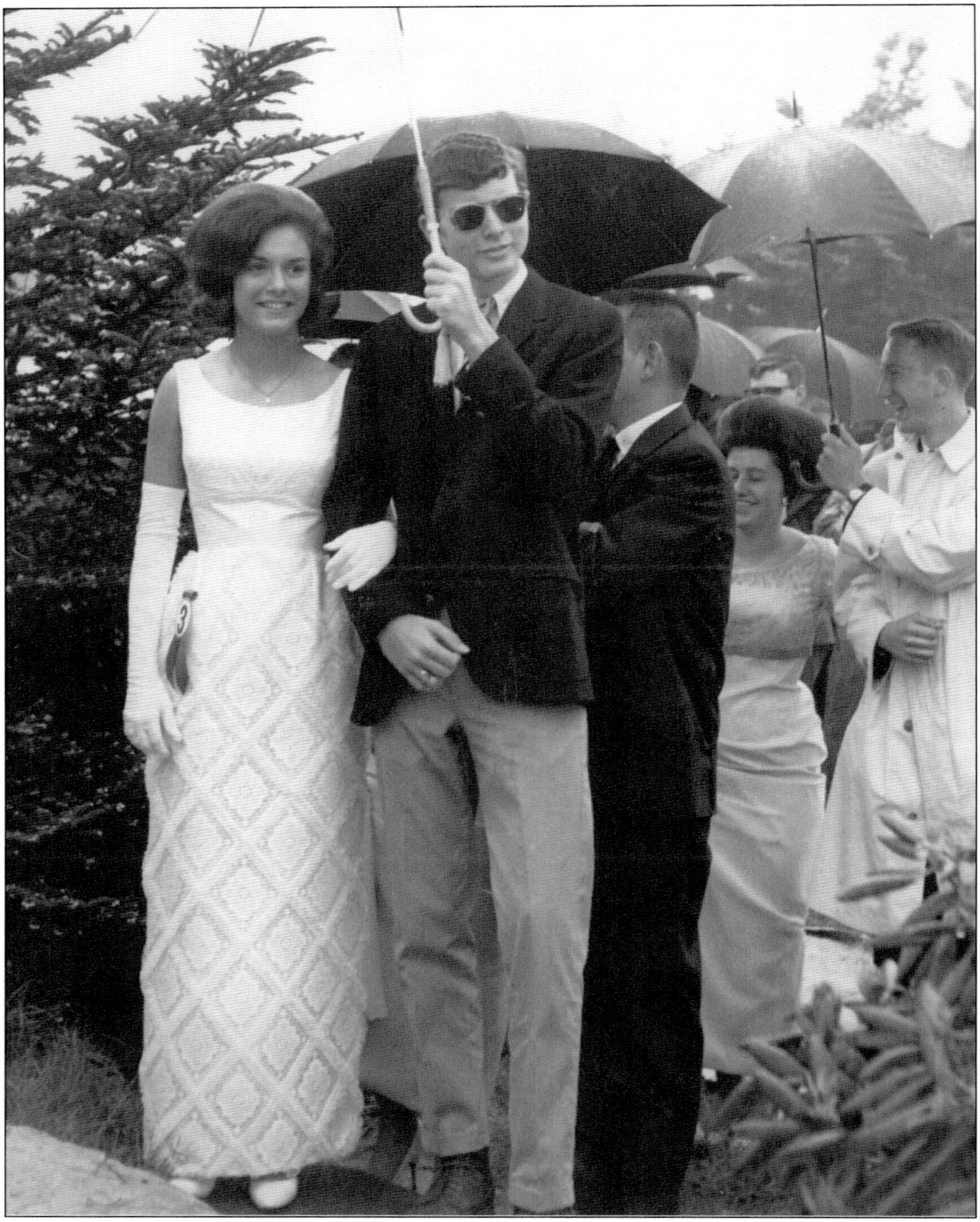

During the 1960s, the happiest young men in Bakersville were those chosen as escorts for visiting queens and contestants vying for the title of North Carolina rhododendron queen. They were present during the festivities atop Roan Mountain as well as the Rhododendron Ball, held later the same evening. (Courtesy of the Barron Collection.)

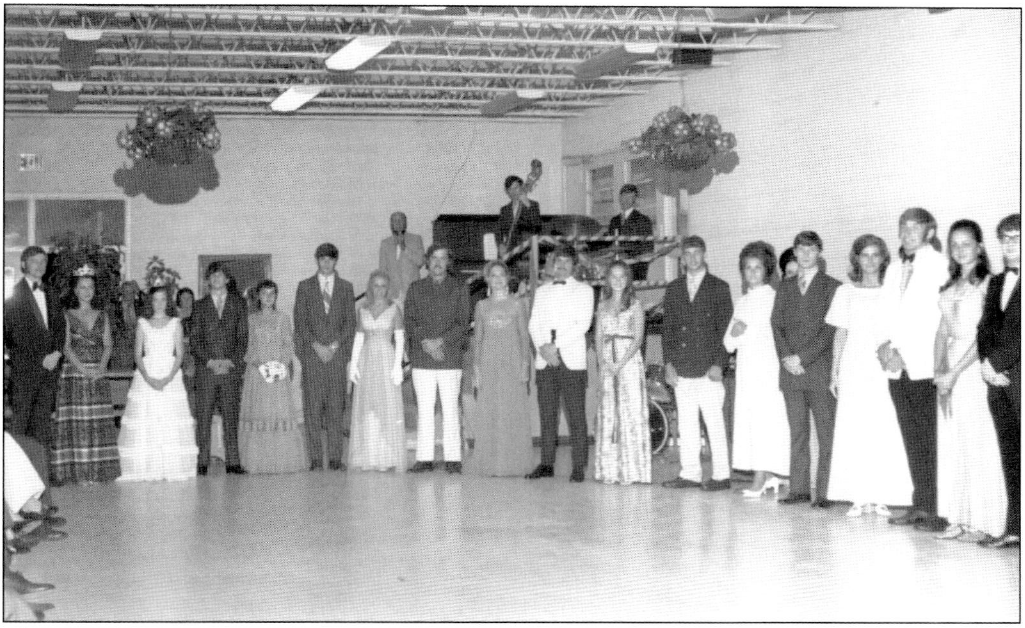

The same fortunate young men who served as escorts for visiting queens and contestants during the crowning ceremony on Roan Mountain had the pleasure of accompanying the contestants to the annual Rhododendron Ball, an event that was discontinued in the 1970s. (Courtesy of Barron and Wilson Collections.)

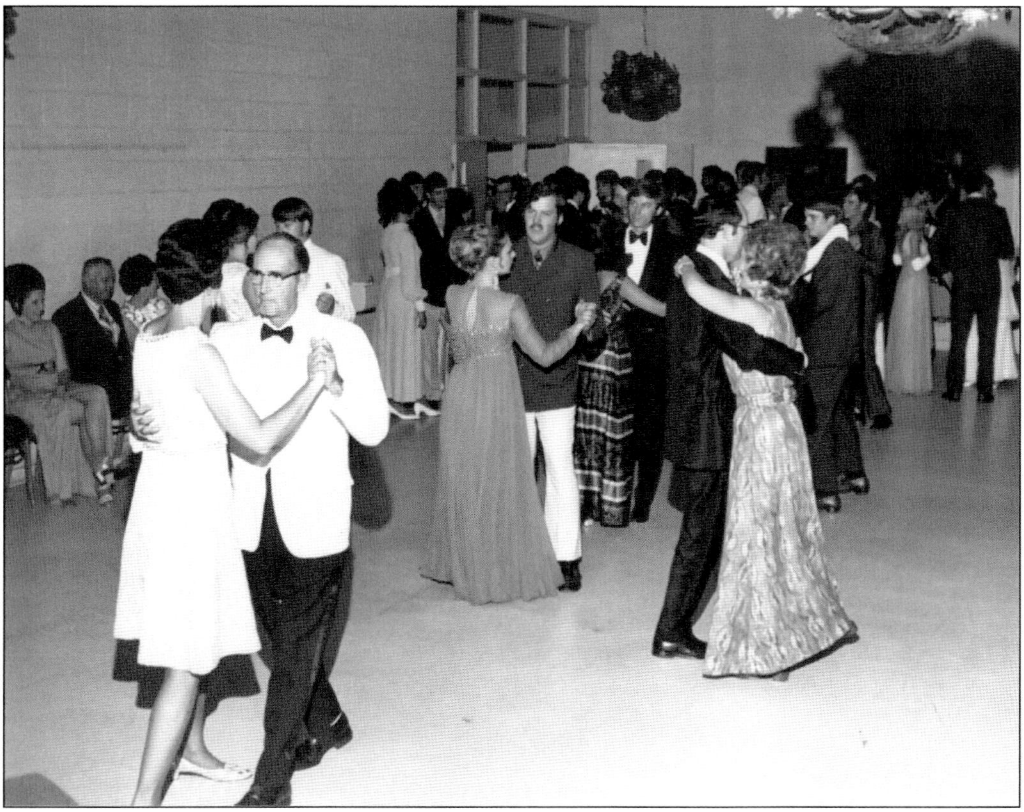

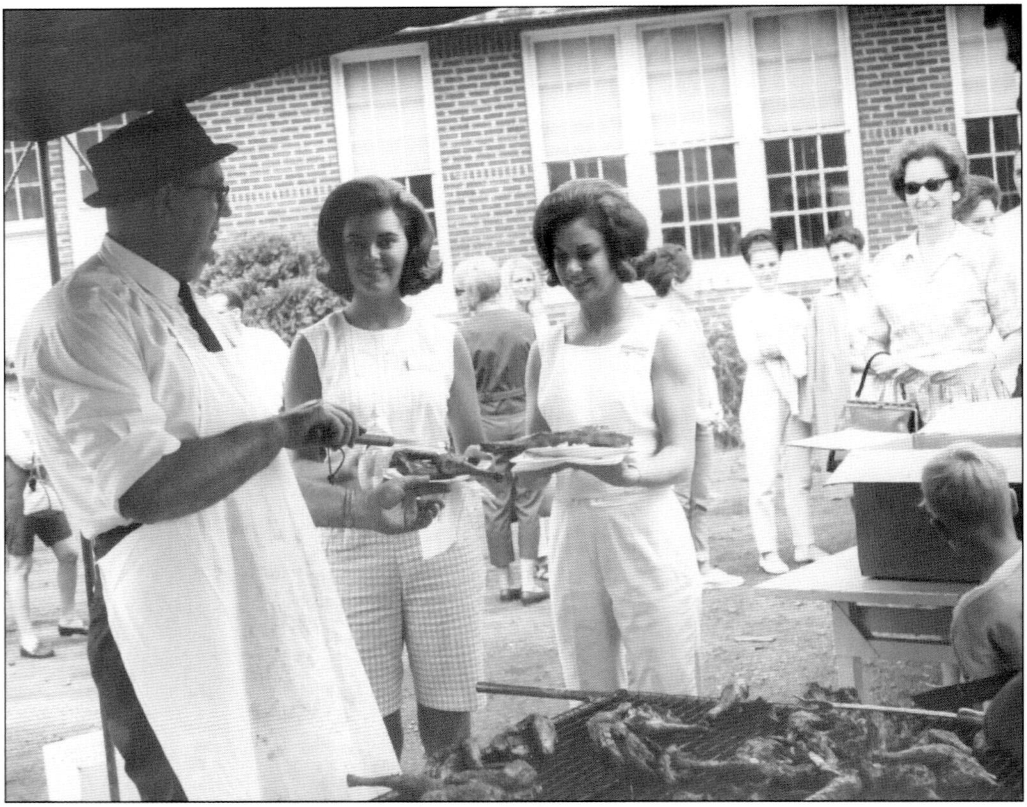

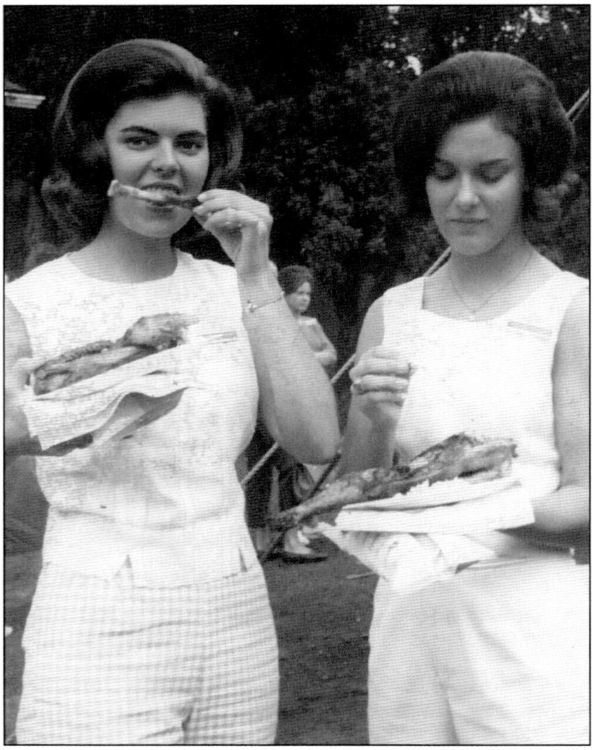

For a period of time in the 1960s, Holly Farms Famous Bar-b-q Chicken sponsored a luncheon for contestants, chaperones, and festival officials. Contestant Linda Blair (left), who would ultimately be the winner of the pageant, enjoys a tasty meal with her fellow contestants. (Above, courtesy of Theresa Matthews; left, courtesy of the Barron Collection.)

The 1967 queen, Linda Blair, participated in a number of parades during her year's reign. One in particular was memorable because the hosts of the event provided her with a float that featured the misspelling "rhododendren." (Courtesy of the Wilson Collection.)

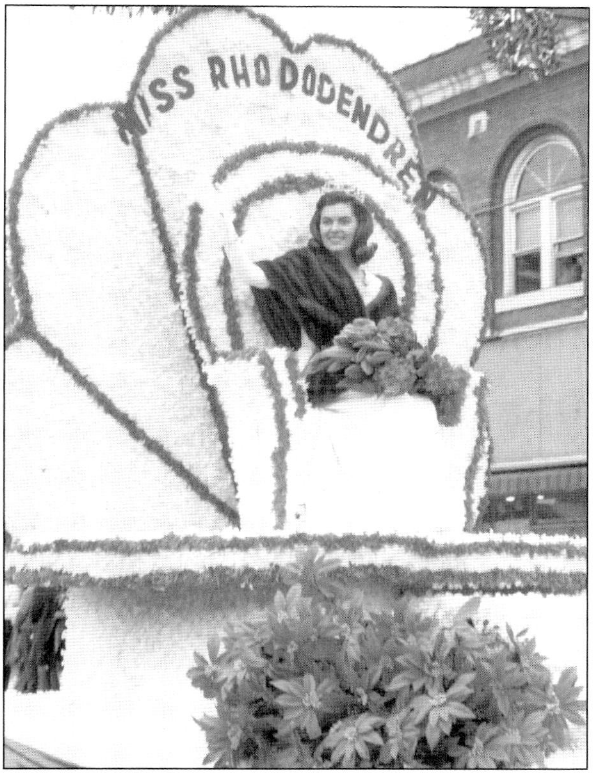

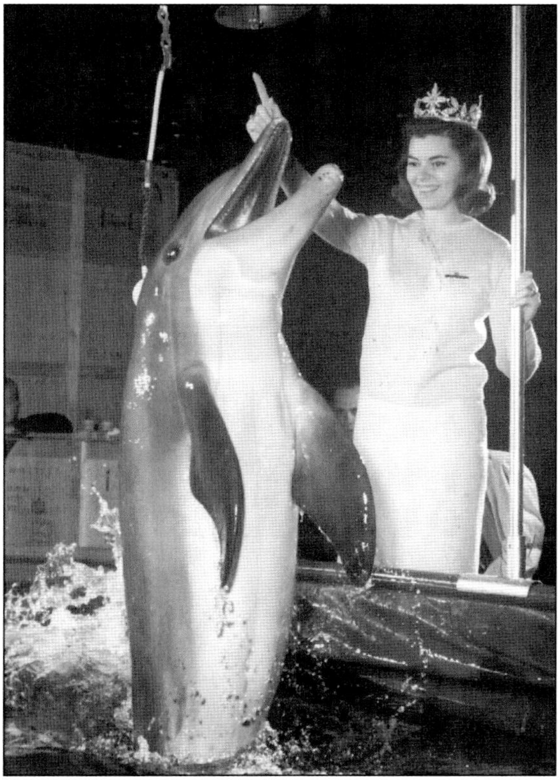

In February 1967, Linda Blair represented North Carolina at the International Travel and Vacation Show held in Jacksonville, Florida, where an estimated 75,000 people visited the North Carolina Variety Vacationland booth. Blair assisted Sinbad, a 325-pound trained porpoise in ringing the bell that officially opened the show. (Courtesy of the Barron Collection.)

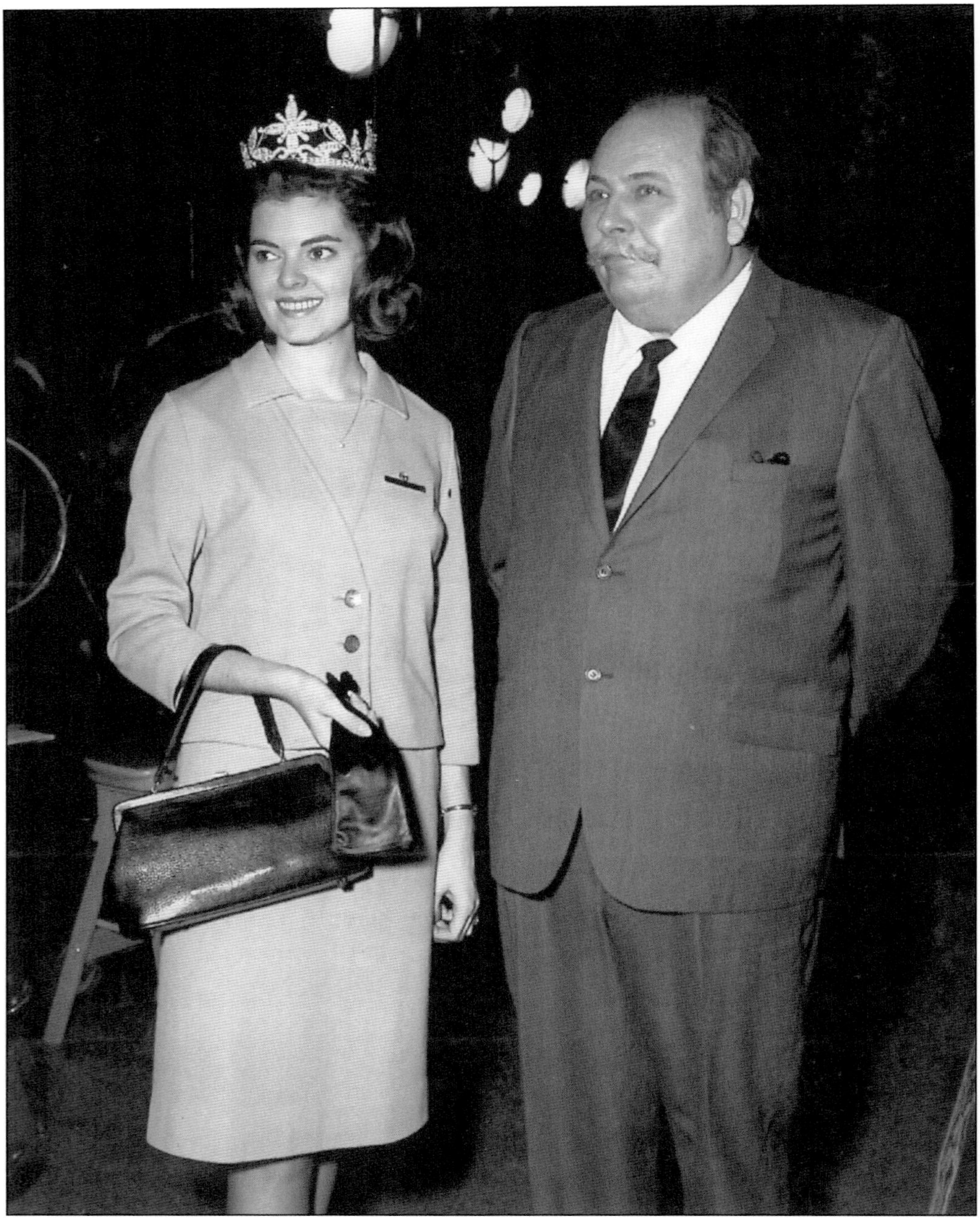

Linda Blair, the 1967 North Carolina rhododendron queen, traveled extensively while representing Bakersville and Roan Mountain. During a trip to California, she was a guest on the set of the Disney movie *Blackbeard's Ghost*, starring Peter Ustinov, Dean Jones, and Suzanne Pleshette. While on set, Linda had the opportunity to meet Dan Stahl, author of the book upon which the movie was based. (Courtesy of the Barron Collection.)

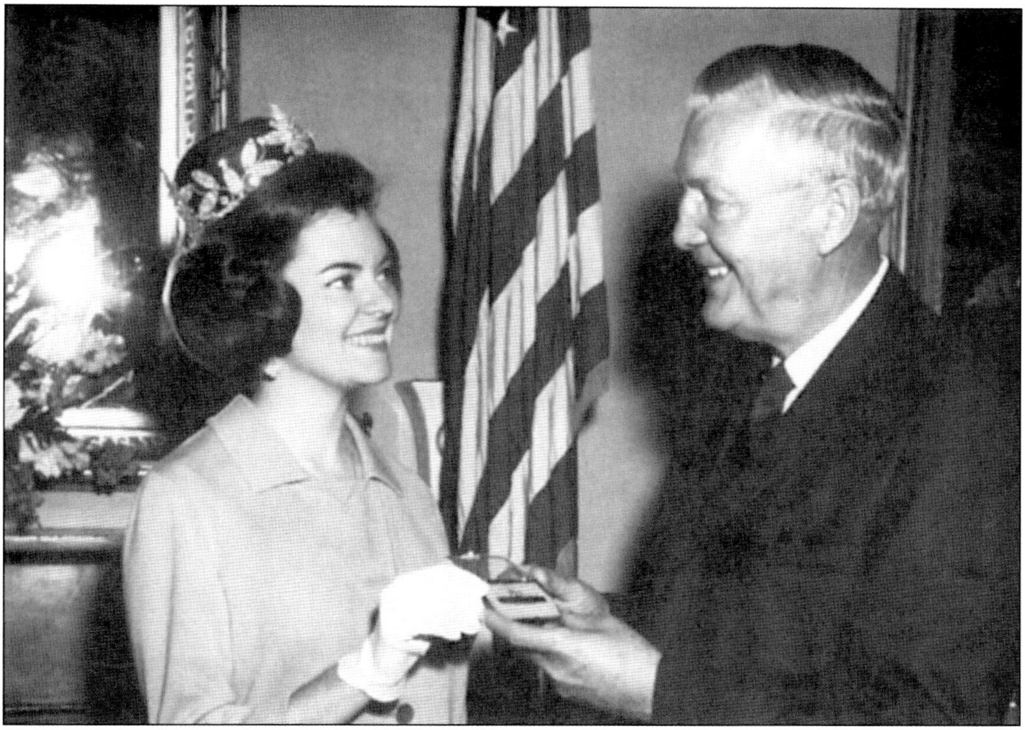

Blair was invited to the state capitol in Raleigh, where Gov. Dan K. Moore officially presented the North Carolina rhododendron queen of 1967 pin to her. (Courtesy of the Barron Collection.)

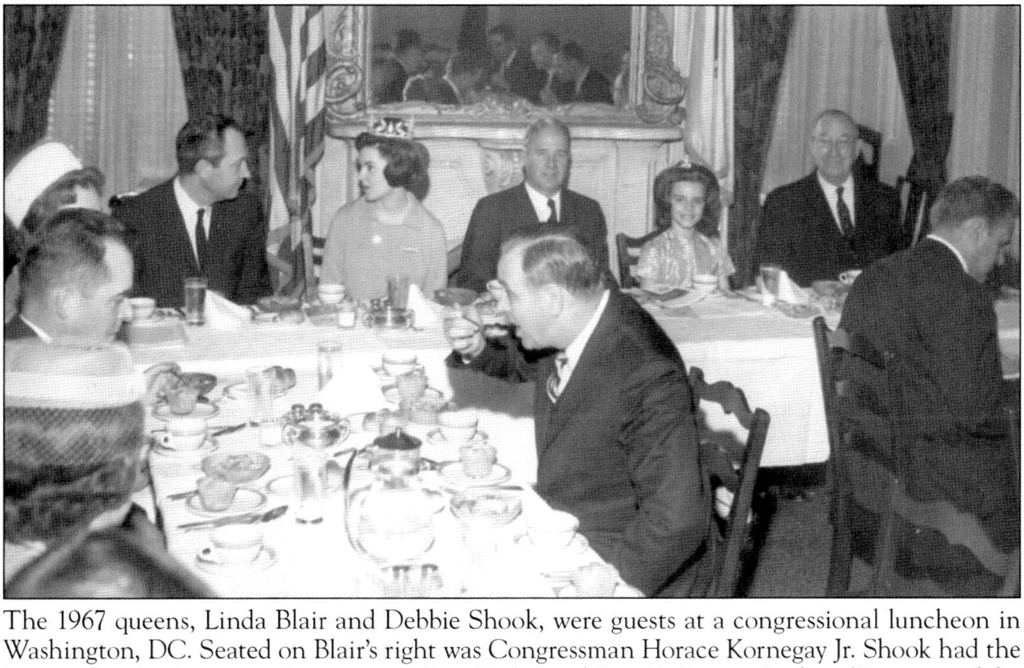

The 1967 queens, Linda Blair and Debbie Shook, were guests at a congressional luncheon in Washington, DC. Seated on Blair's right was Congressman Horace Kornegay Jr. Shook had the honor of sitting between Congressman Roy Taylor and Sen. B. Everett Jordan. (Courtesy of the Barron Collection.)

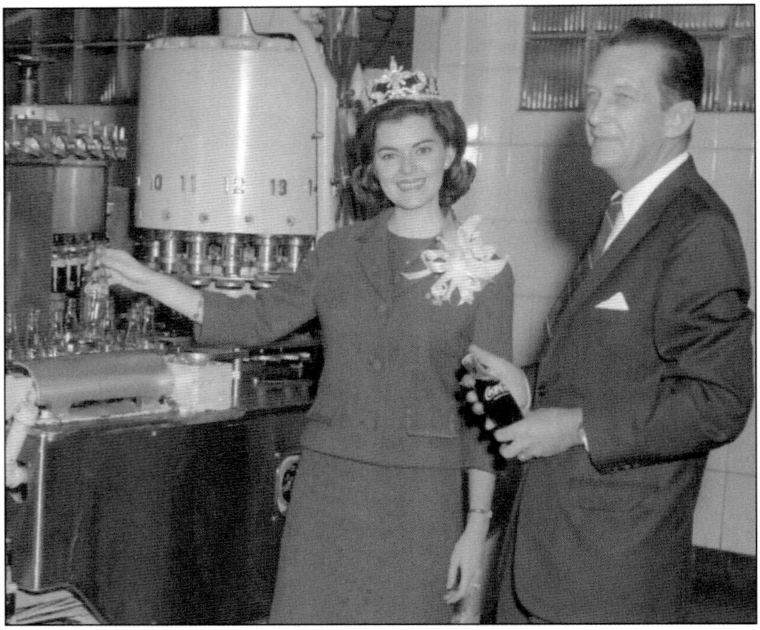

Coca-Cola Bottling Company, a major contributor to the rhododendron festival in the 1960s, sponsored many of the queens' appearances across the Southeast. Linda Blair had the honor of meeting Paul Warlick, president of Coca-Cola, while touring one of the bottling plants. (Courtesy of the Barron Collection.)

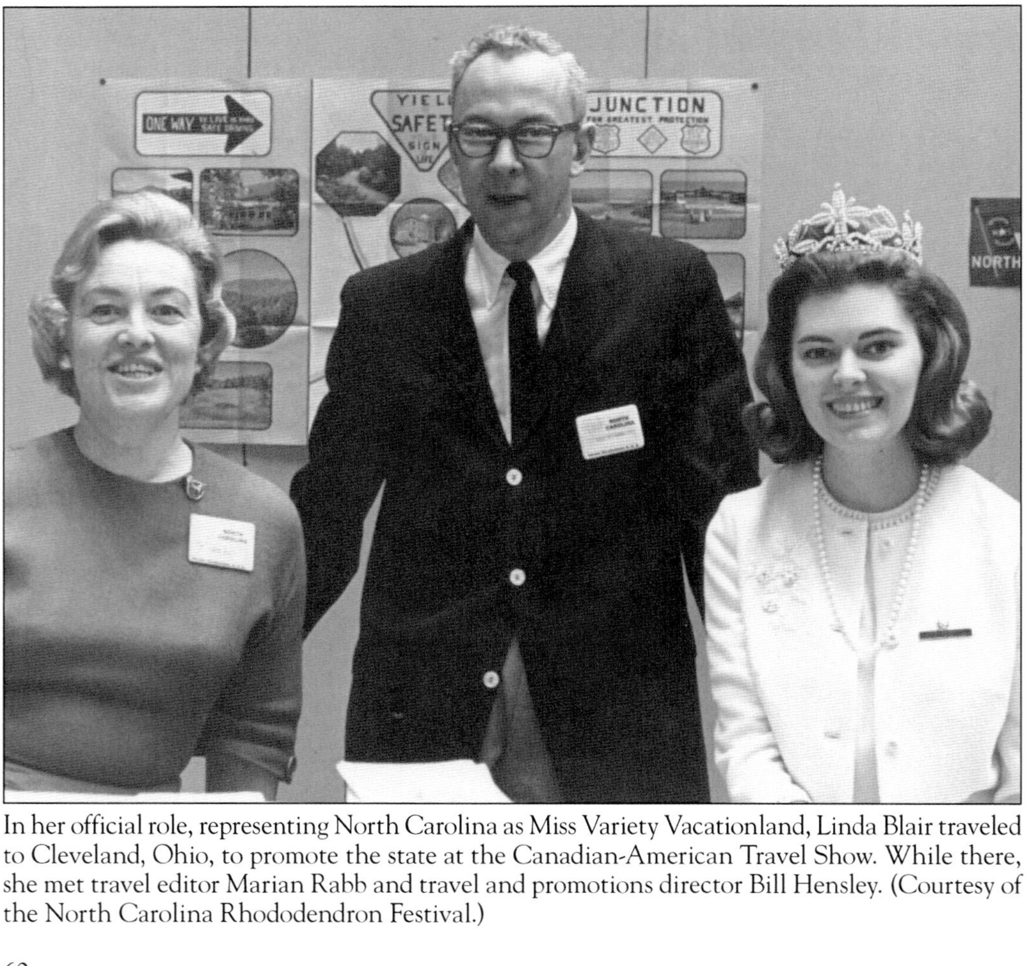

In her official role, representing North Carolina as Miss Variety Vacationland, Linda Blair traveled to Cleveland, Ohio, to promote the state at the Canadian-American Travel Show. While there, she met travel editor Marian Rabb and travel and promotions director Bill Hensley. (Courtesy of the North Carolina Rhododendron Festival.)

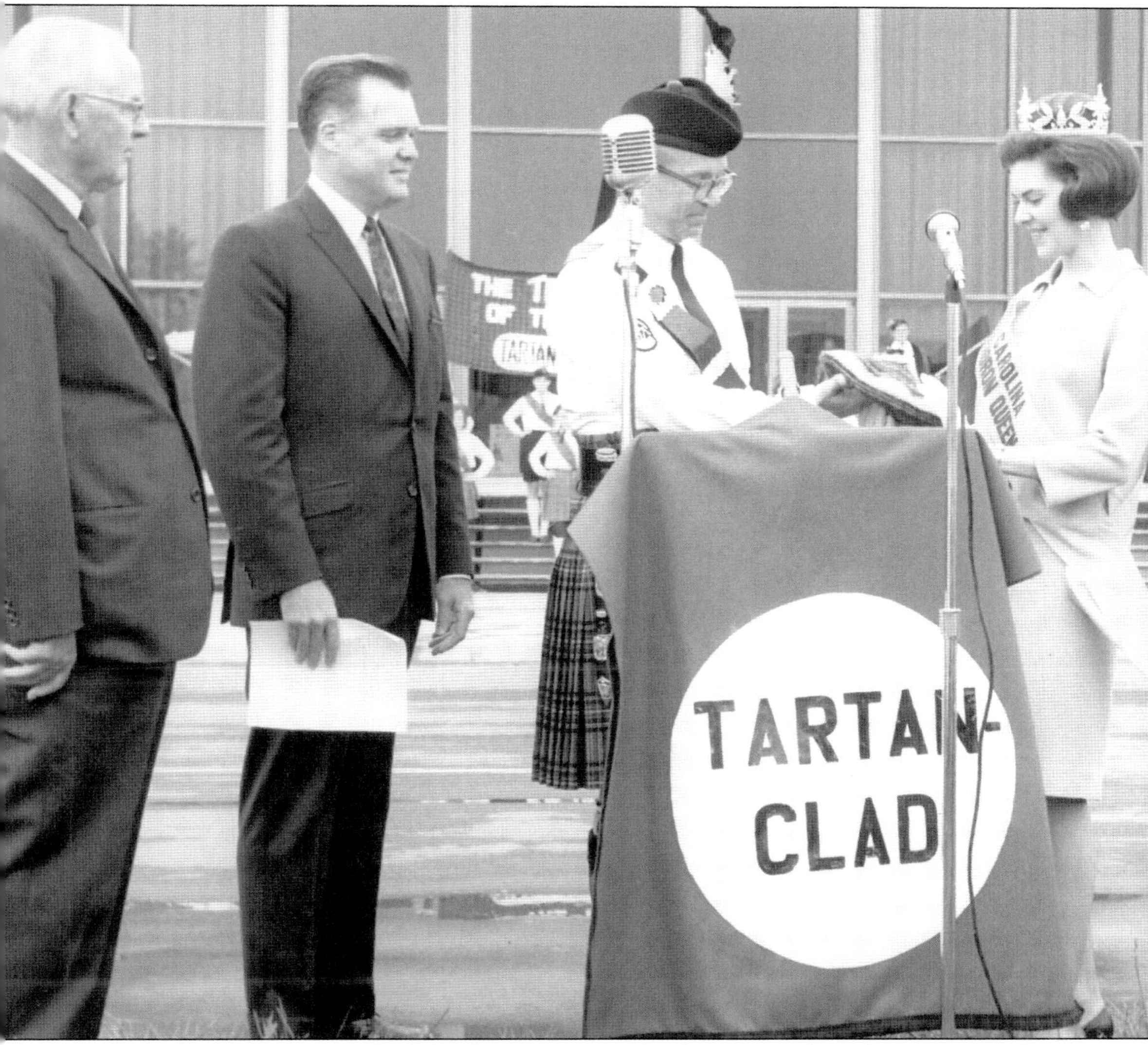

Shortly after being crowned rhododendron queen, Linda Blair was made an honorary member of the Charlotte Caledonian Pipe Band. J.E. Broyhill (far left), president of Broyhill Furniture Company, was present for the award. (Courtesy of the Barron Collection.)

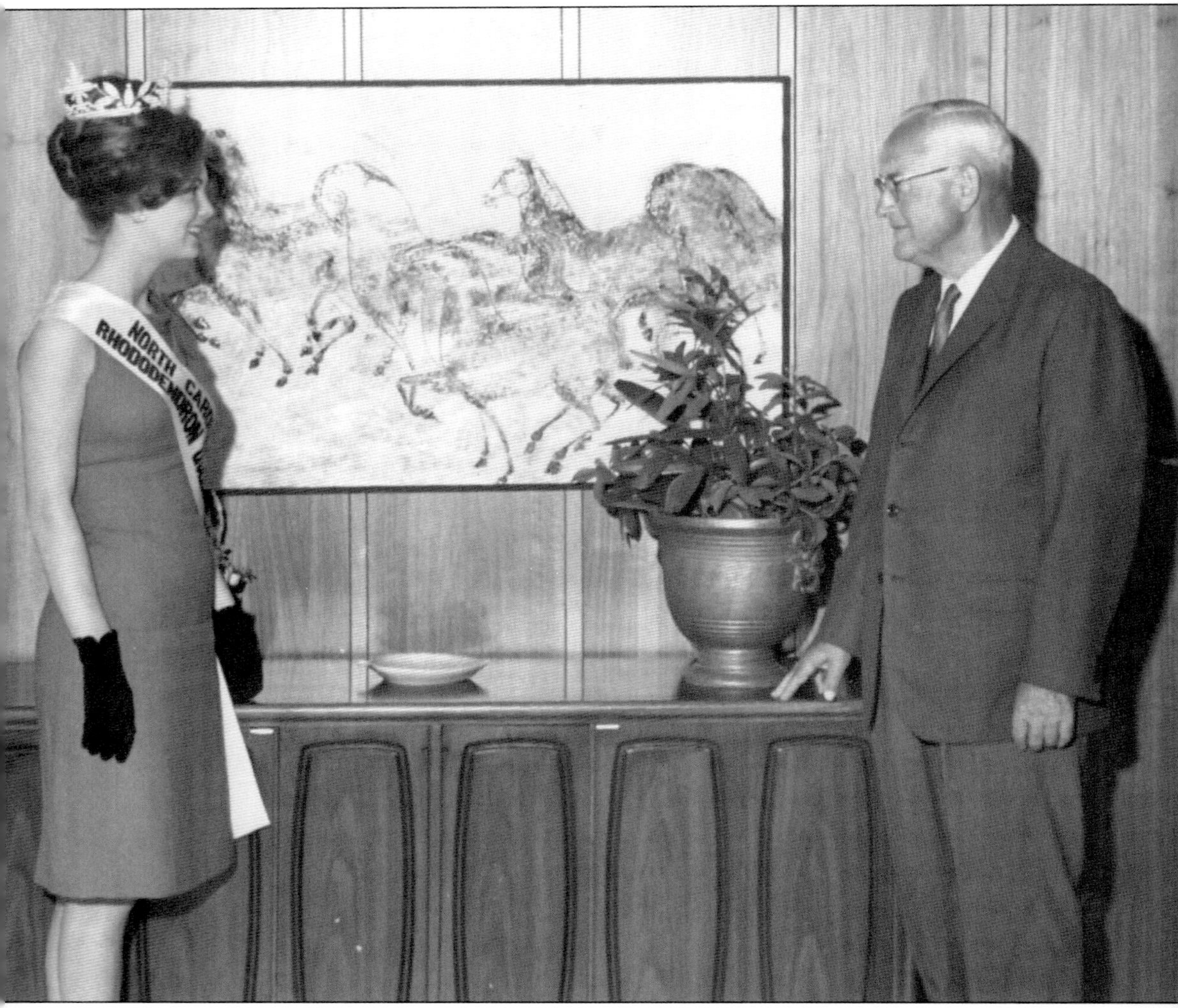

For many years, the Broyhill Foundation generously provided a $1,000 scholarship for the rhododendron queen. Jean Rhodes, the 1966 queen, had the opportunity to visit with J.E. Broyhill while touring Broyhill Industries. He was a longtime advocate and supporter of higher education and the founder of the Broyhill Foundation. Broyhill passed away in 1988. (Courtesy of the Barron Collection.)

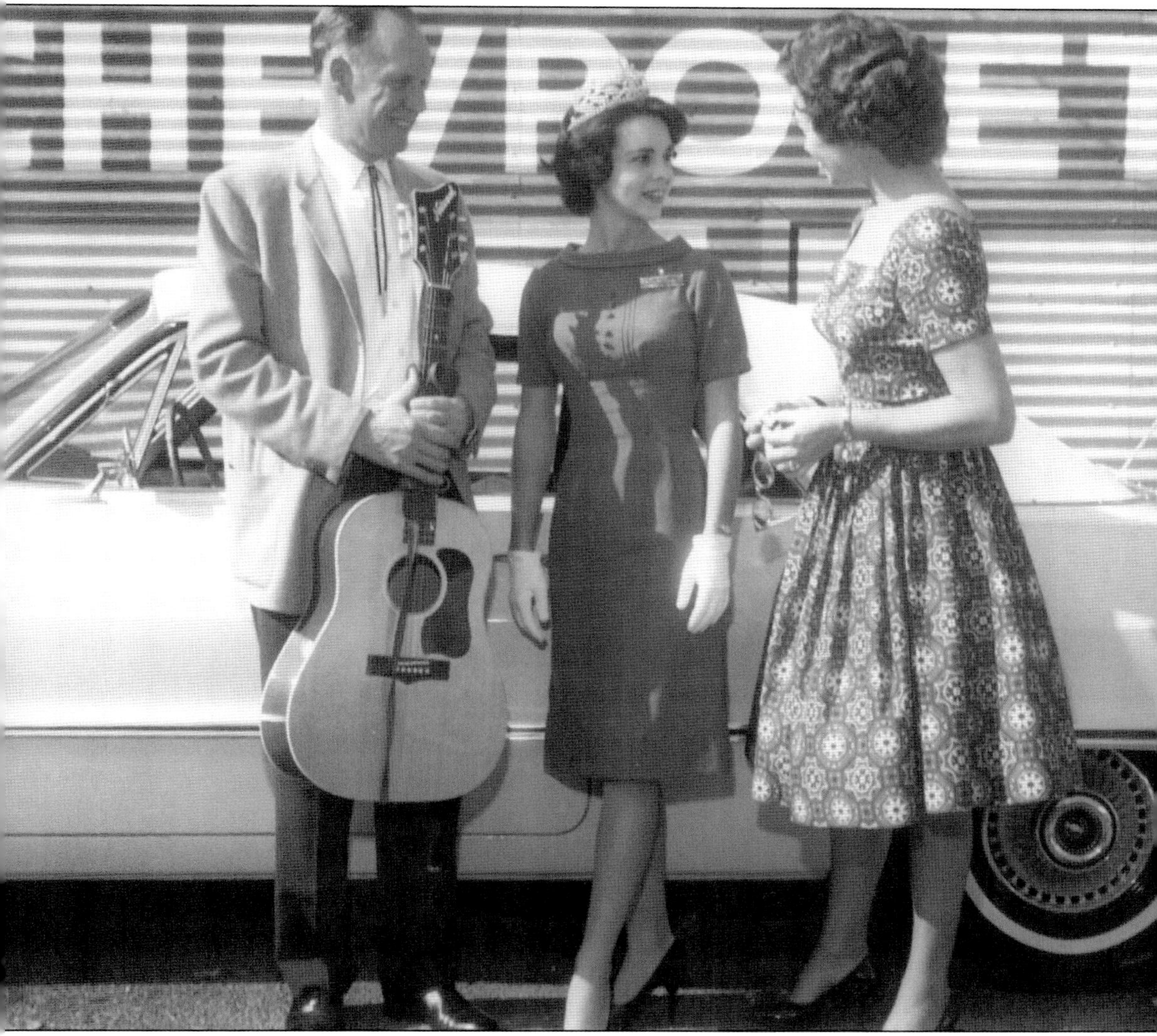

"On the lofty peaks of Roan, where the hand of God alone grew a garden such as man has seldom seen." These words are the opening lines of a song penned by singer and songwriter Scotty Wiseman in 1966, titled "Rhododendron Queen." Wiseman was half of the legendary country music team known as Lulu Belle and Scotty. They were one of the major county music acts of the 1930s and 1940s and were dubbed the "Sweethearts of Country Music." They were best known for writing the well-known and oft-recorded "Have I Told You Lately That I Love You?" The Wisemans are pictured here with Betty Rae Lawhon, the 1963 rhododendron queen. They were residents of neighboring Avery County and staunch supporters of the North Carolina Rhododendron Festival. The chorus of the song, which is now simply called "The Rhododendron Song," is still sung each year during the crowning of the new rhododendron queen: "She's the queen of Rhododendron. She's the fairest of the fair. On her cheeks the blush of beauty, like the blossoms rich and rare. And her smile is like the sunrise from a lofty mountain seen. Let the whole world sing the praises of our Rhododendron Queen." (Courtesy of Betty Lawhon Deviney.)

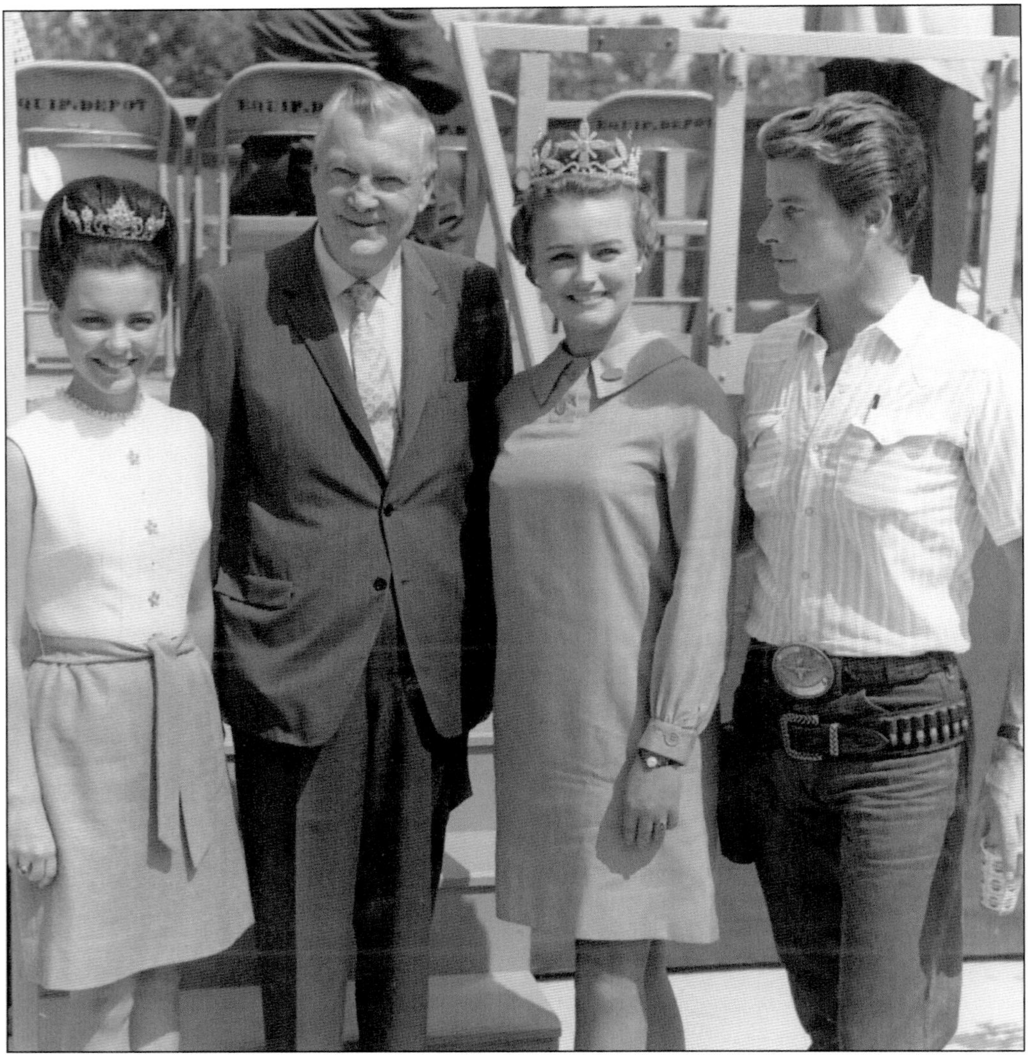

Brenda Heath, the North Carolina rhododendron queen of 1969, had the opportunity to meet with North Carolina governor Dan K. Moore, who served from 1965 to 1969. Also pictured is actor Peter Brown (far right), who was best known for his roles in the television westerns *Lawman* and *Laredo*. Carol Ann Bass (far left), who would capture the title of North Carolina rhododendron queen two years later, was also present. (Courtesy of the Barron Collection.)

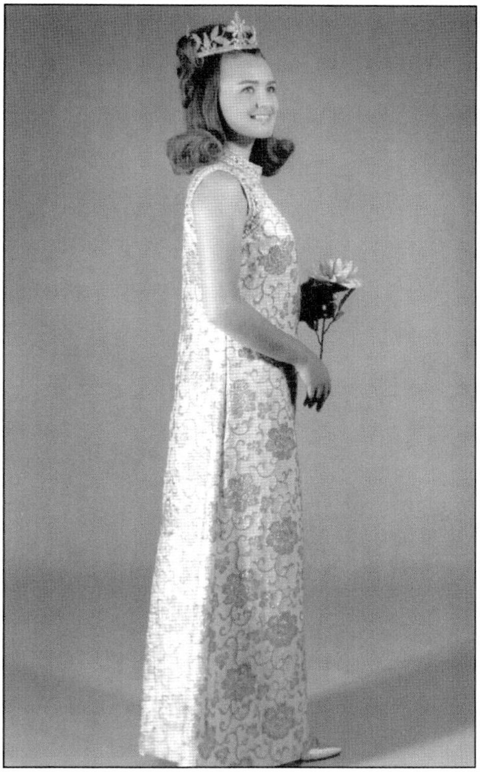

Brenda Faye Heath finished out the decade as the 1969 North Carolina rhododendron queen. Like her predecessors, she traveled far and wide—the fourth queen to receive the 100,000-mile trophy. She made more than 350 appearances worldwide. (Both, courtesy of the North Carolina Rhododendron Festival.)

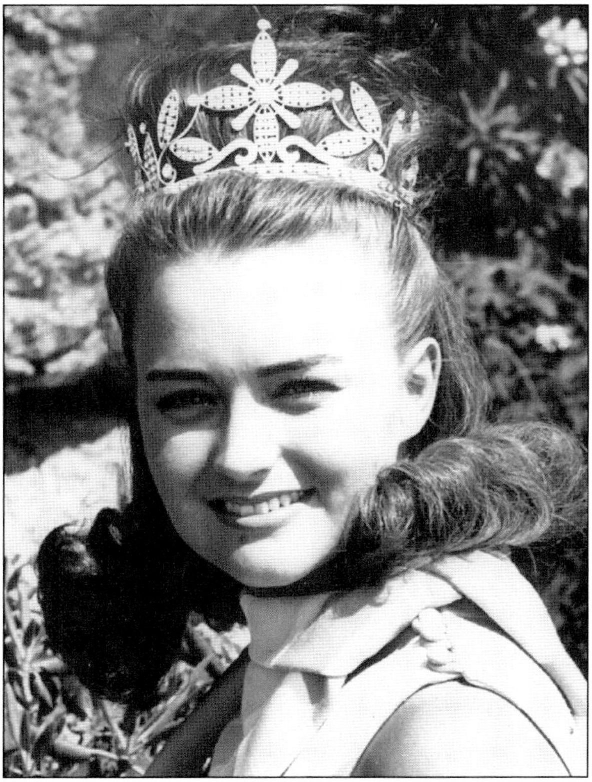

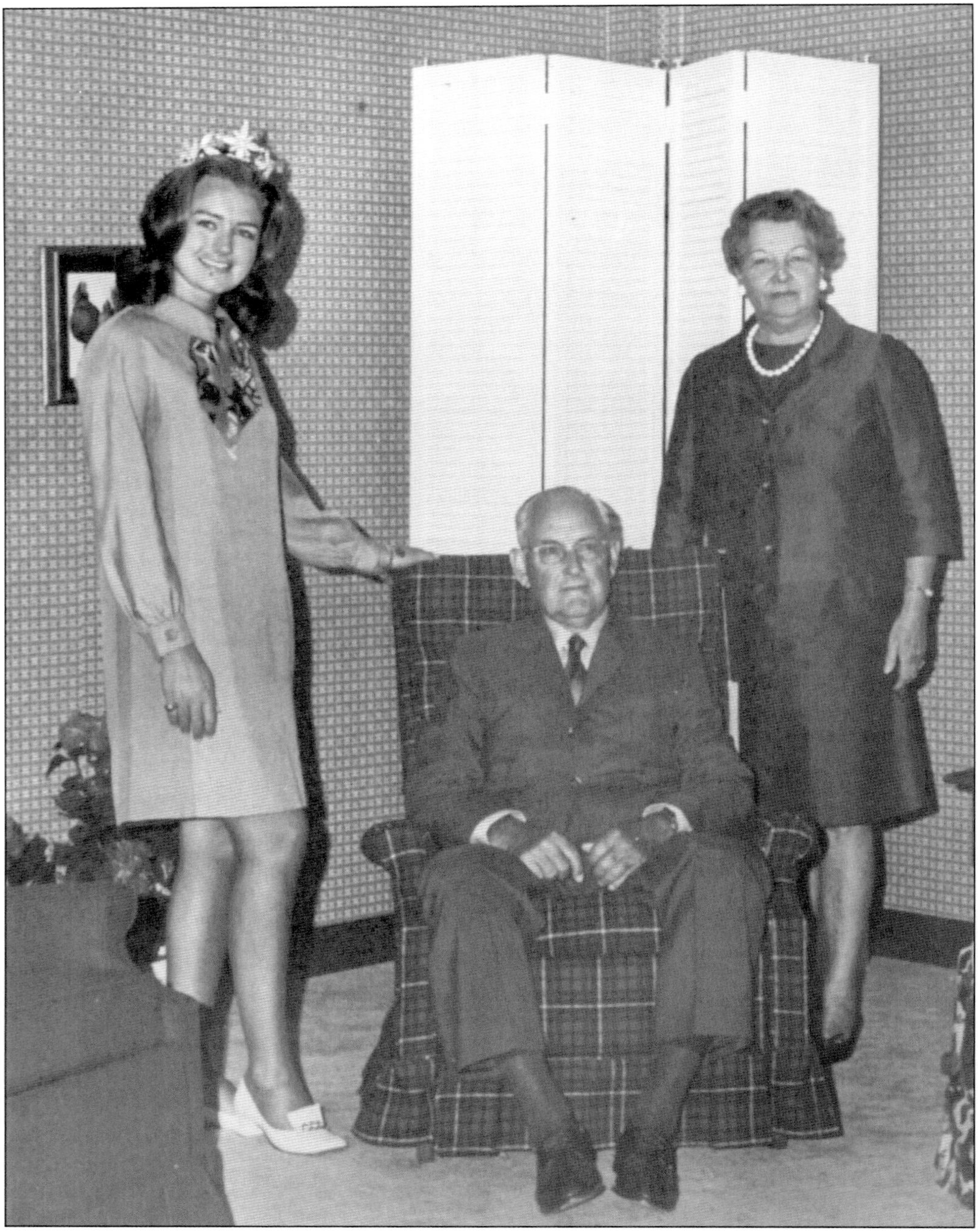

Brenda Heath, the 1969 queen, is pictured here with Mr. and Mrs. J.E. Broyhill at the Broyhill Furniture Industries showroom. For many years, the Broyhill Foundation was an annual donor of a $1,000 scholarship for the rhododendron queen. (Courtesy of the North Carolina Rhododendron Festival.)

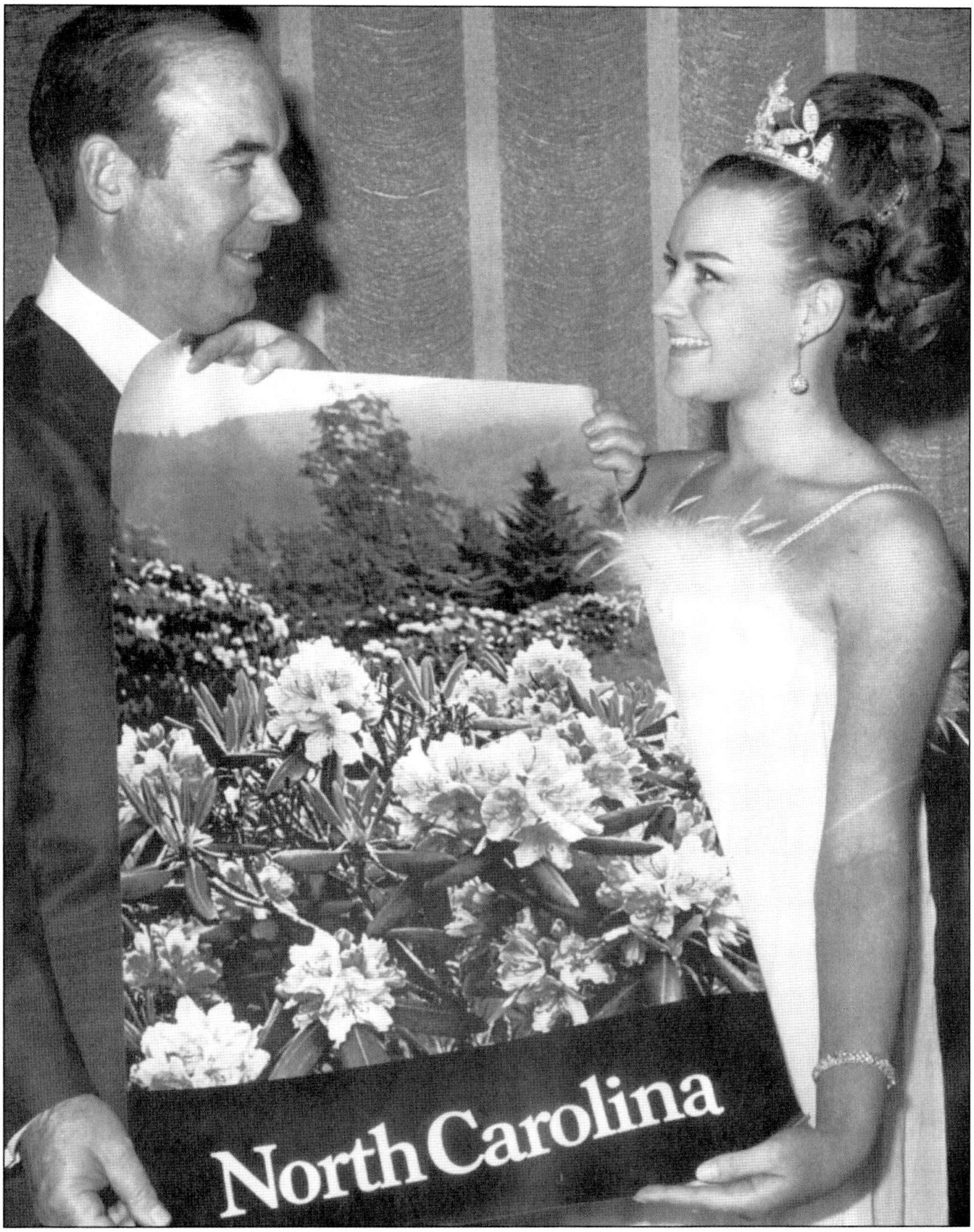

During an appearance tour in California, Brenda Heath presented a full-color picture of Roan Mountain to Evelle J. Younger, a Los Angeles district attorney. Younger was the prosecuting attorney in the Sirhan Sirhan trial for the murder of Robert Kennedy. Heath made the presentation on behalf of the director of the North Carolina Travel Council. (Courtesy of the Barron Collection.)

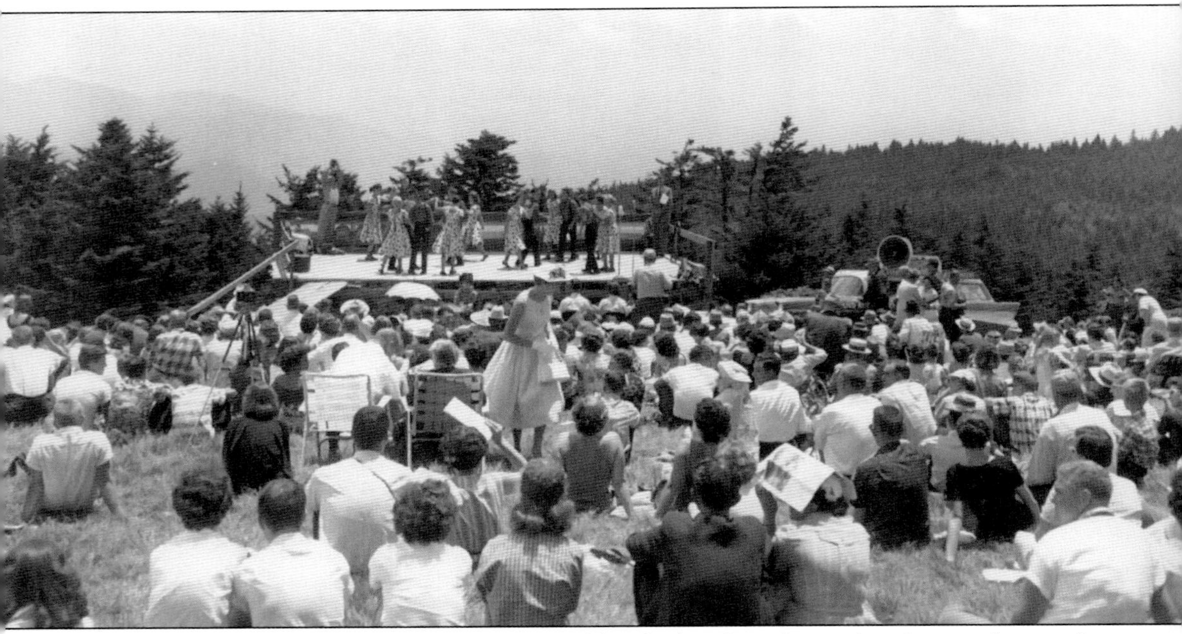

Special entertainment by visiting queens and local talent has always played a significant role in the production of the festival pageant. This photograph, taken in the late 1960s or early 1970s, shows a local square-dance team providing entertainment for an appreciative crowd atop Roan Mountain just prior to the crowning ceremony of the new rhododendron queen. (Courtesy of the Barron Collection.)

Four

The More Things Change . . .

Seven Decades of Legacy

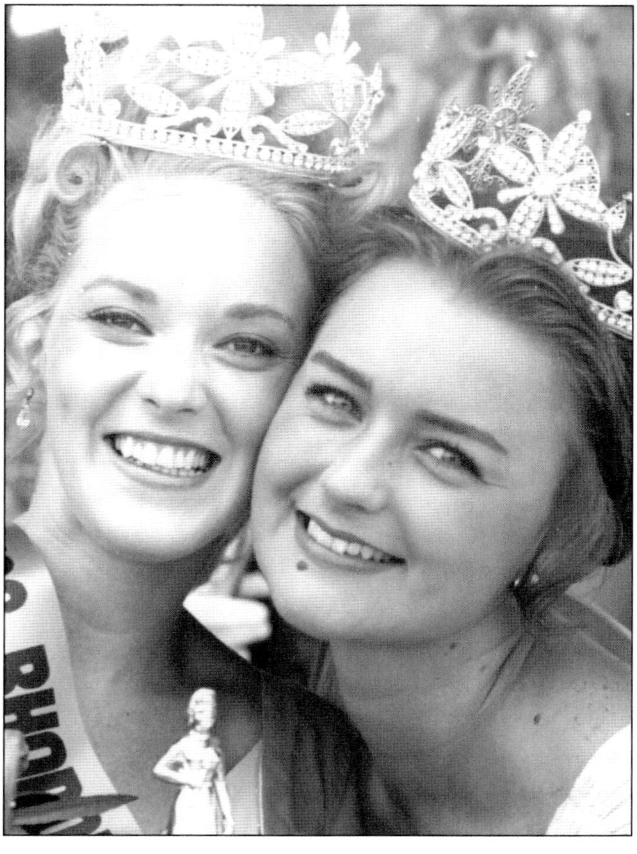

The advent of the 1970s brought many changes for the North Carolina Rhododendron Festival. Among the new events were a golf tournament at Grassy Creek Golf and Country Club and a 5K run in downtown Bakersville. Years later, an arts and crafts event was added to the lineup. Even with the changes, many things prevail. One of the most enduring events is the street dance that takes places during Friday and Saturday nights of the festival. Bakersville's main thoroughfare is closed, and attendees enjoy dancing in the street to music by a live bluegrass band. The Rhododendron Ball was discontinued in the early 1970s. Mary Selene Duncan (pictured on the left) was crowned the first North Carolina rhododendron queen of the 1970s by retiring queen Brenda Faye Heath. (Courtesy of the Barron Collection.)

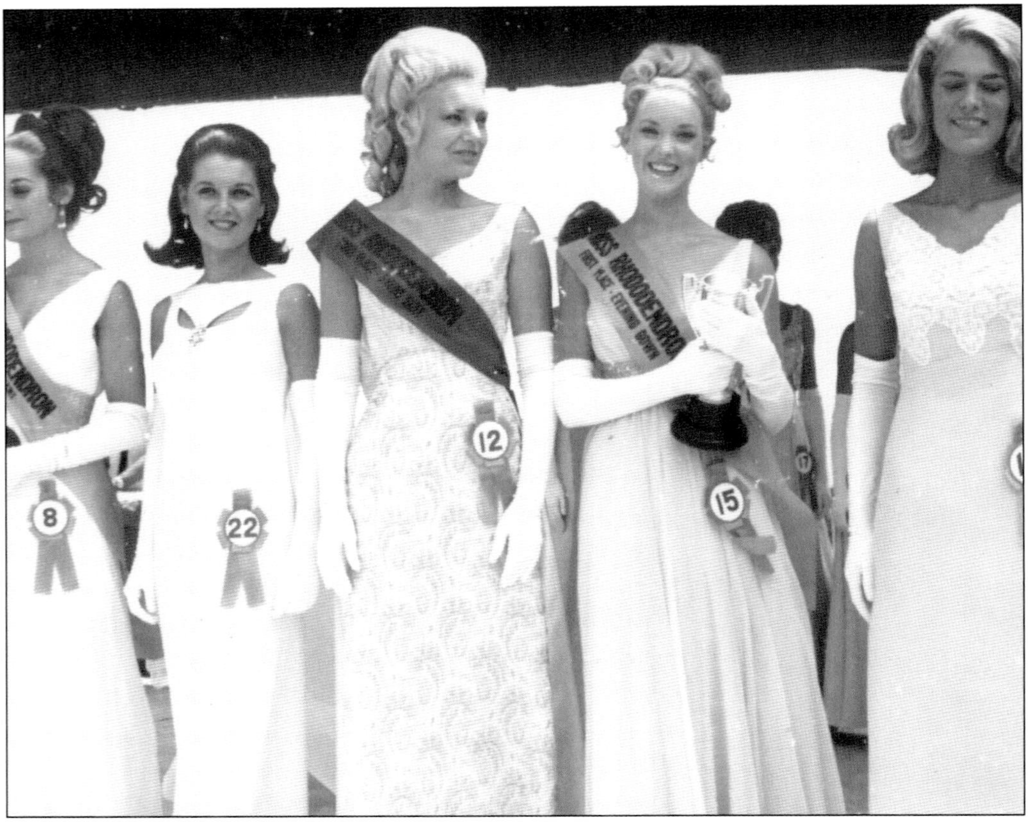

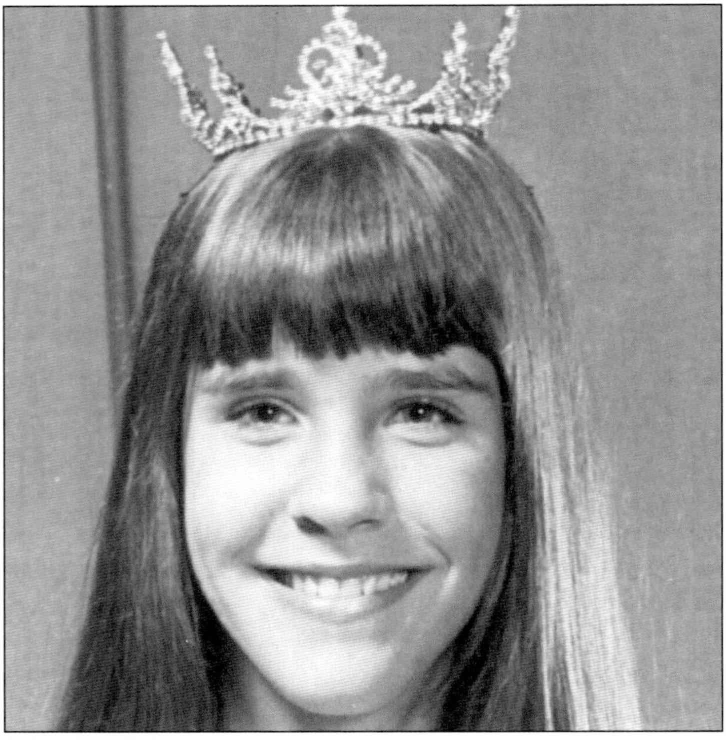

Mary Selene Duncan's crowning ceremony was one of the last to be held atop Roan Mountain. Evangeline Roberts won the title of junior rhododendron queen for 1970. (Both, courtesy of the North Carolina Rhododendron Festival.)

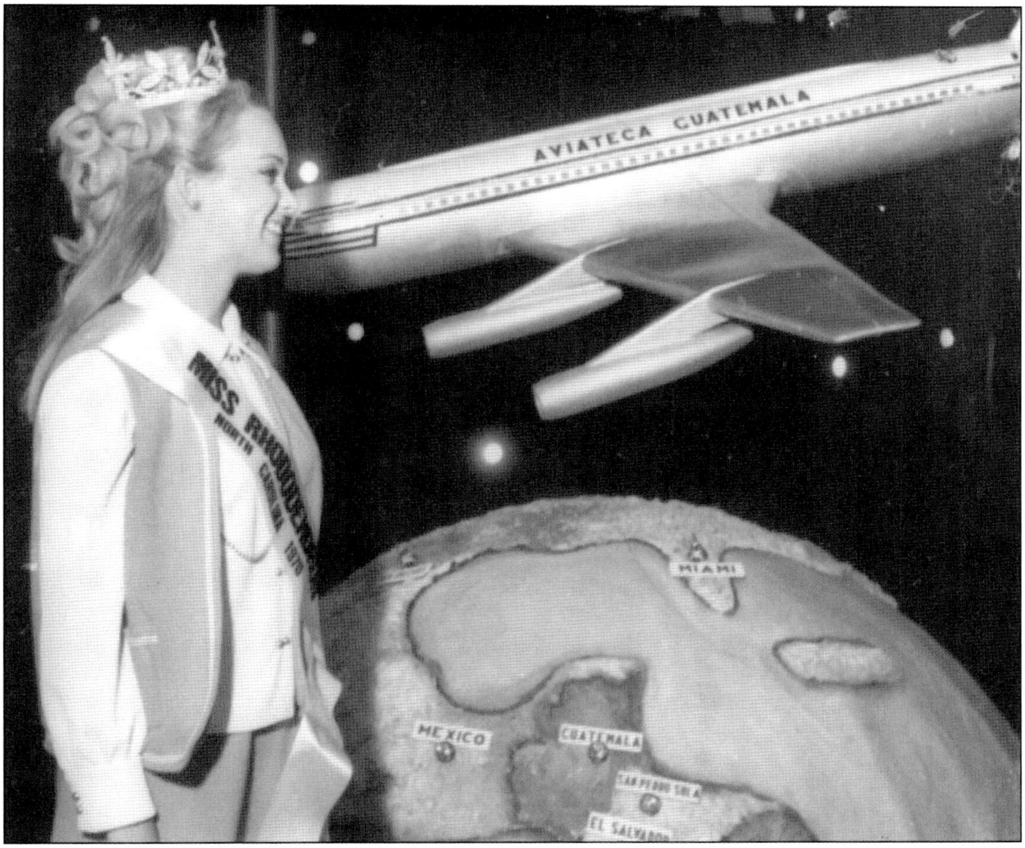

Mary Selene Duncan made over 300 personal appearances during her reign, including a trip to the International Trade Fair in Guatemala. She is pictured here at the AVIATECA Airline Booth. She also made appearances closer to home, including Grandfather Mountain and the famous mile-high swinging bridge. (Above, courtesy of the Barron Collection; below, courtesy of the Wilson Collection.)

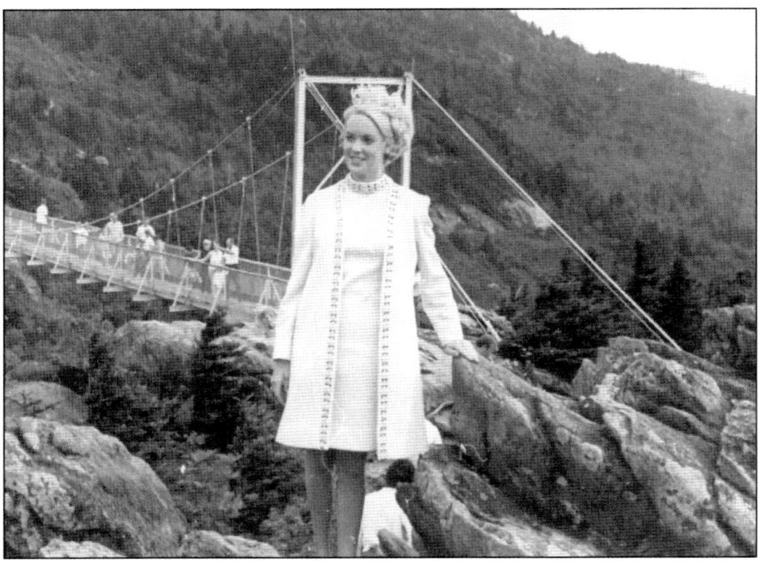

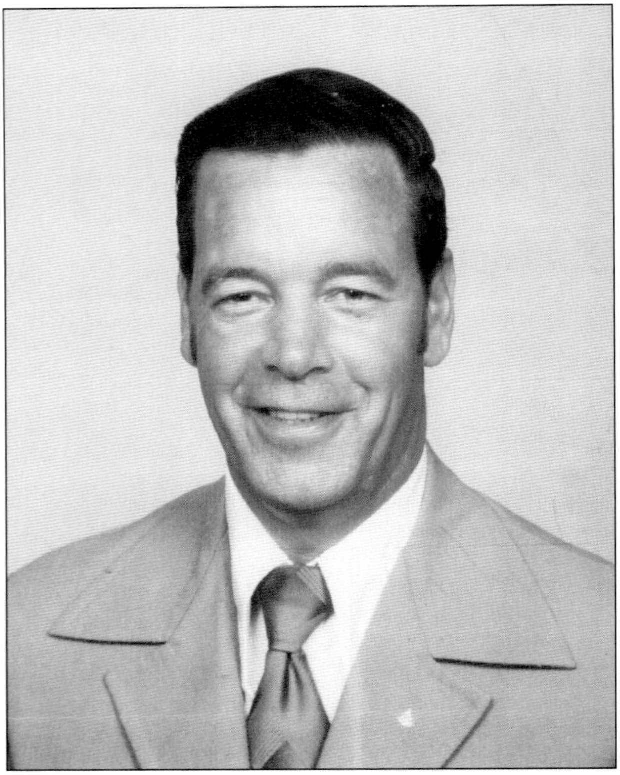

After O.D. Calhoun's resignation from the role of business manager, Don Brewer, a native of Bakersville, stepped in to the position. (Courtesy of Geneva Brewer.)

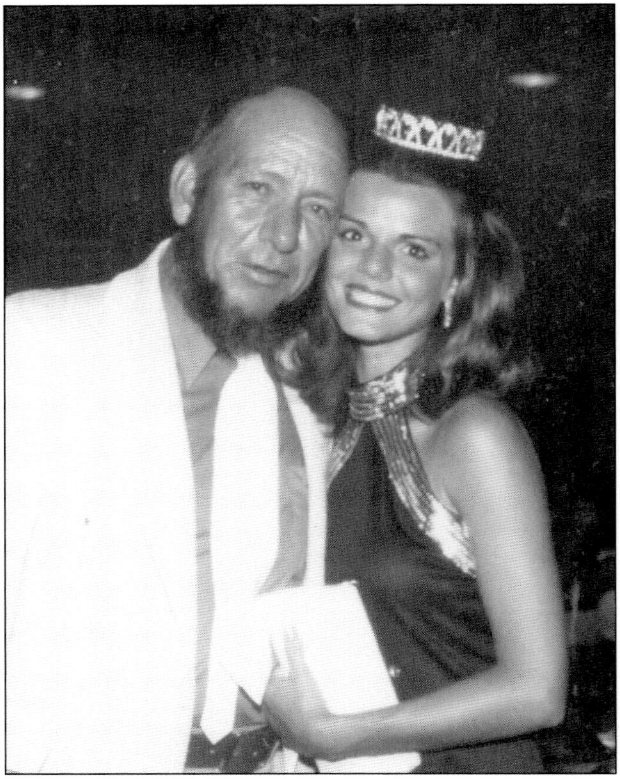

Brewer was succeeded a few years later by Ed Wilson, also of Bakersville, shown here with the 1977 rhododendron queen, Debbie Shook. (Courtesy of the Wilson Collection.)

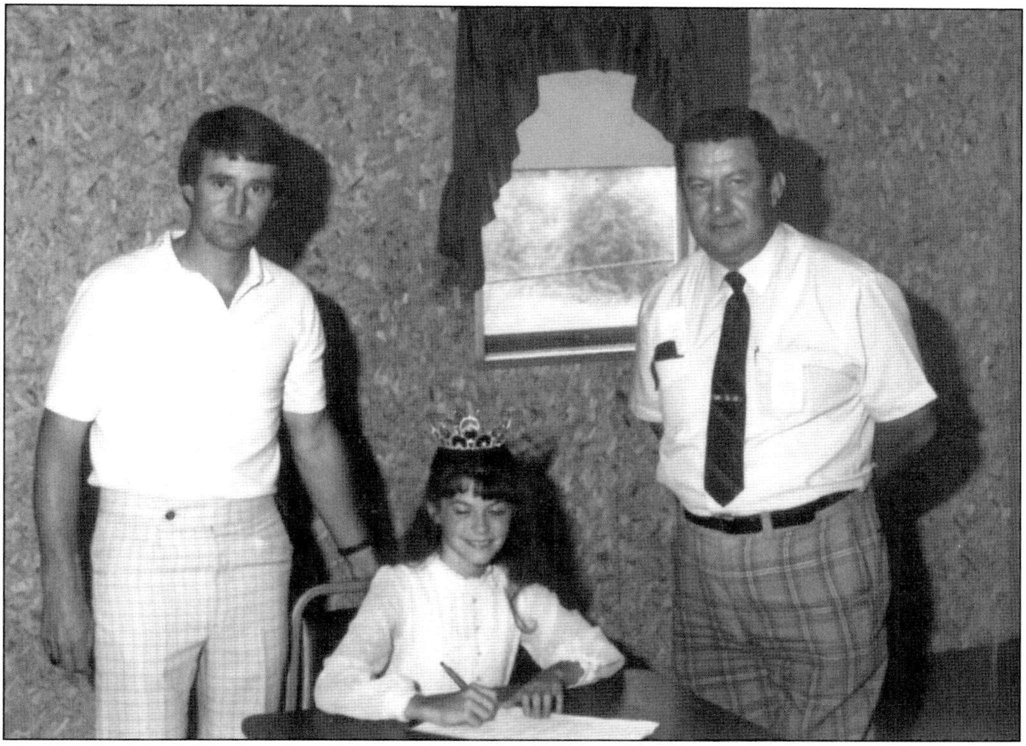

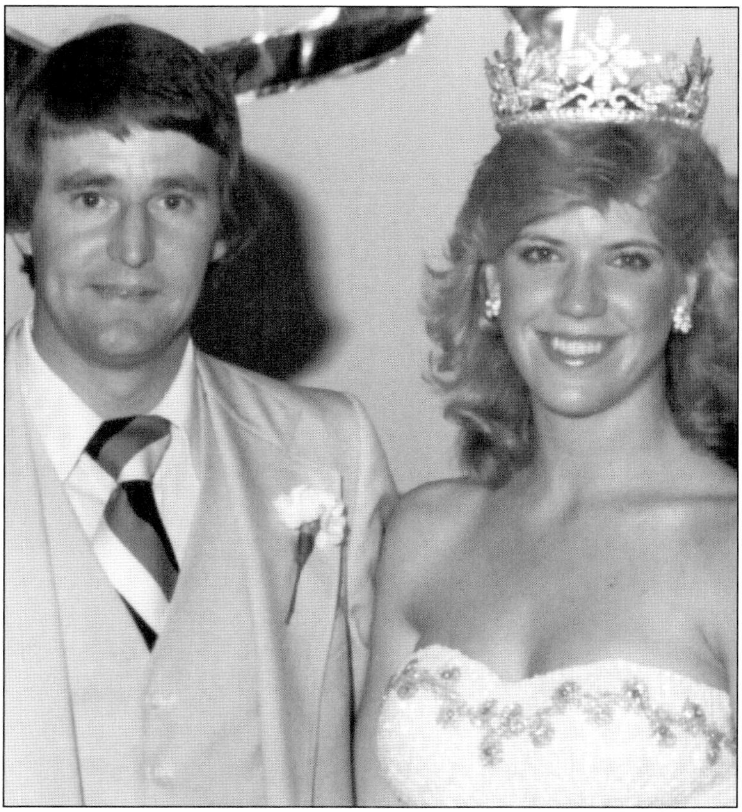

The role of business manager for the rhododendron queen has changed hands several times over the years. Gene Edwards stepped into the position in the mid-1980s. He is pictured here at the contract signing of the 1984 junior rhododendron queen, Kara White, along with North Carolina state representative Monroe Buchanan and Betsy Jones, the 1983 queen. (Above, courtesy of the Wilson Collection; right, courtesy of the North Carolina Rhododendron Festival.)

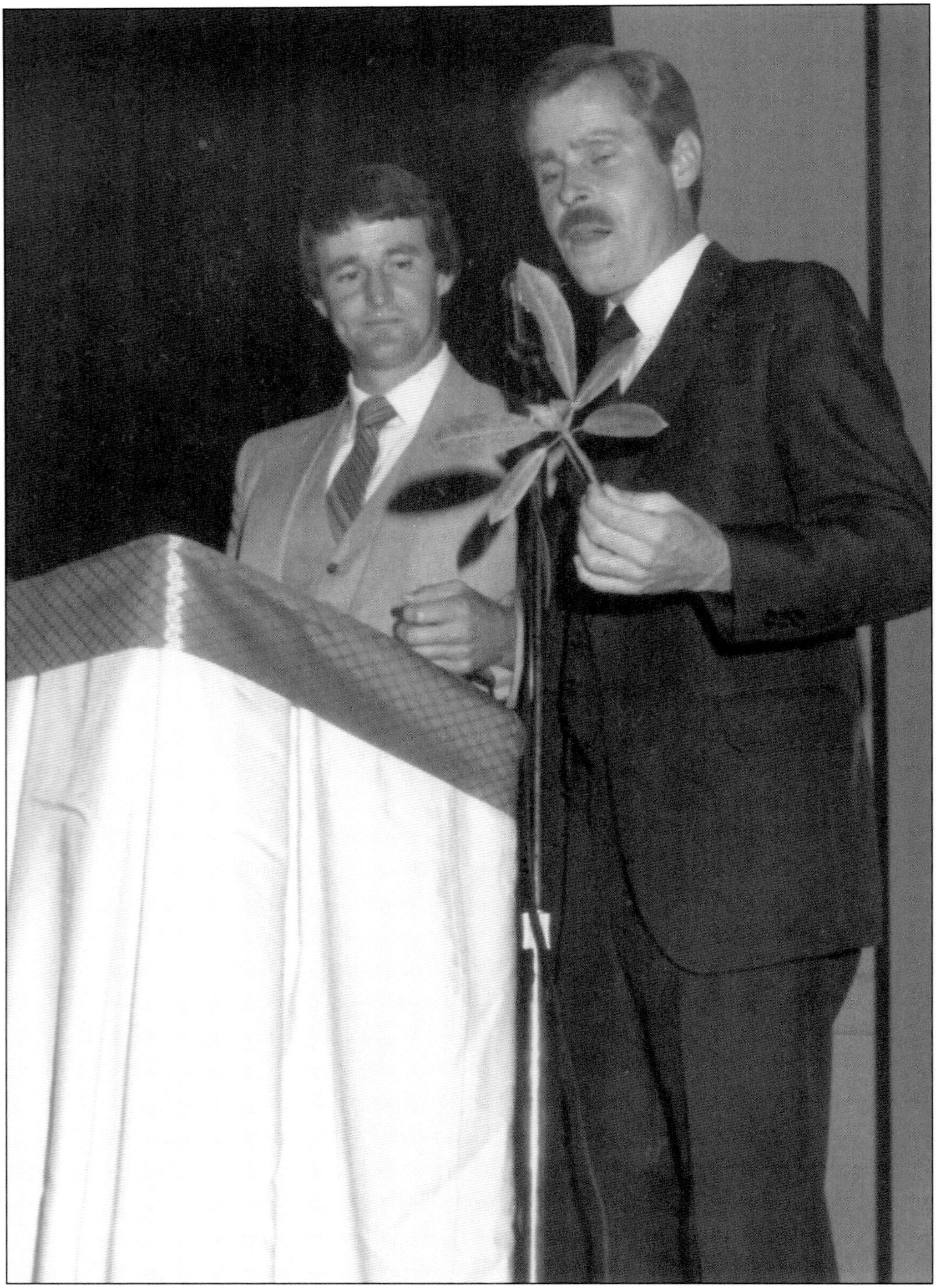

Dr. Charles Nash succeeded Gene Edwards as business manager. When he stepped down in 1998, Bob Hensley assumed the responsibility and still holds the position today. Hensley also serves as master of ceremonies for the rhododendron festival pageant. He is pictured here on stage with Gene Edwards (left) during a pageant in the 1980s. (Courtesy of the North Carolina Rhododendron Festival.)

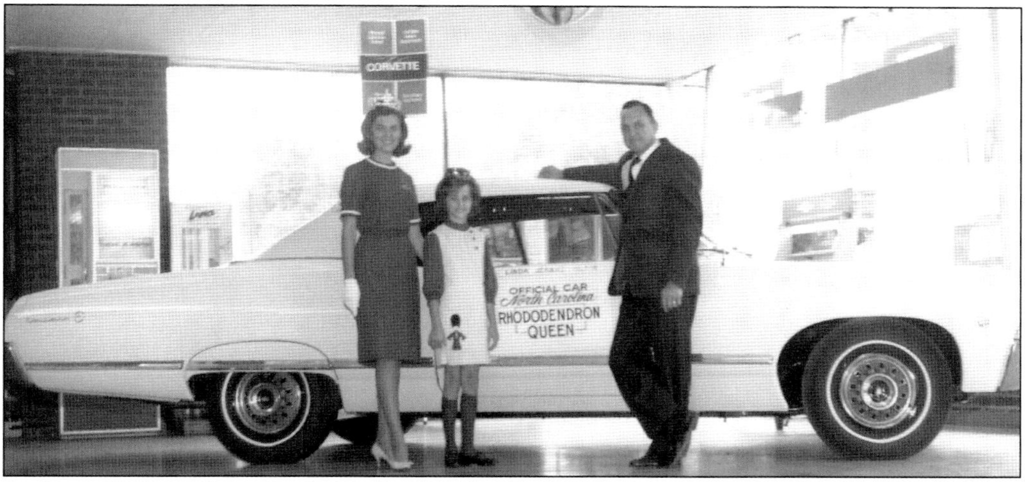

In the early days of the rhododendron festival, Claude Greene of Claude Greene Chevrolet in neighboring Spruce Pine provided the North Carolina rhododendron queen with the use of a car for her year's reign. The 1967 queens, Linda Blair and Debbie Shook, pose with Greene after receiving the keys for the official rhododendron car. (Courtesy of the Barron Collection.)

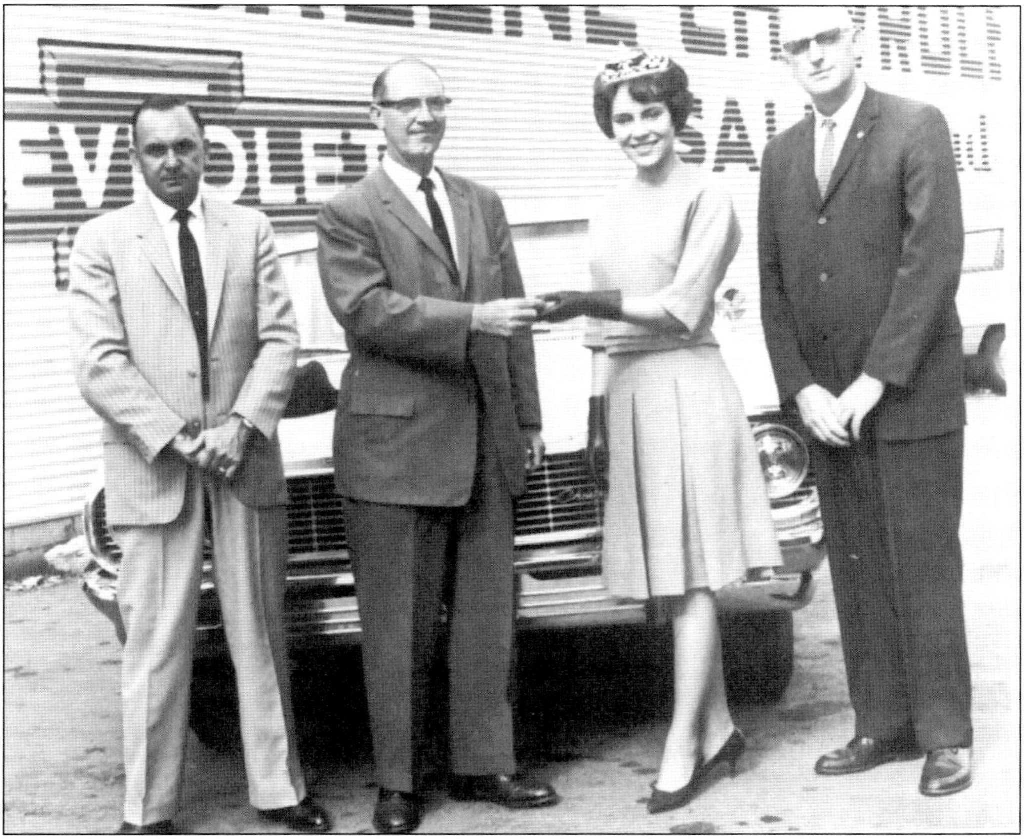

Brenda Bost, the 1964 North Carolina rhododendron queen, was presented with the keys to her official rhododendron car by representatives from Greene Chevrolet. Rhododendron festival committee member Marcus Blanton (far right) was also in attendance. (Courtesy of the Barron Collection.)

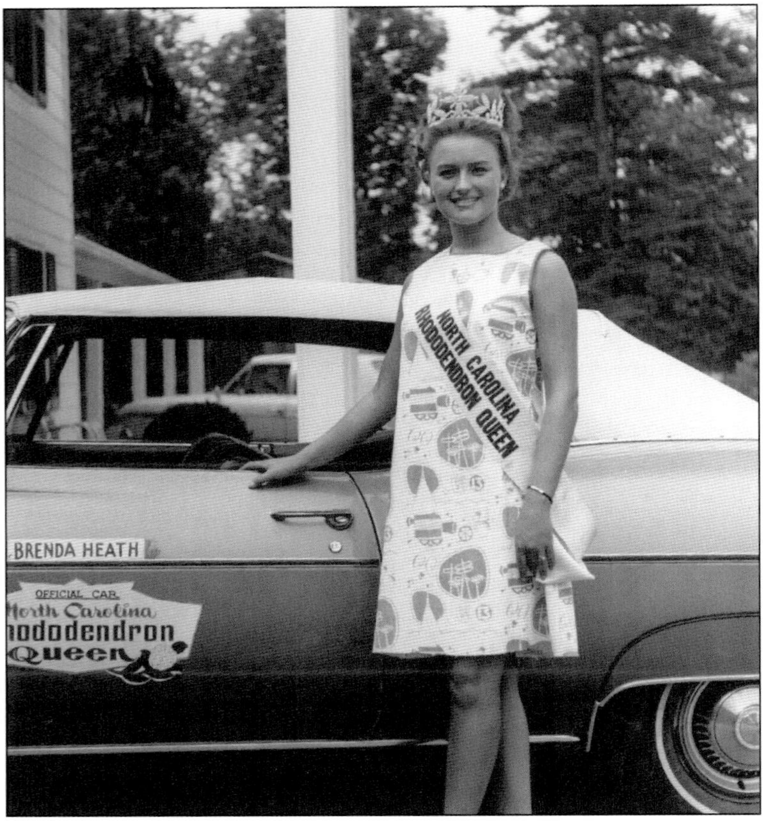

Brenda Heath, the 1969 rhododendron queen, poses with her car. Heath was the fourth North Carolina rhododendron queen to receive the 100,000-mile award for her travel during personal appearances. (Courtesy of the Barron Collection.)

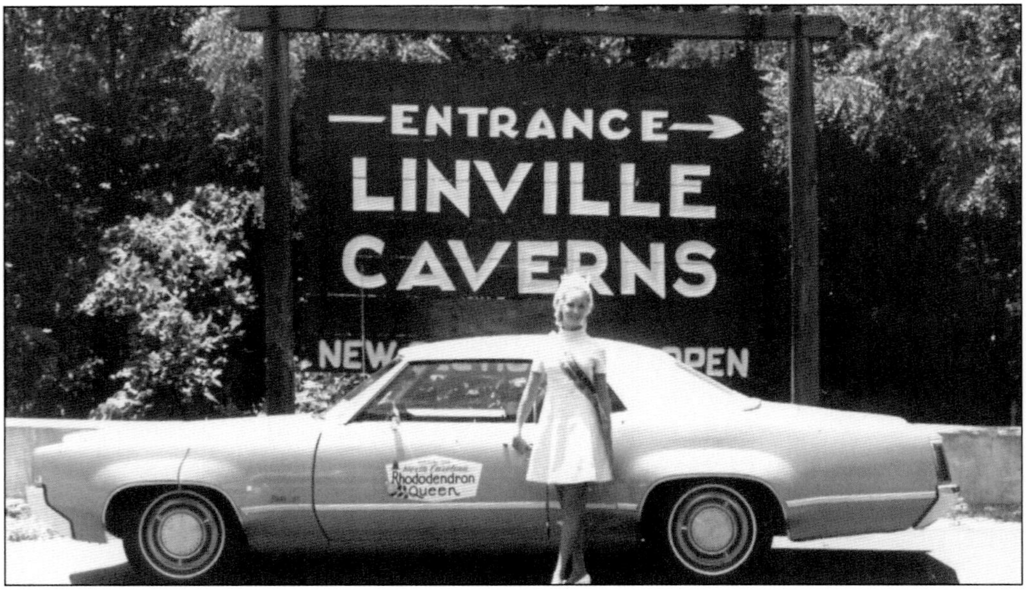

Mary Selene Duncan made an appearance at Linville Caverns, proudly posing by her new car. Duncan established a new travel record as North Carolina rhododendron queen by traveling over 10,000 miles during the first 30 days of her reign. (Courtesy of the Barron Collection.)

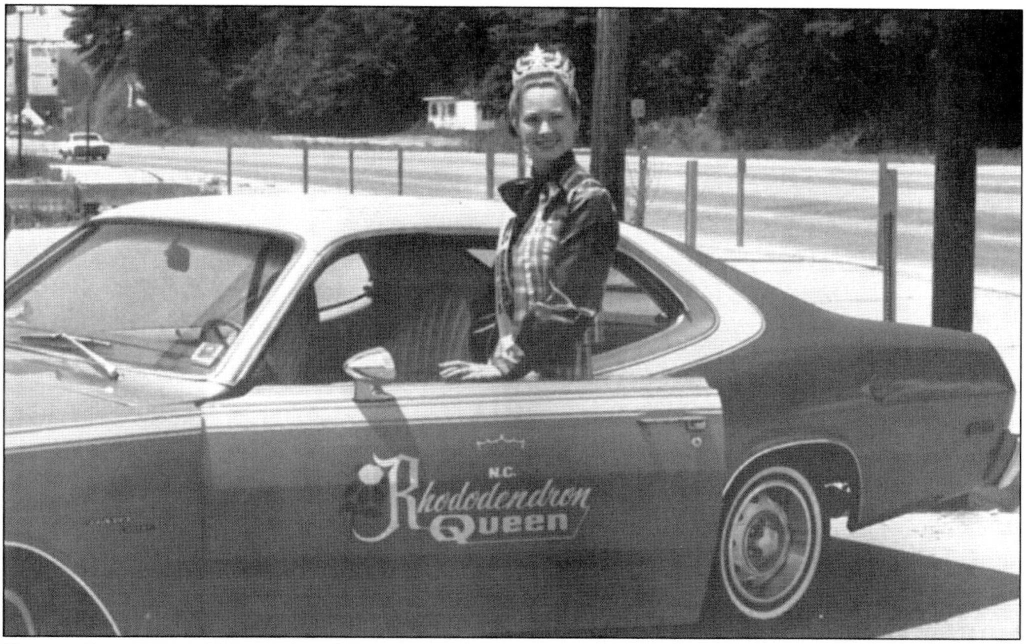

During the 1970s, 1980s, and early 1990s, Buchanan & Young, a local Chrysler-Plymouth dealership, provided the rhododendron queen with the use of a car for her appearances throughout her year's reign. Betsy Jo McDonald, the 1975 queen, was granted the use of a new Dodge Dart. (Courtesy of the North Carolina Rhododendron Festival.)

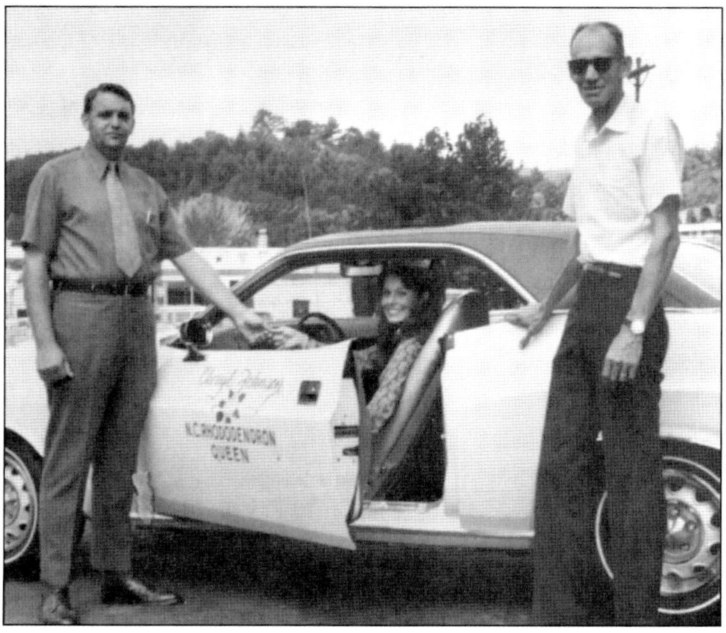

Warren Buchanan (left) and Joe Young presented Cheryl Sue Johnson with the keys to the car she would drive during her tenure as the 1972 North Carolina rhododendron queen. (Courtesy of the North Carolina Rhododendron Festival.)

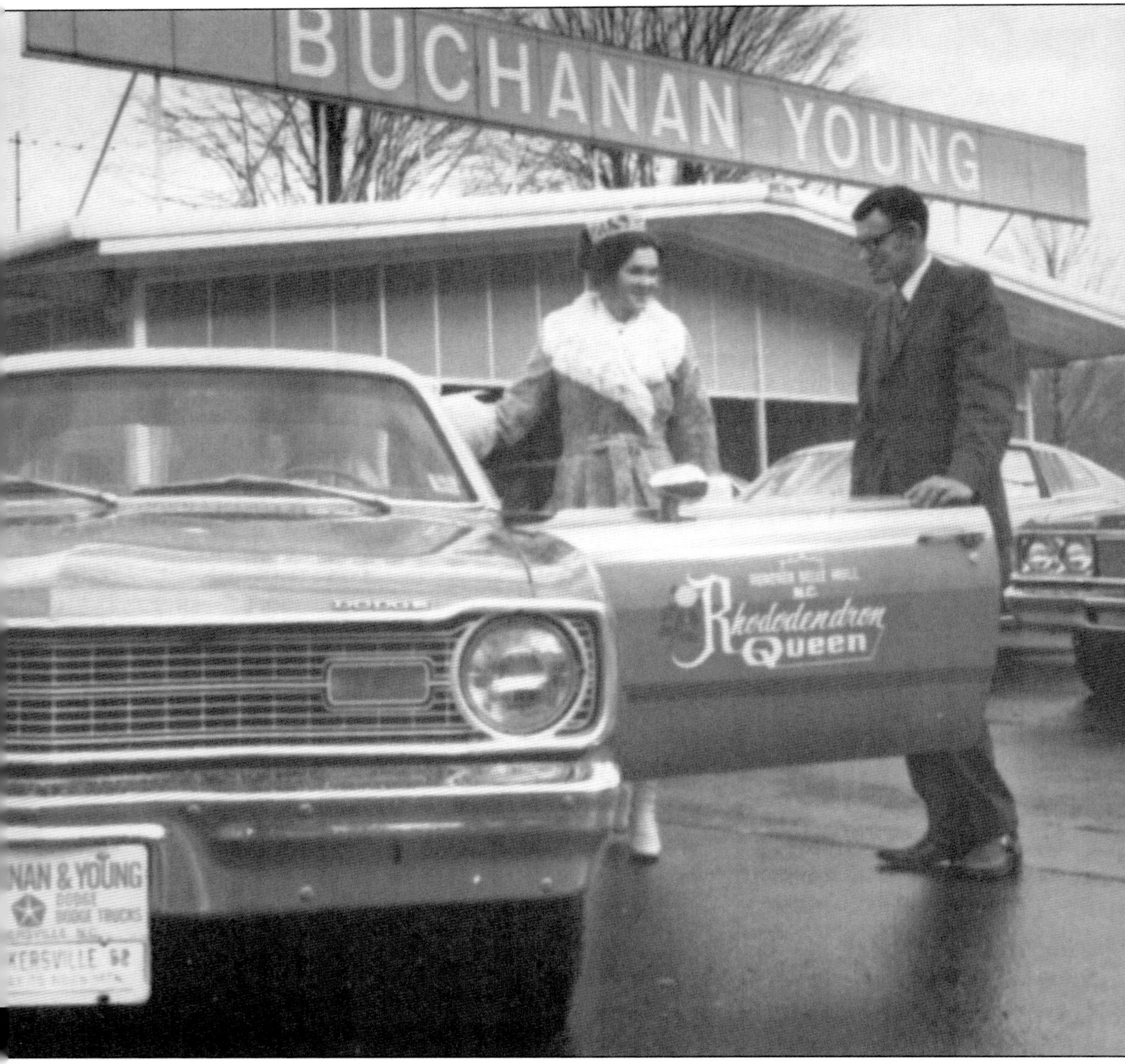

Andrea Mull, the 1974 queen, poses with Joe Young of Buchanan and Young Chrysler Plymouth after being presented the keys to her official rhododendron car. (Courtesy of the Wilson Collection.)

Ed Wilson, serving in the role of business manager for the 1971 queen, Carol Ann Bass, posed with her the day she received the keys to her car. (Courtesy of the Wilson Collection.)

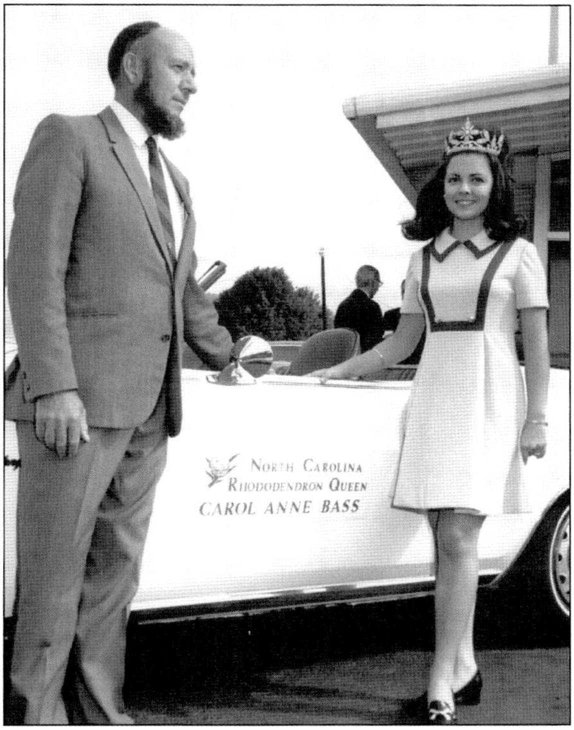

Business manager Gene Edwards presented a very happy Betsy Jones with keys to her new car. (Courtesy of the Barron Collection.)

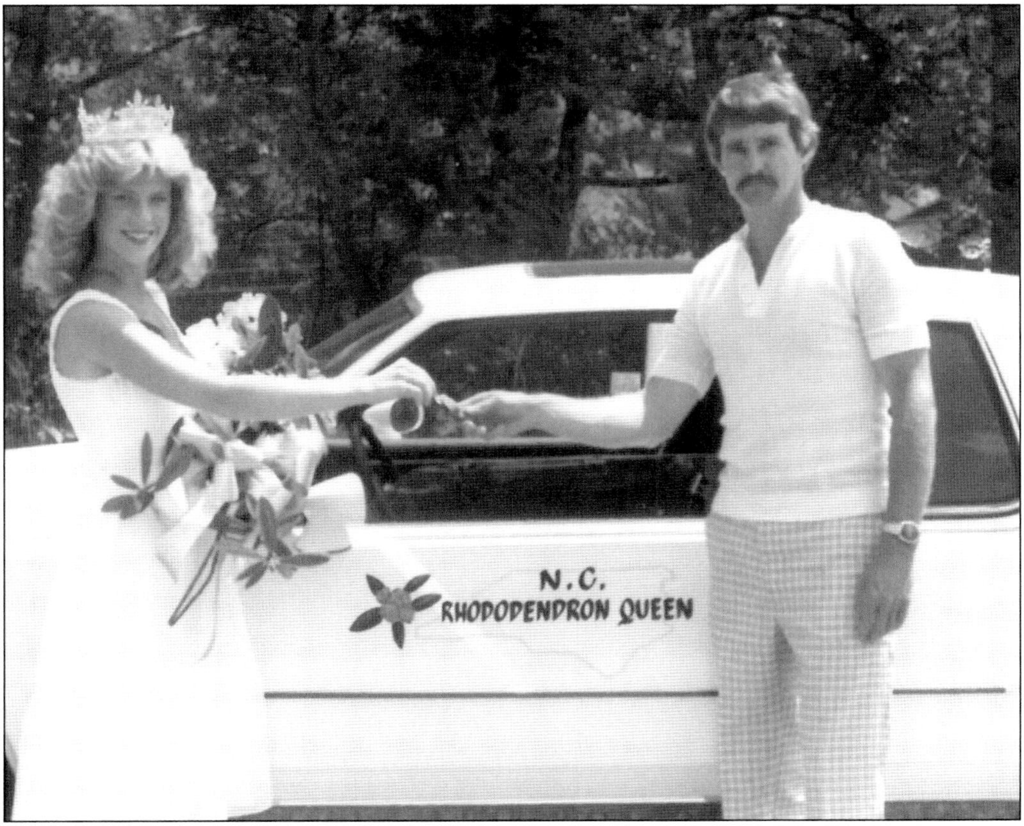

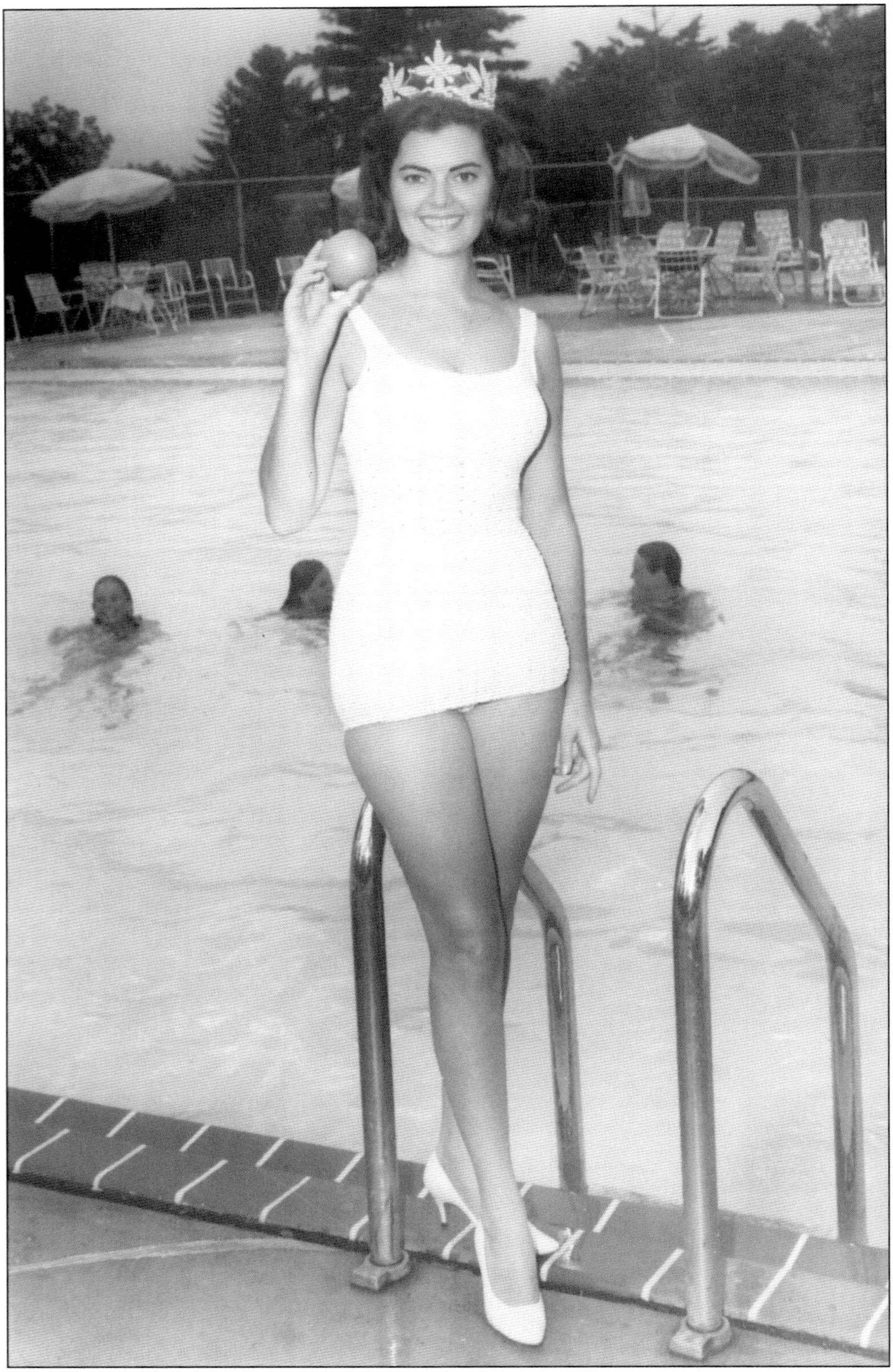

The phases of competition for the title of North Carolina rhododendron queen have evolved over the years. The interview aspect is heavily weighted, since the title requires the ability to be both ambassador and spokesperson. Talent and swimsuit competitions are audience favorites. Linda Blair, the 1967 queen, exhibits a beautiful example of 1960s style. (Courtesy of the Barron Collection.)

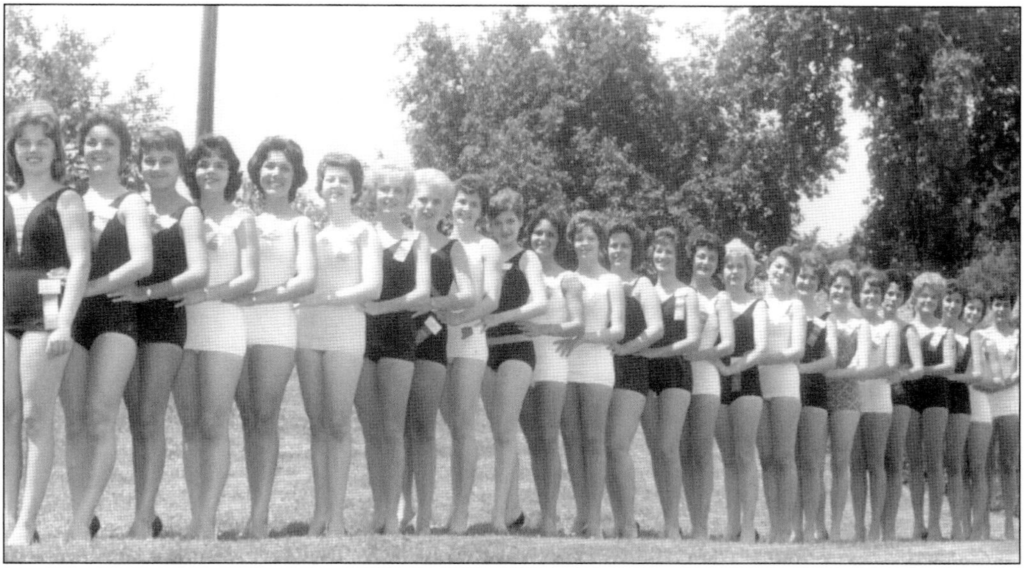

In addition to winning the title of 1963 North Carolina rhododendron queen, Betty Rae Lawhon also won the swimsuit phase of the competition. She is pictured here (11th from left) with the 24 other contestants vying for the title and crown. (Courtesy of Betty Lawhon Deviney.)

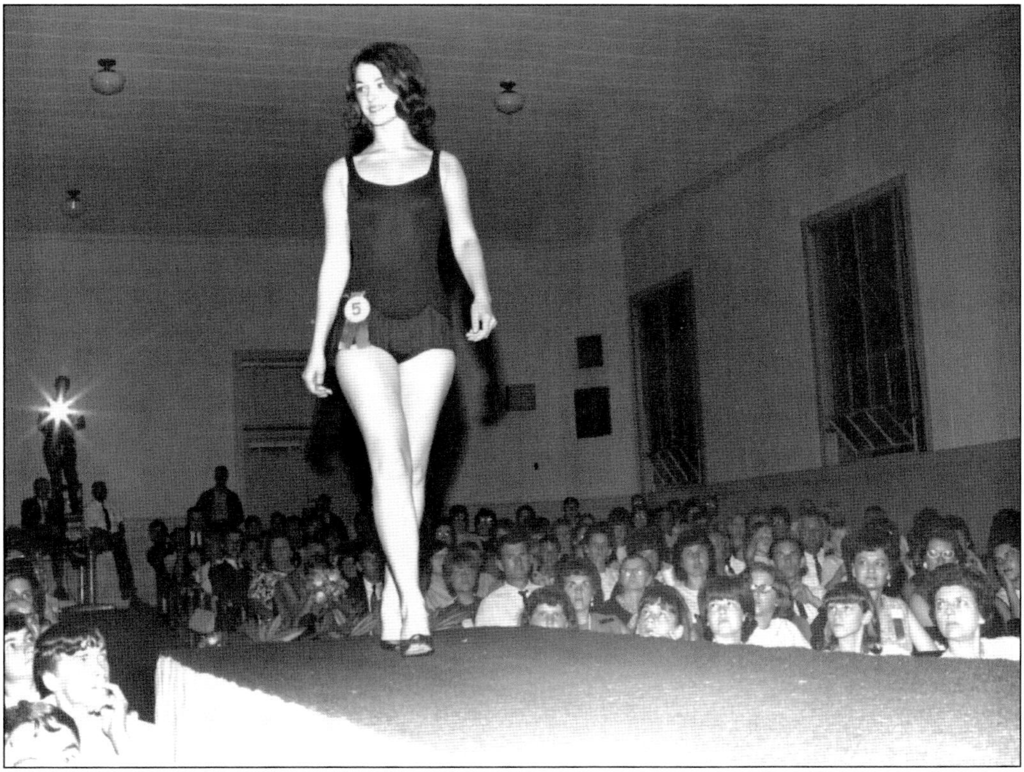

It is a long walk down that ramp. The swimsuit competition, though an audience favorite, can be quite intimidating for the contestants. It takes courage to appear onstage and walk down the ramp. A brave contestant smiles for the crowd during a 1960s rhododendron pageant. (Courtesy of Theresa Matthews.)

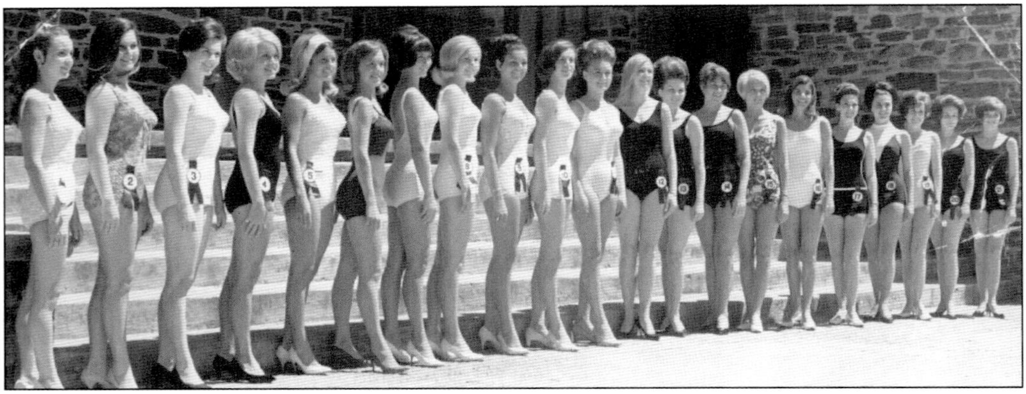

Contestants pose for a formal swimsuit shot on the steps of the Bowman auditorium in the late 1960s. Brenda Heath (11th from left) was the pageant winner. (Courtesy of the Wilson Collection.)

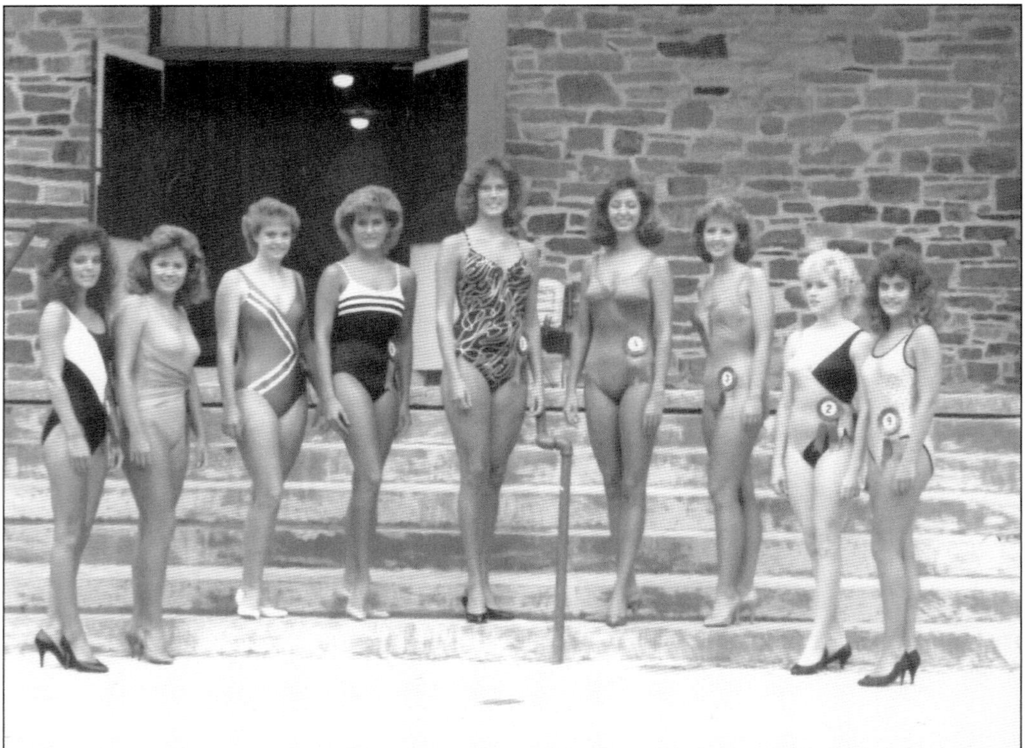

Almost 20 years later, those same steps provided an ideal setting for that perfect shot. Tracey Russell (fourth from left) would ultimately win the title of 1988 North Carolina rhododendron queen. (Courtesy of Bob Hensley.)

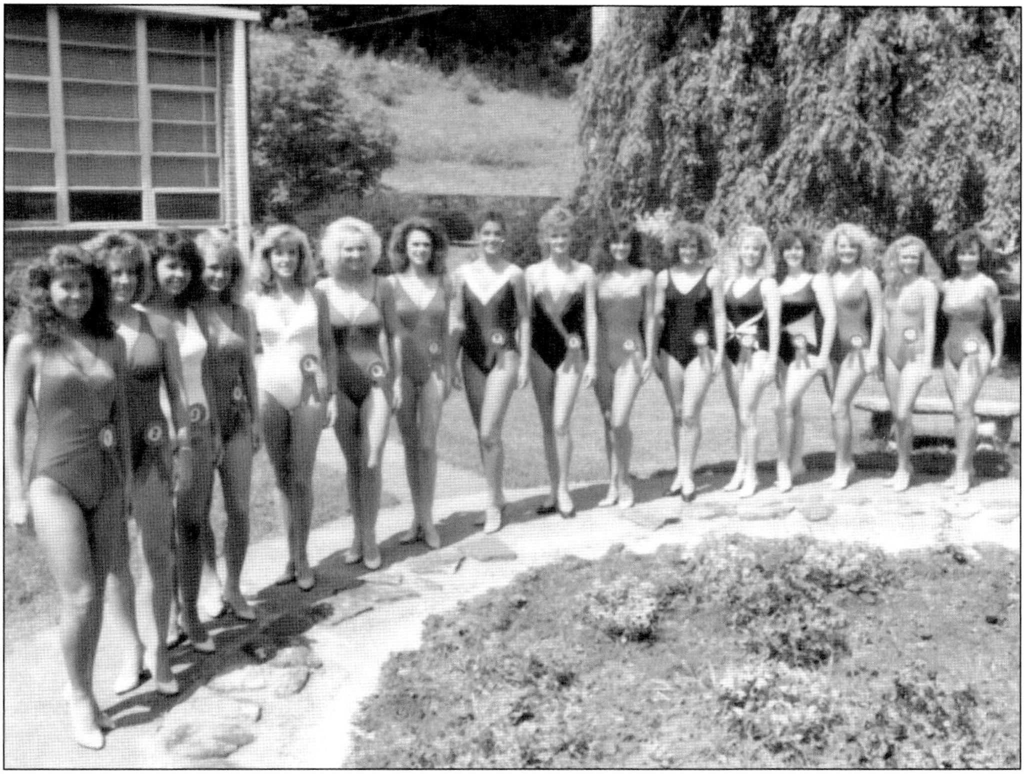

These two photographs, taken in 1989 and 2014 in the Bowman courtyard just outside the auditorium, beautifully depict how styles have evolved through the years. (Both, courtesy of Bob Hensley.)

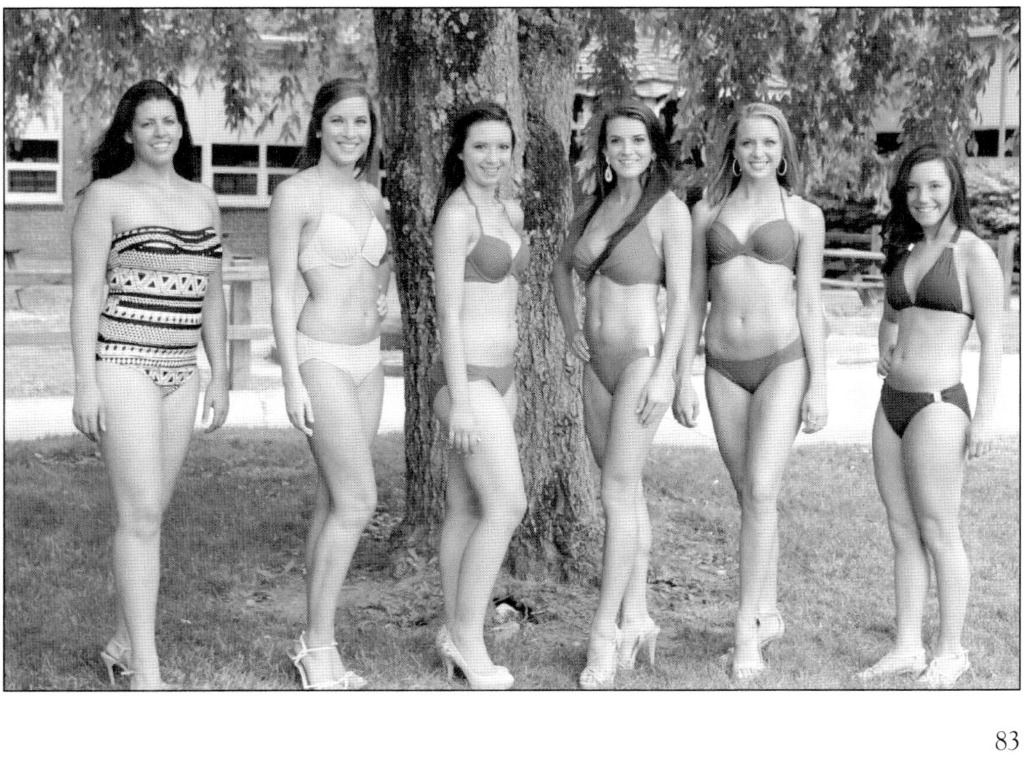

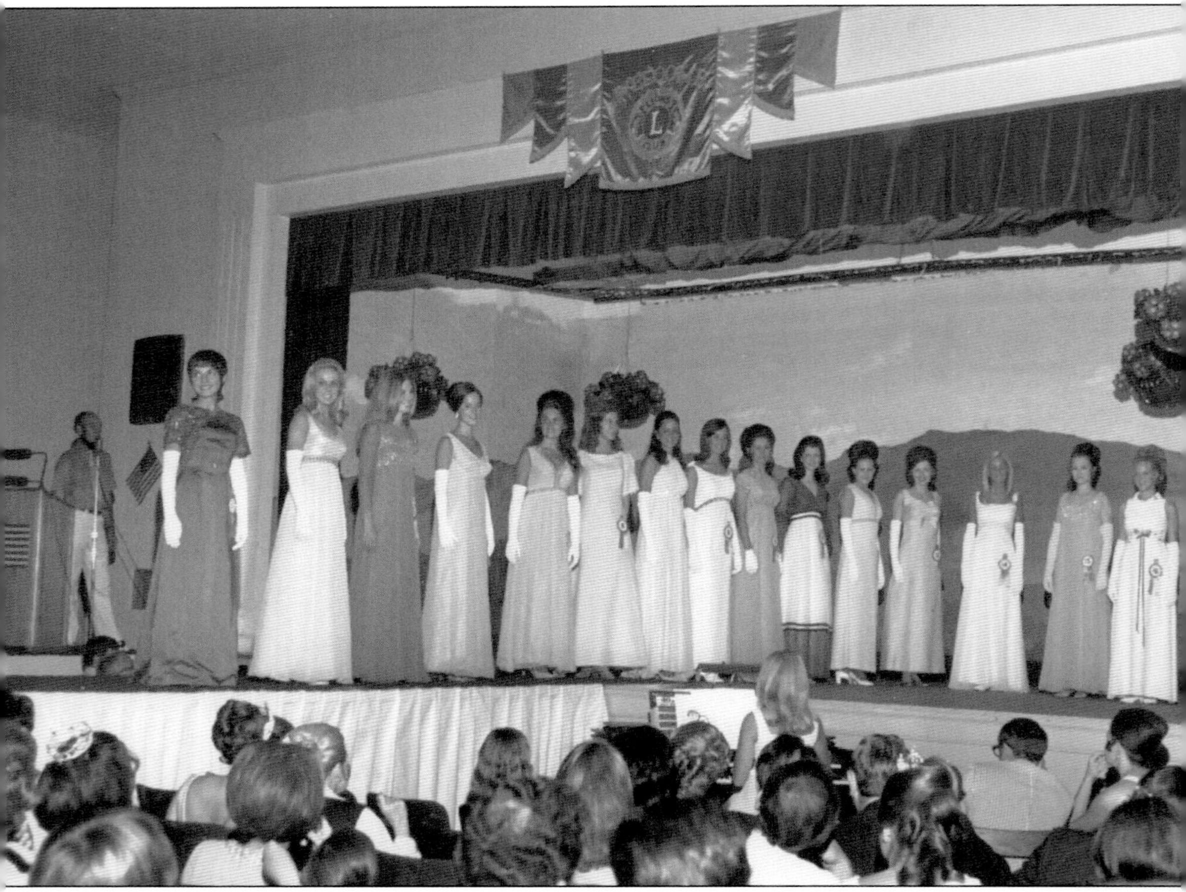

The evening gown competition, an ongoing tradition for both the queen and junior contestants, requires both poise and elegance. (Courtesy of the North Carolina Rhododendron Festival.)

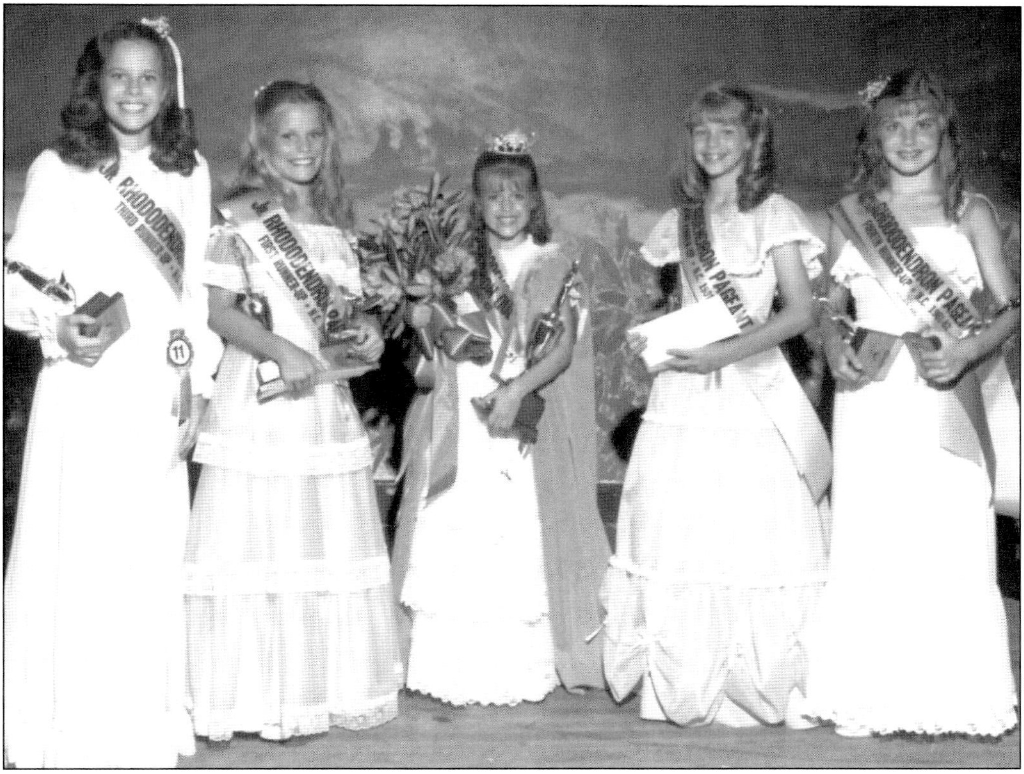

Jennifer Carroll was elated after winning the title of 1982 junior rhododendron queen. She poses for official shots in evening dress with runners-up shortly after crowning. (Courtesy of Geneva Brewer.)

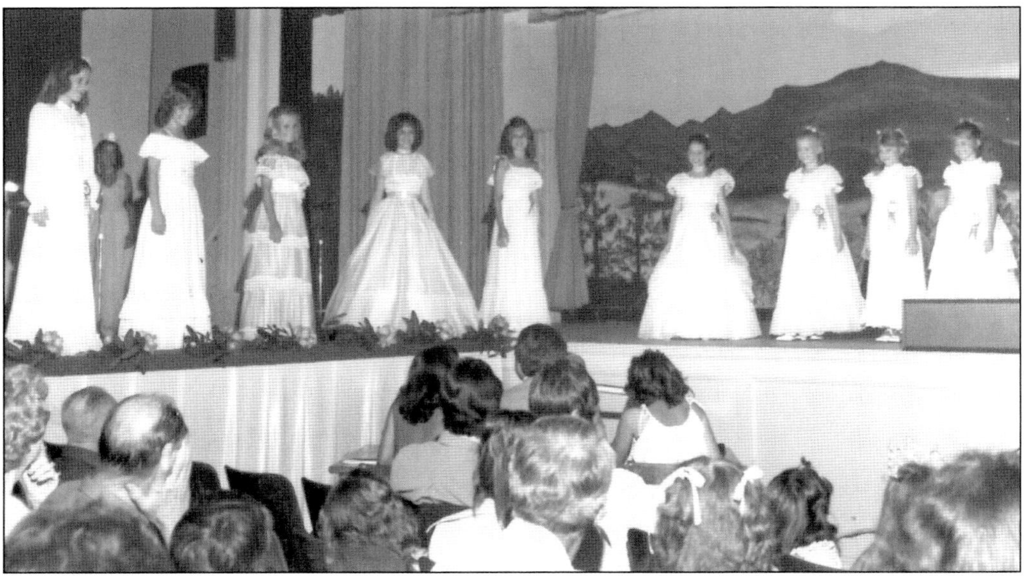

Contestants vying for the title of 1982 North Carolina junior rhododendron queen modeled for the audience and judges during the evening gown competition. Collective judging in the evening gown competition is no longer practiced during today's festival pageant. (Courtesy of Geneva Brewer.)

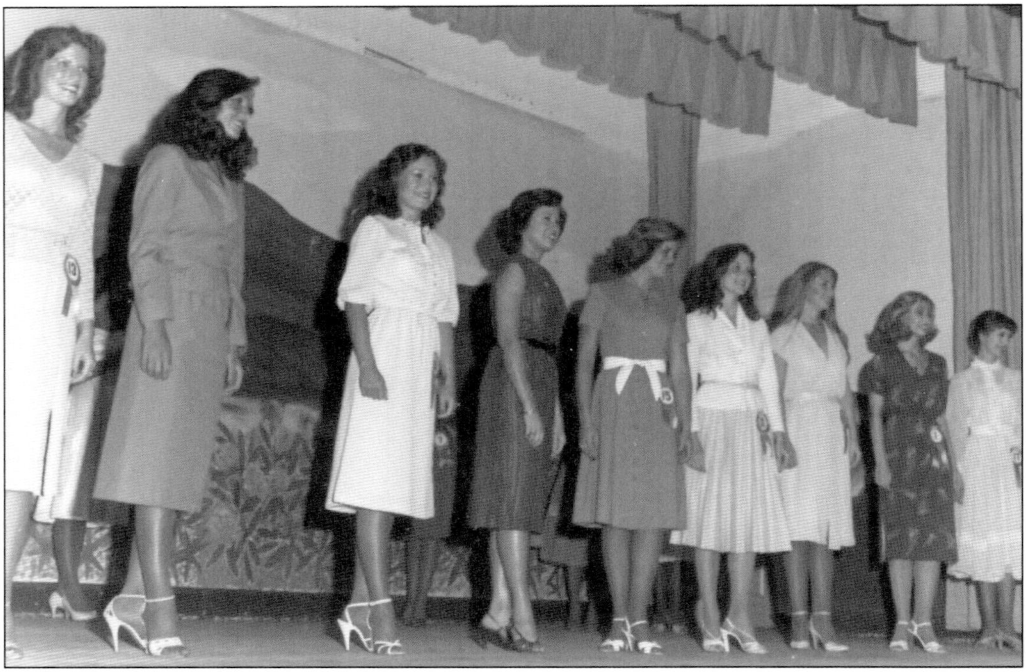

Queen contestants pose on stage in 1981, modeling interview wear. (Courtesy of Geneva Brewer.)

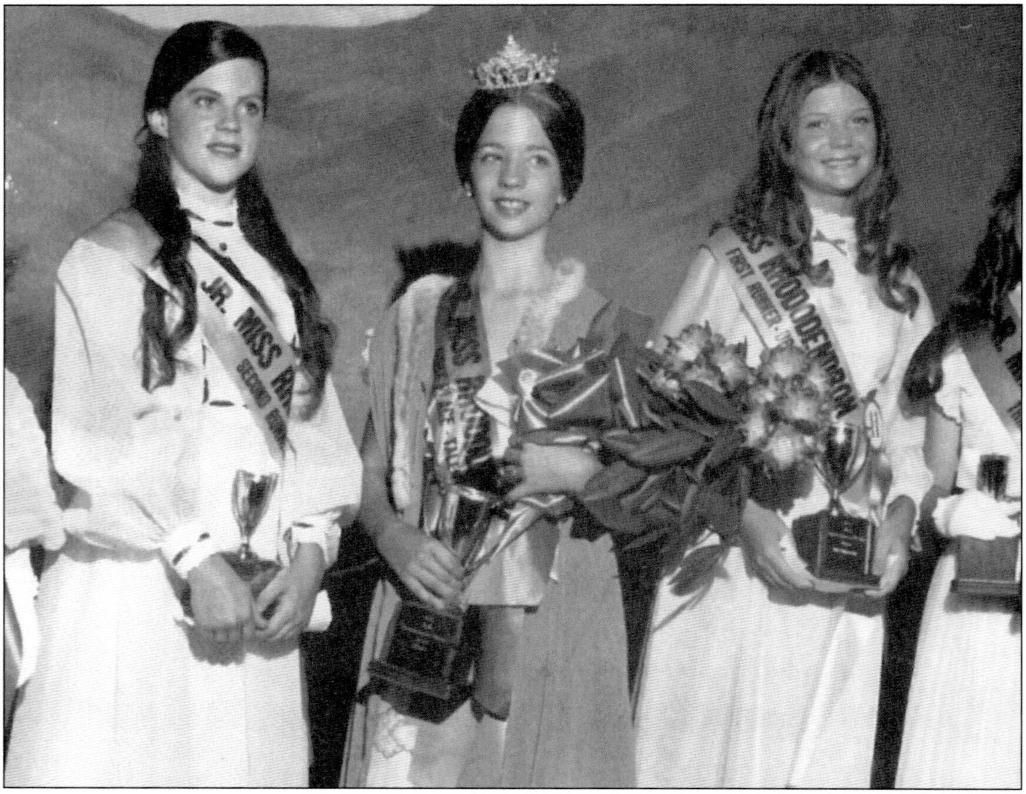

The 1974 junior rhododendron queen, April Myers, poses in evening dress with her runners-up. (Courtesy of the North Carolina Rhododendron Festival.)

Melissa Bass (right) congratulates her successor, Tracey Russell, on winning the title of 1988 North Carolina rhododendron queen. (Courtesy of Geneva Brewer.)

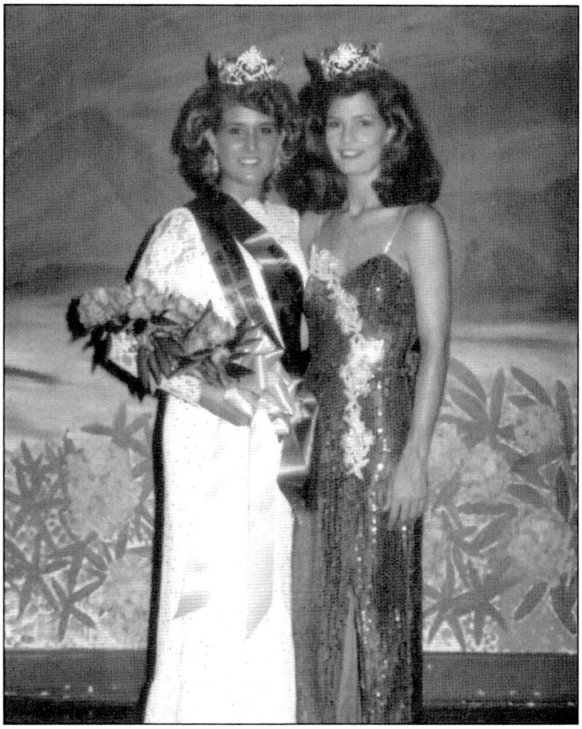

Lori Boggs (fourth from left) competes in the evening gown competition before being named the 1982 North Carolina rhododendron queen. A few years after serving as rhododendron queen, Boggs went on to compete in and win the title of Miss North Carolina. (Courtesy of Geneva Brewer.)

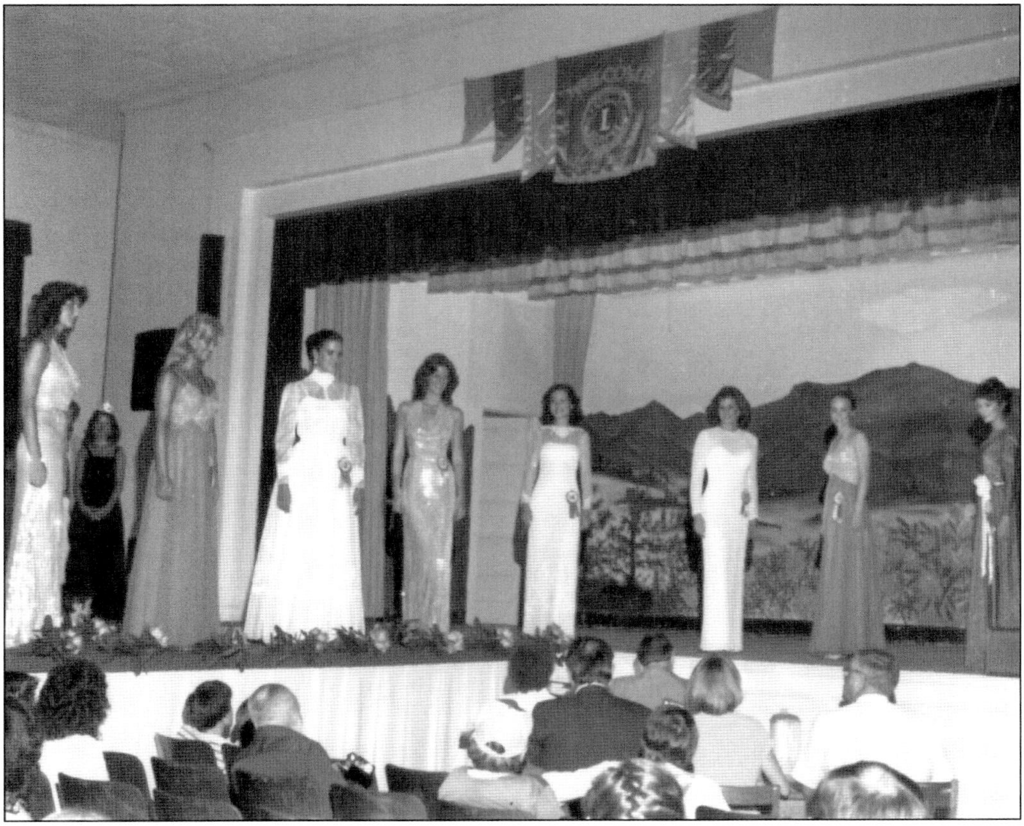

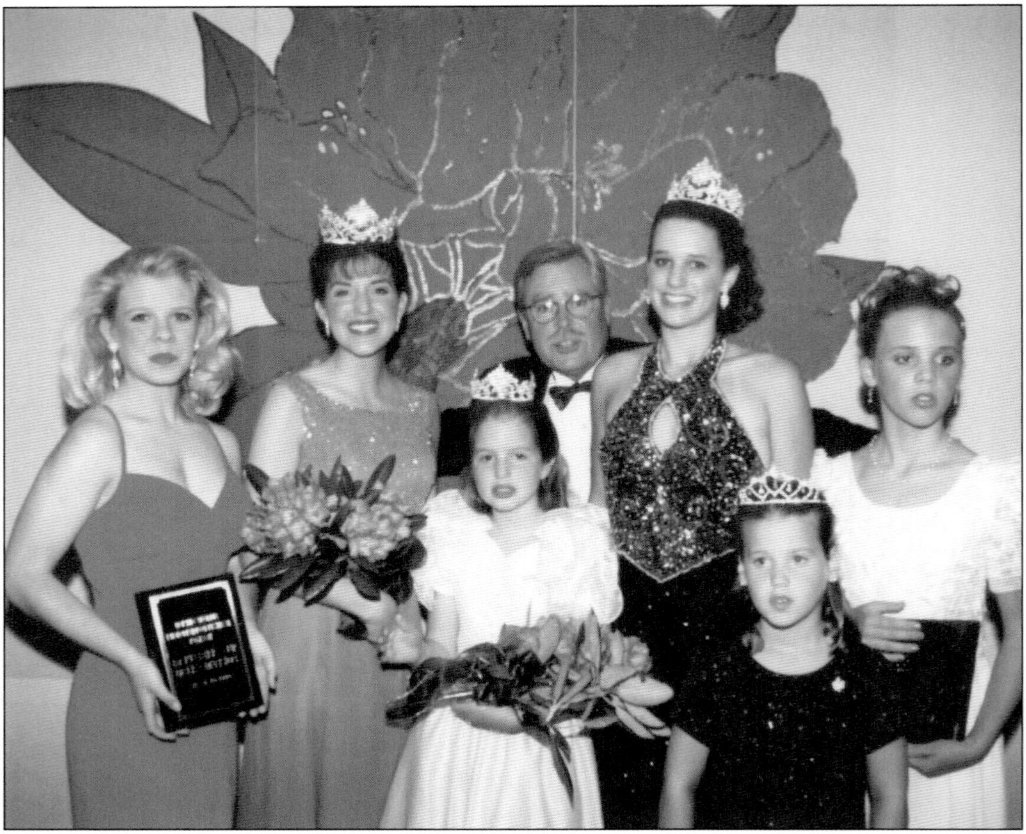

Audrey Thayer (second from left) and Lyndsay Watson (center front) pose on stage with business manager and master of ceremonies Bob Hensley, runners-up, and visiting queens shortly after being crowned the first rhododendron queens of the new millennium. (Courtesy of Bob Hensley.)

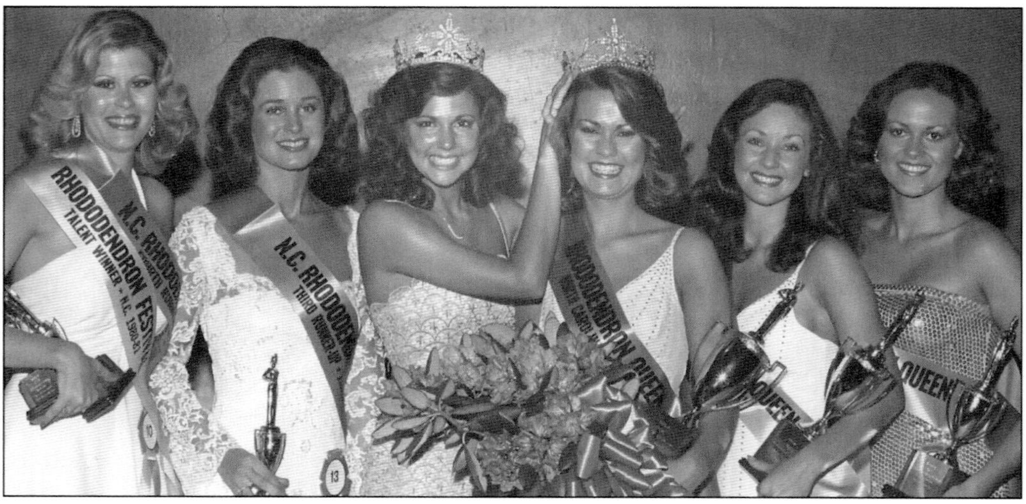

Tammy Roberts, the 1980 rhododendron queen, crowns Teresa Strawser. They are pictured here with the runners-up competing for the 1981 title. (Courtesy of Tammy Roberts Preusse.)

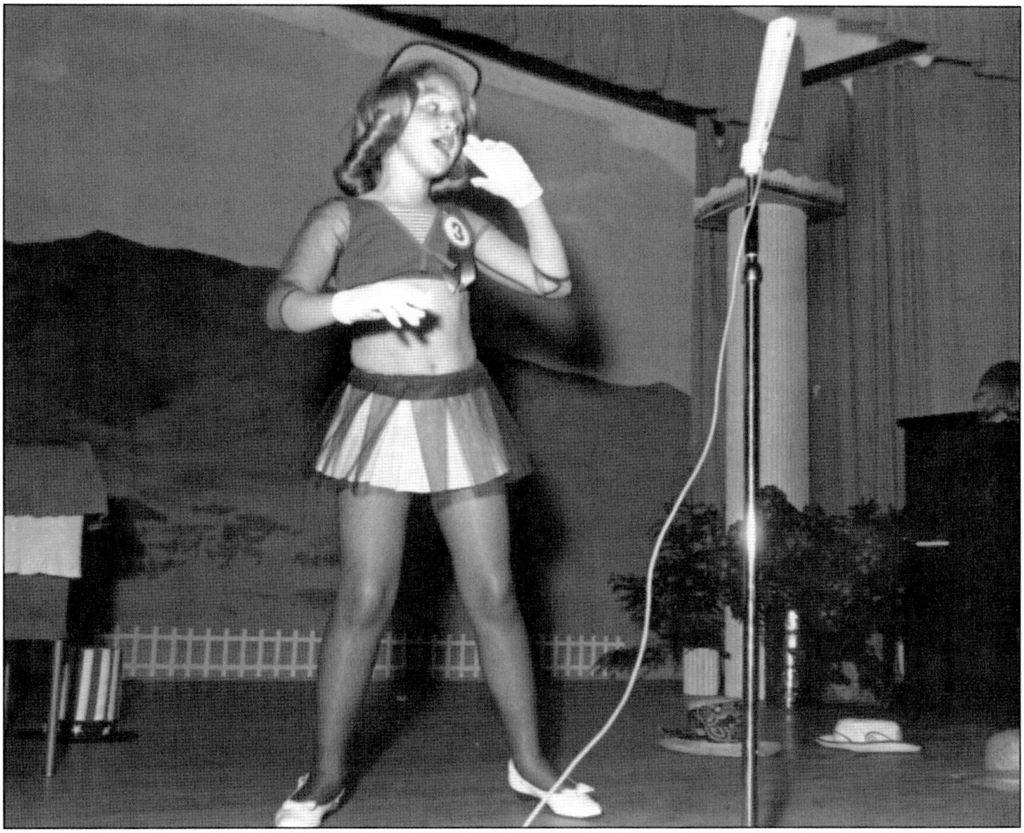

The talent phase of the competition is a favorite among audience members. A contestant entertains the crowd while competing for the junior title. (Courtesy of the Wilson Collection.)

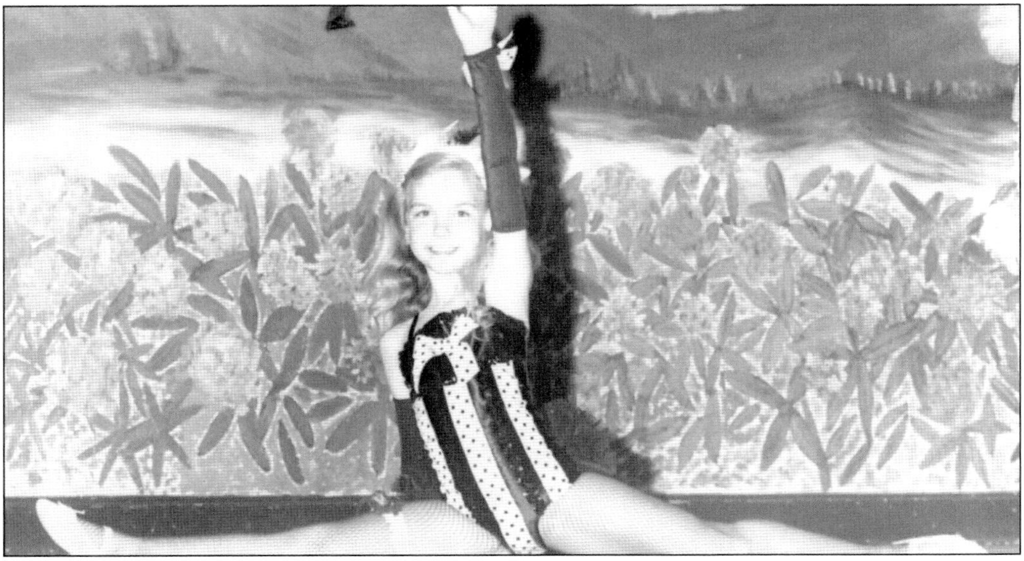

Donna Hursey, the 1979 North Carolina junior rhododendron queen, was a crowd favorite during the talent portion of the competition. (Courtesy of the Wilson Collection.)

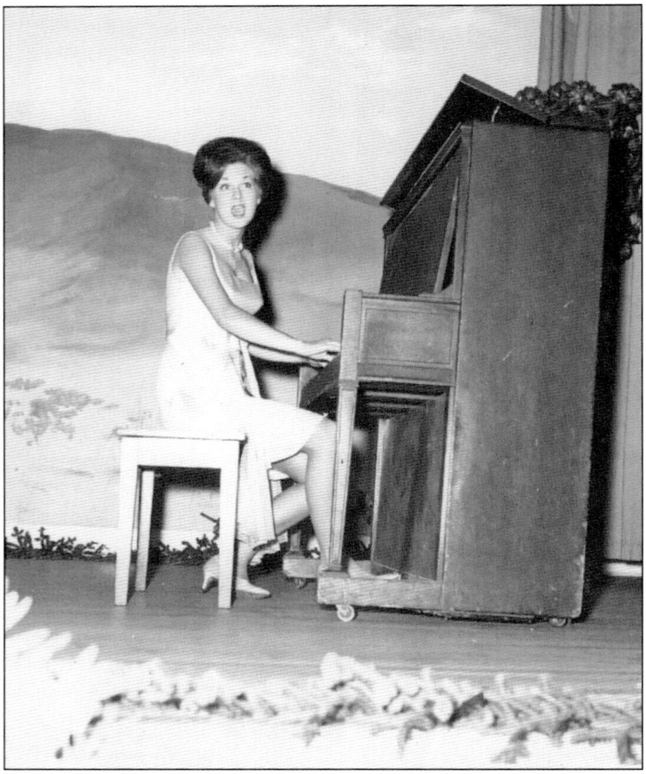

Talent is not just a phase of competition; it is a requirement for the rhododendron queen. During hectic personal appearance tours, the rhododendron queen is often asked to perform at festivals and pageants throughout the state. Jean Rhodes, the 1966 queen, entertains the crowd while competing in the talent portion of the pageant. (Courtesy of the Barron Collection.)

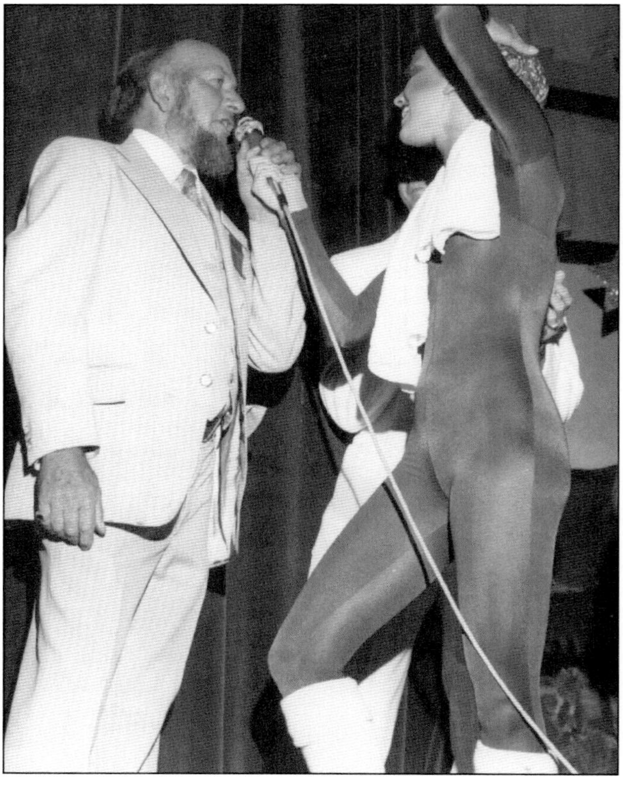

Kim Morgan Greene, the 1979 queen, chats with Ed Wilson after performing for the crowd. Greene went on to have a successful career in the entertainment field, acting and producing. She is well known for her roles in *The Colbys* and *Another World* and has had roles in numerous other television shows and movies. In 2002, she played the role of Roxie Hart in the musical *Chicago* at the North Shore Music Theatre outside of Boston. (Courtesy of the Wilson Collection.)

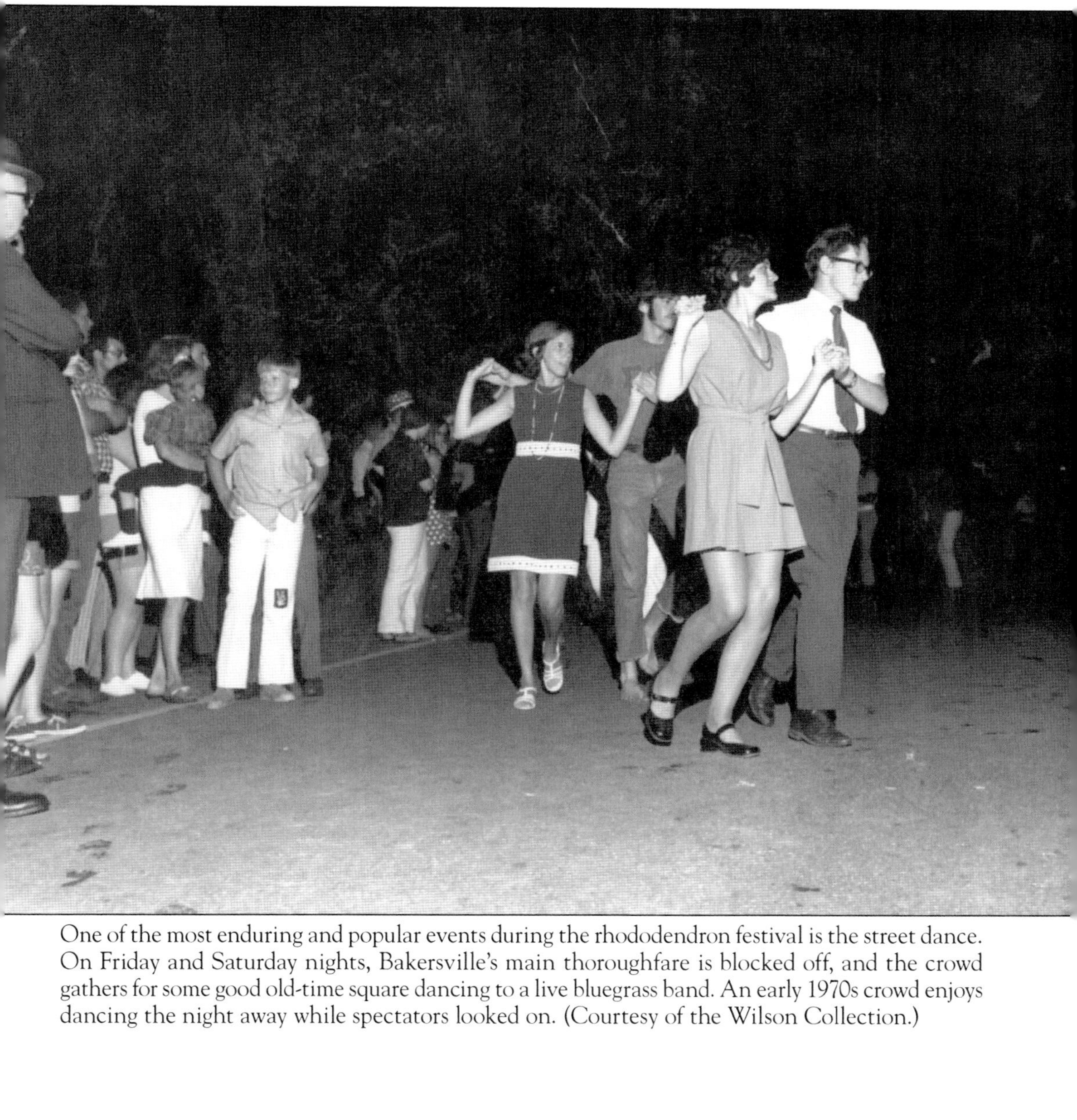

One of the most enduring and popular events during the rhododendron festival is the street dance. On Friday and Saturday nights, Bakersville's main thoroughfare is blocked off, and the crowd gathers for some good old-time square dancing to a live bluegrass band. An early 1970s crowd enjoys dancing the night away while spectators looked on. (Courtesy of the Wilson Collection.)

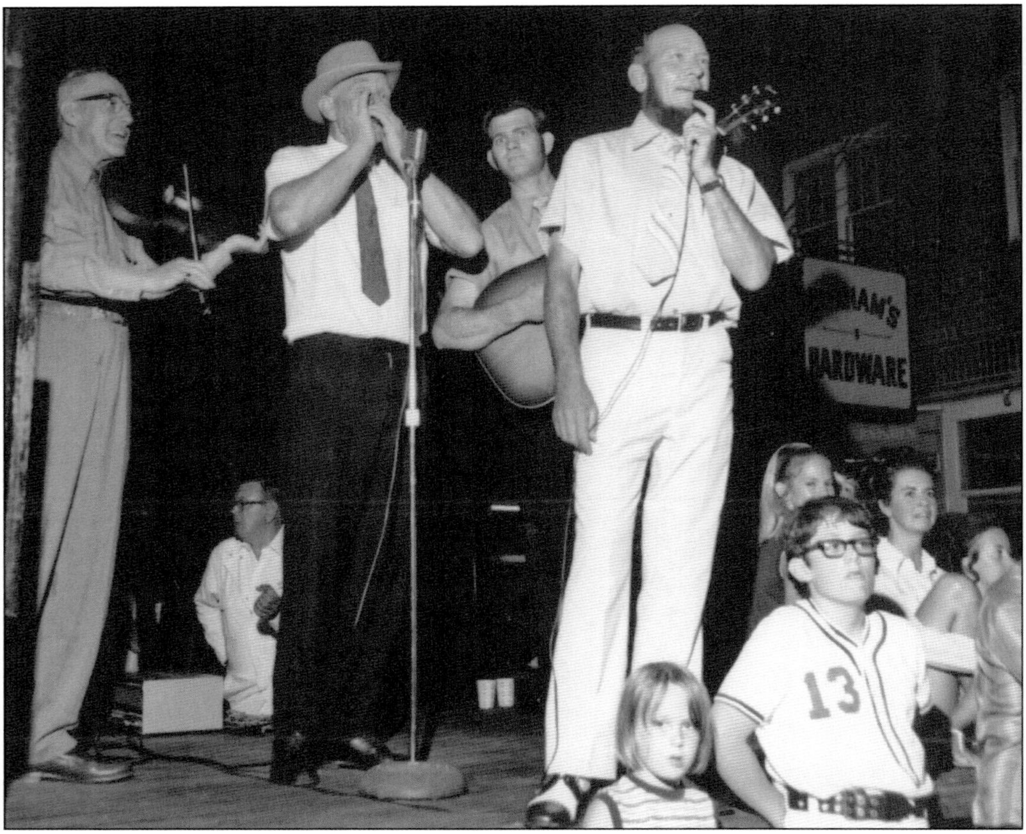

This photograph, taken sometime in the late 1960s or early 1970s, features rhododendron queen business manager Ed Wilson as he welcomes the street dance crowd from the bandstand. (Courtesy of the Wilson Collection.)

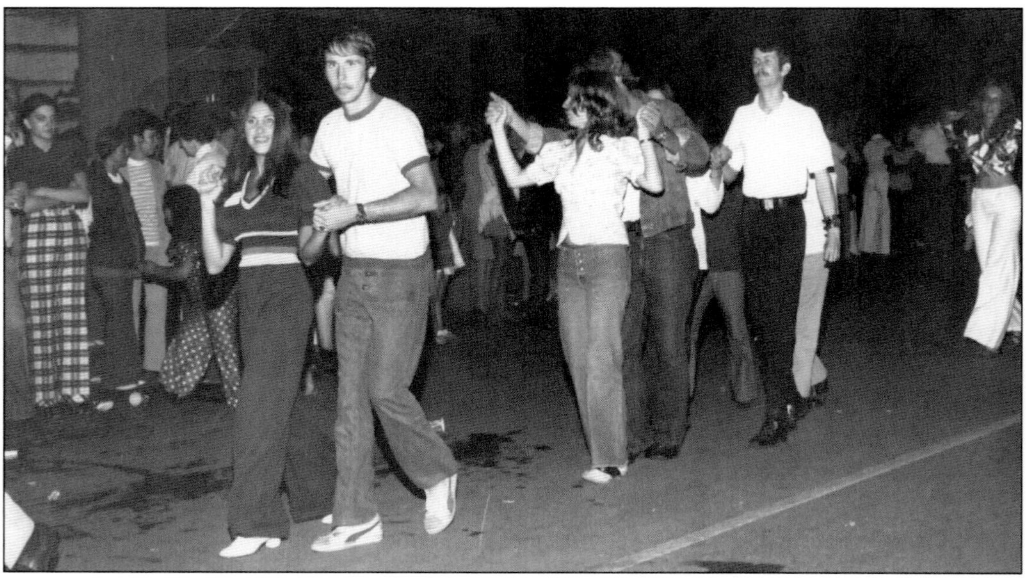

A mid-1980s crowd enjoys the music and the dancing. Local young men have always looked forward to dancing with pageant contestants and visiting queens. (Courtesy of Geneva Brewer.)

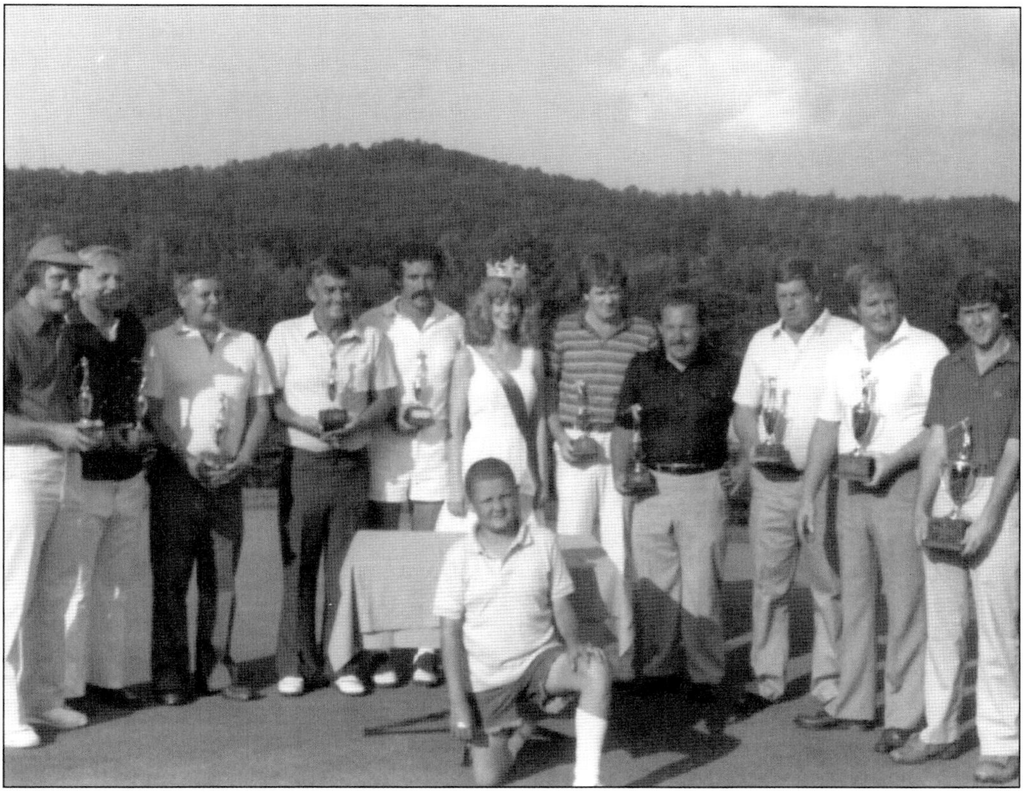

An annual event that coincides with the rhododendron festival is the golf tournament, which takes place at Grassy Creek Golf and Country Club in neighboring Spruce Pine. The 1983 rhododendron queen, Betsy Jones, poses with the participants and had the honor of making the presentation to the tournament winner. (Both, courtesy of the Barron Collection.)

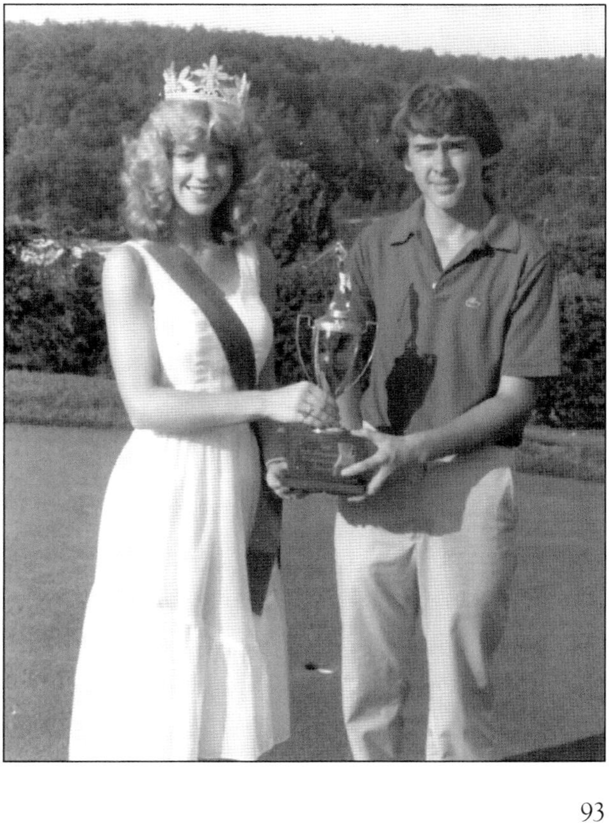

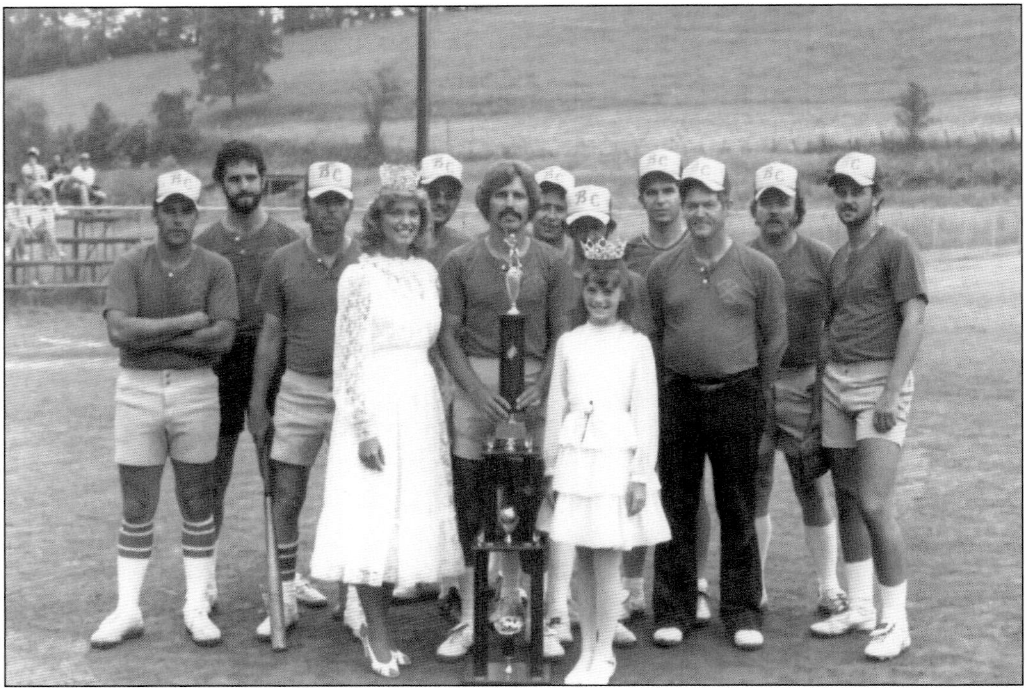

The 1984 rhododendron queens, Donna Wilson (front left) and Kara White, were on hand to meet the participants and present the awards during the Rhododendron Golf Tournament. (Courtesy of the Barron Collection.)

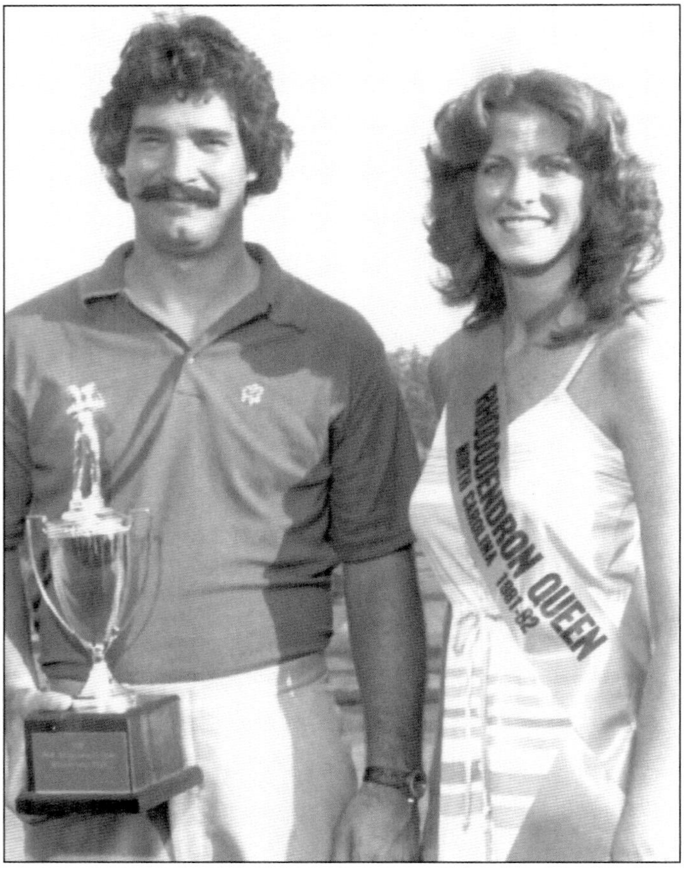

Lori Boggs, the 1982 North Carolina rhododendron queen, presents the award to the tournament winner. (Courtesy of Geneva Brewer.)

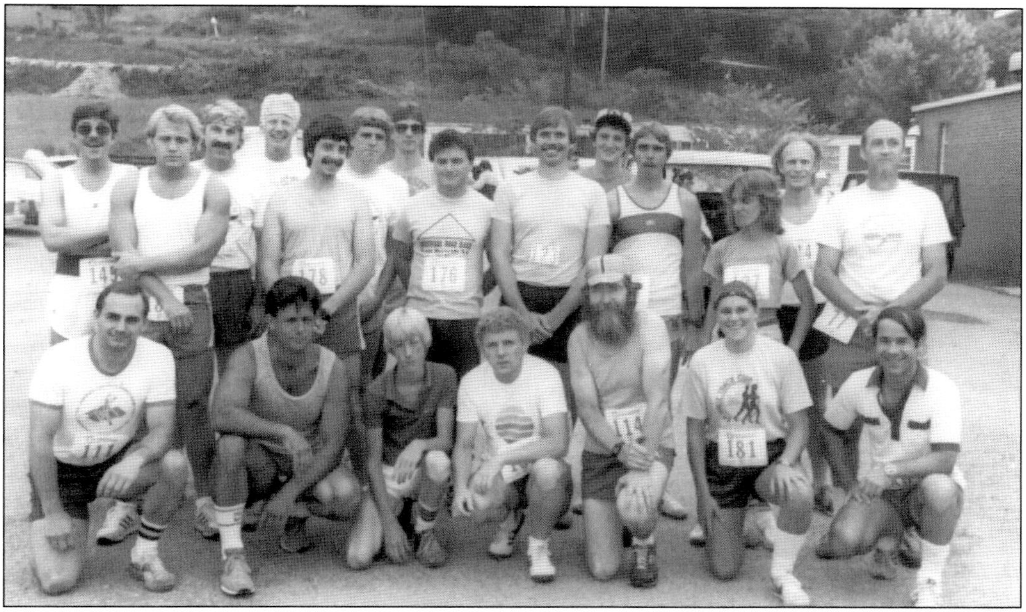

The Rhododendron Run, an annual event that coincides each year with the rhododendron festival, celebrated its 37th year in 2014. The course run is a US track-and-field-certified 10 kilometer course, sanctioned by the State of Franklin Track Club for king, queen, and team of the road competition. Attracting avid runners from all over the Southeast, the run has come to be known as a premier competition for dedicated runners. The event has always attracted local runners. This photograph, taken sometime in the 1980s, captures a group of Mitchell County participants. (Courtesy of the North Carolina Rhododendron Festival.)

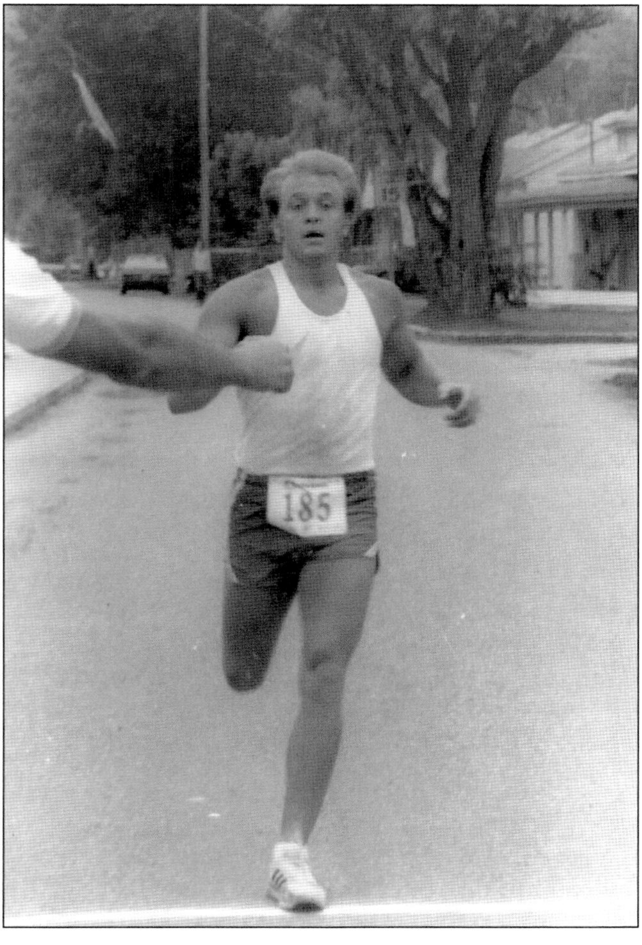

A tired runner crossed the finish line amidst cheers and congratulations from the crowd. (Courtesy of the North Carolina Rhododendron Festival.)

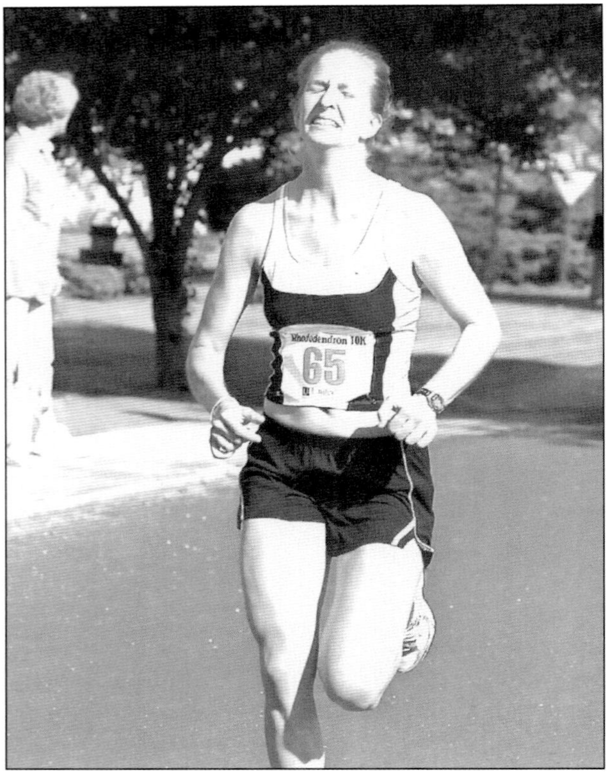

The emotions displayed on the faces of the runners crossing the finish line often range from relieved to jubilant. (Both, courtesy of Terry Campbell.)

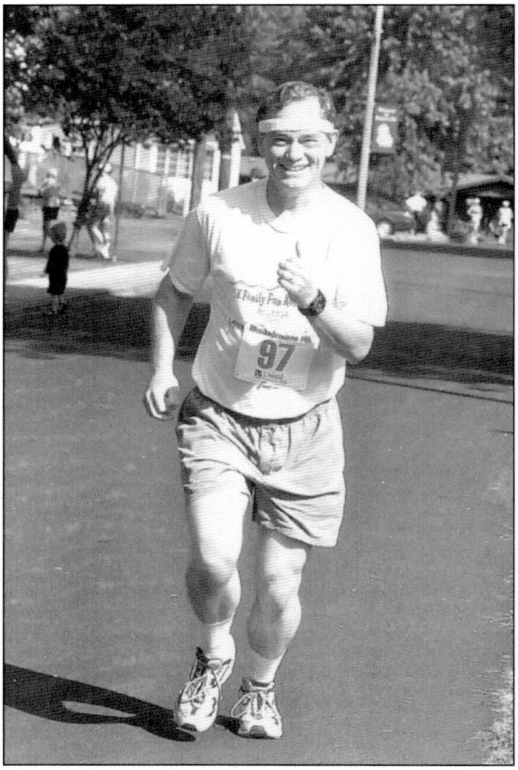

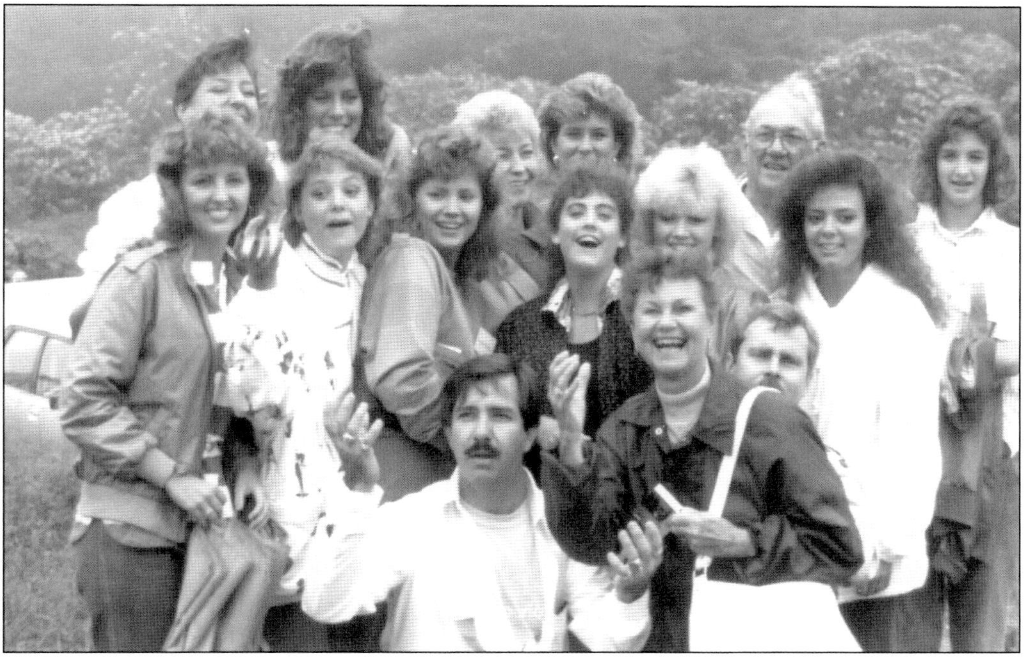

Representatives from visiting festivals are always in attendance. Since the first festival, visiting queens and festival officials from all over the state have joined pageant contestants on a tour of Roan Mountain and the famous Rhododendron Gardens. This tradition continues today. This 1980s photograph was taken during a foggy tour of the gardens and features contestants, judges, and pageant master of ceremonies Bob Hensley. (Courtesy of Bob Hensley.)

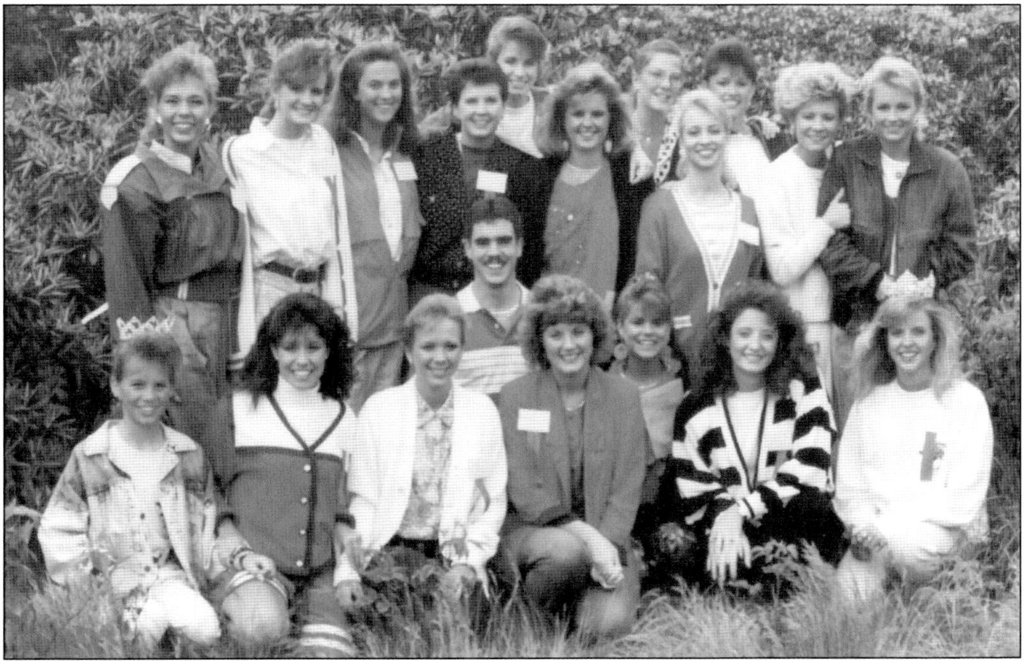

In 1990, Melissa Crouse (front row, far right), retiring rhododendron queen, and newly crowned junior rhododendron queen Heather Boone (front row, far left) pose with contestants competing for the 1991 title during a tour of Roan Mountain. (Courtesy of Bob Hensley.)

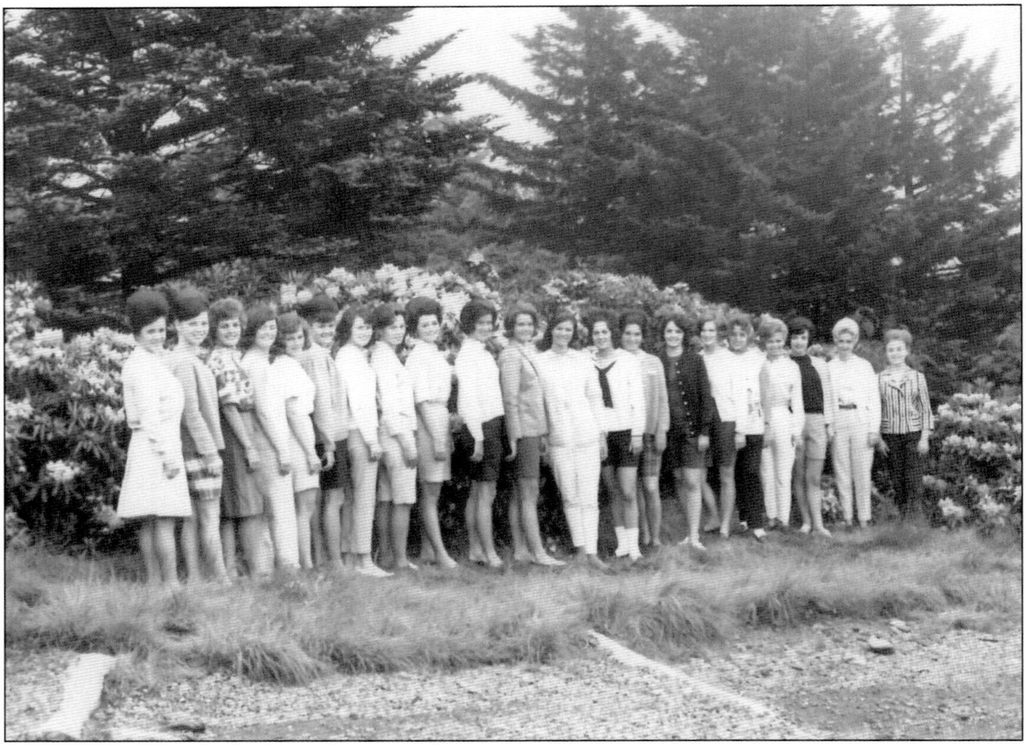

A mid-1960s group of hopeful contestants smile for the camera during a tour of the Rhododendron Gardens. (Courtesy of Bob Hensley.)

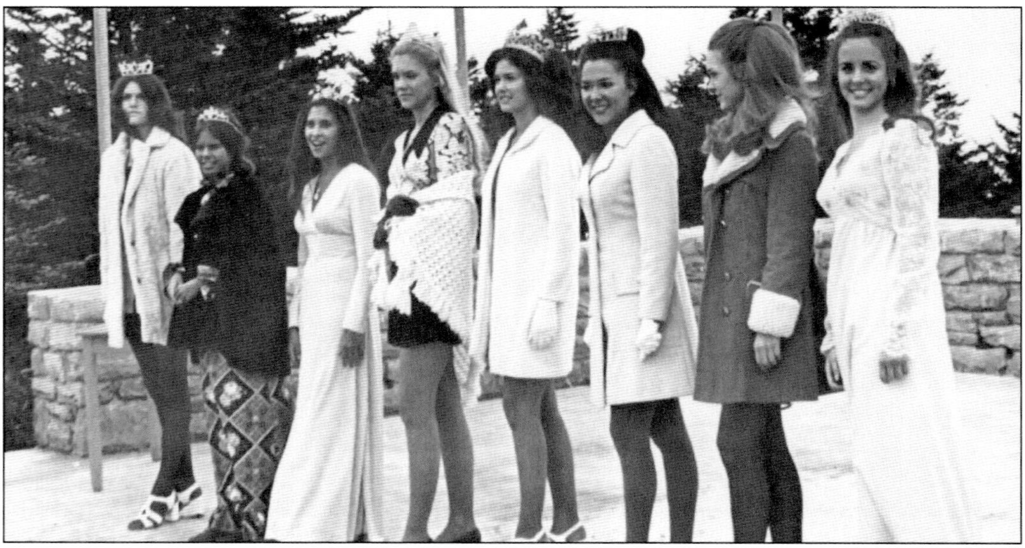

A group of visiting queens pose on the platform once used for the rhododendron queen crowning ceremony. (Courtesy of the Wilson Collection.)

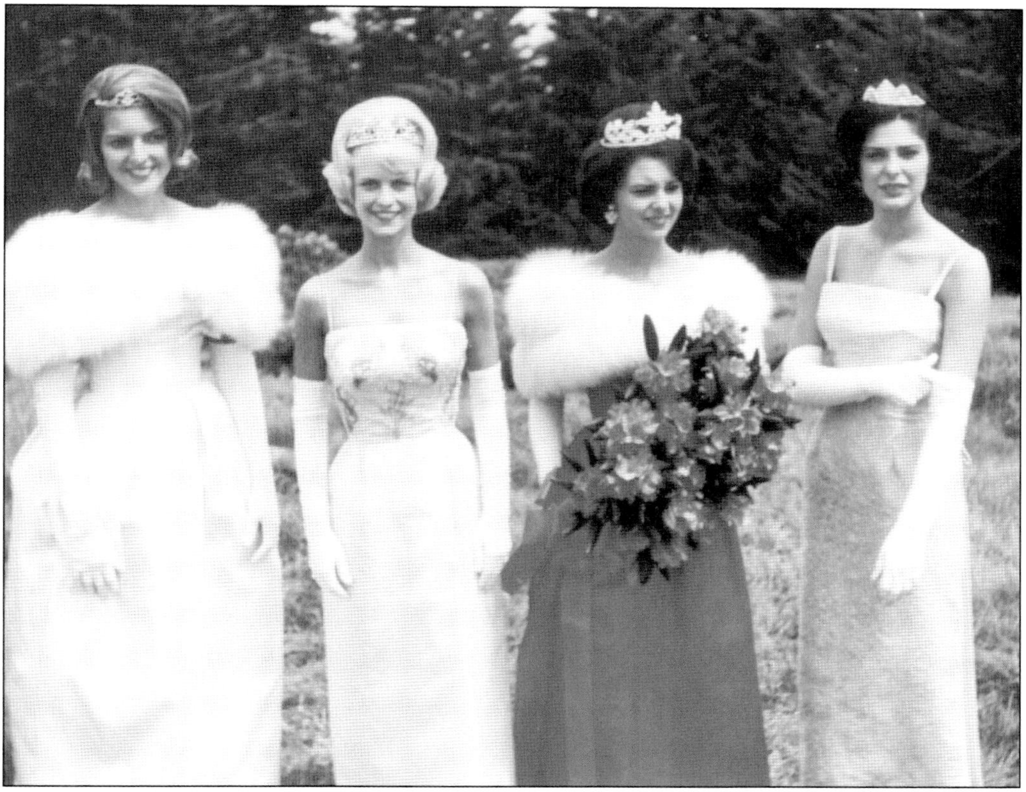

Betty Rae Lawhon (second from right), the 1963 North Carolina rhododendron queen, welcomes visiting queens atop majestic Roan Mountain. (Courtesy of Betty Lawhon Deviney.)

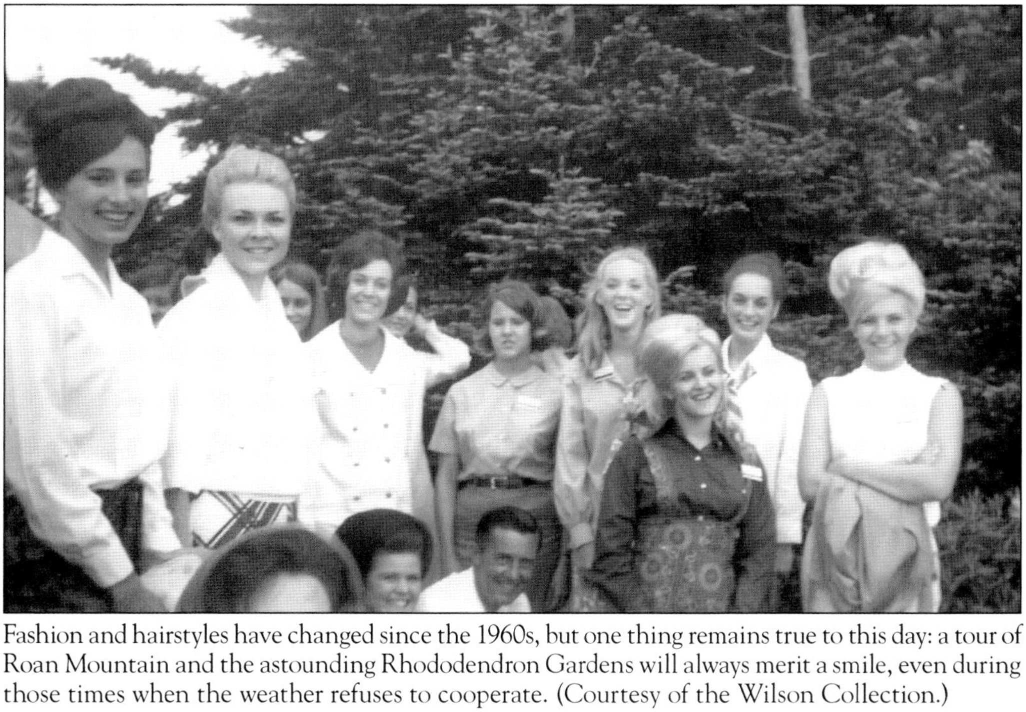

Fashion and hairstyles have changed since the 1960s, but one thing remains true to this day: a tour of Roan Mountain and the astounding Rhododendron Gardens will always merit a smile, even during those times when the weather refuses to cooperate. (Courtesy of the Wilson Collection.)

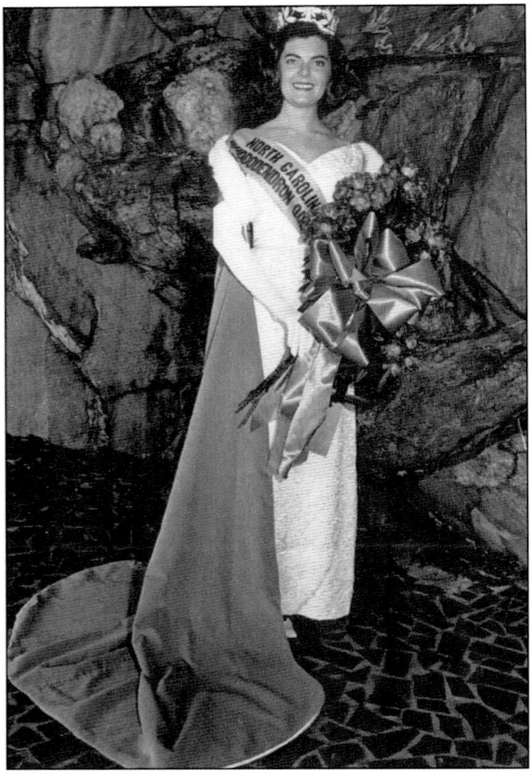

Yes, it is true; the more things change, the more they stay the same. Linda Blair wore the official rhododendron robe in 1967. The very same garment was worn beautifully and regally by Amelia Wilson, the 2013 rhododendron queen, on the same day she relinquished her crown. Amelia is the granddaughter of Ed and June Wilson. Ed served for a number of years as business manager for the rhododendron queen. Amelia holds the distinction of holding both the titles of rhododendron queen and junior rhododendron queen; she was junior queen in 2005. Her younger sister Alora won the title of 2011 junior rhododendron queen. (Left, courtesy of the Barron Collection; below, courtesy of Amelia Wilson.)

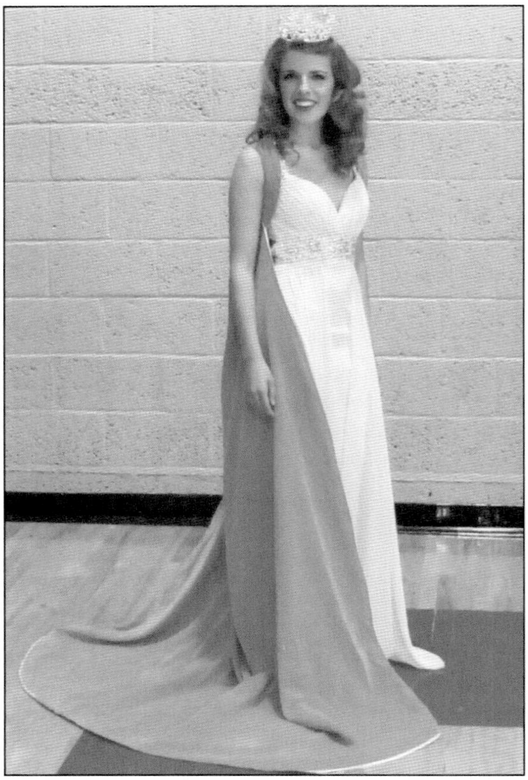

Five

The Rhododendron Family

The Ties That Bind

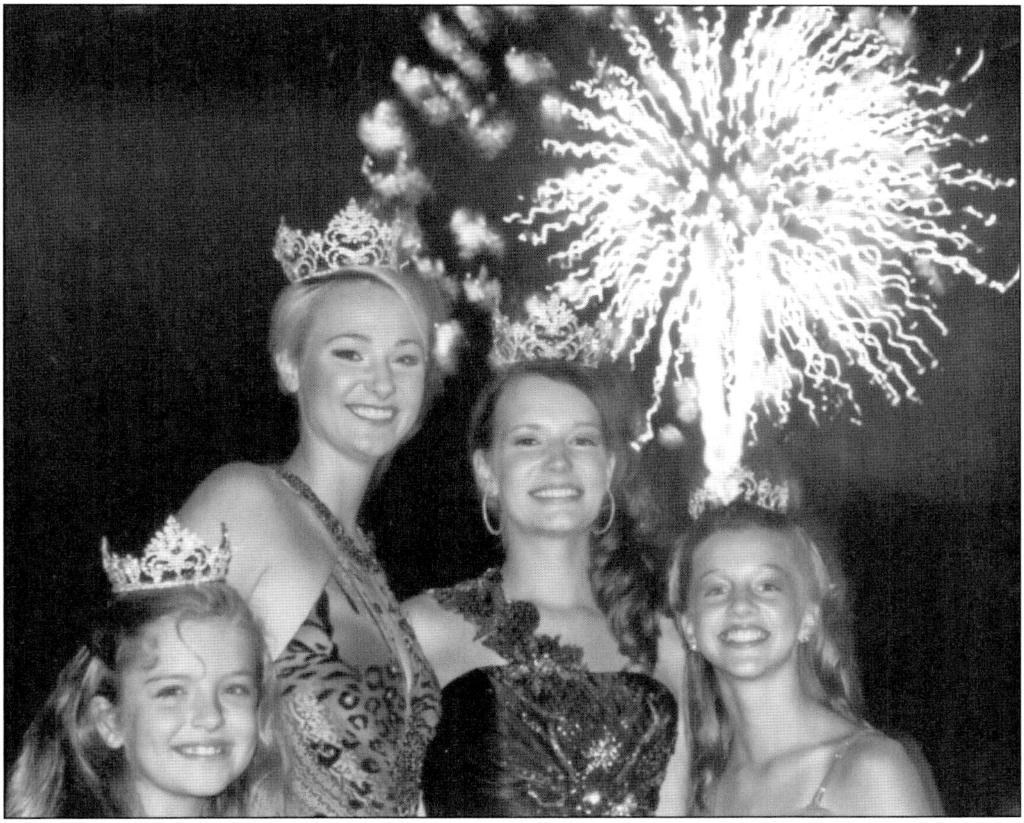

To have been touched by the rhododendron experience is to know and understand the true meaning of the phrase "rhododendron family." The North Carolina Rhododendron Festival is one of many festivals celebrated each year throughout the state. The rhododendron queens form lasting friendships with other festival queens during their reign. In September 2010, North Carolina rhododendron queen Rosa Creech (back left) and junior rhododendron queen Alora Wilson (front left) traveled to Hampstead, North Carolina, to celebrate the North Carolina Spot Festival. They are pictured here with 2010 Spot Festival queen Lauren Vann (back right) and Spot Festival princess Kathleen Berger (front right) during the annual fireworks display. (Courtesy of Bob Hensley.)

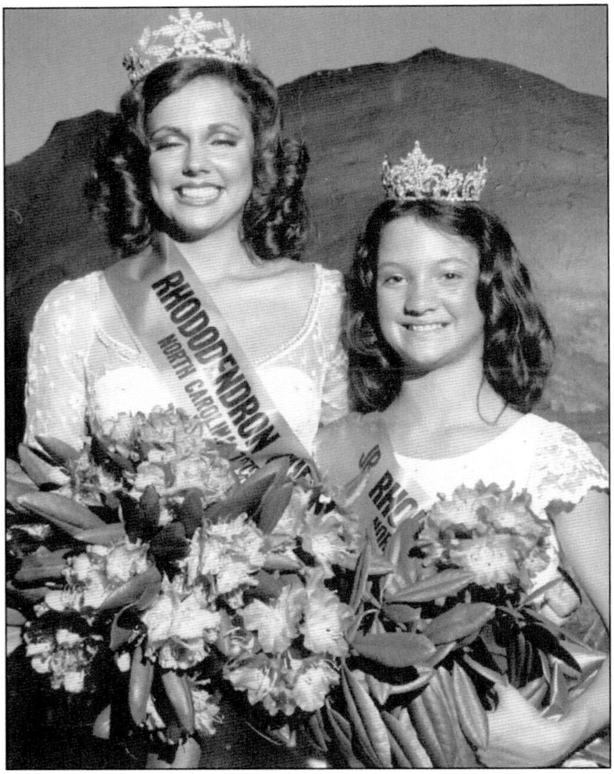

Since 1961, when O.D. Calhoun's inspiration for a junior pageant became reality, the young ladies who have worn the rhododendron crown have formed relationships with the junior queens that have often been equated with that of sisters. Tammy Roberts (left), the 1980 rhododendron queen, has many wonderful memories of her year, many of them involving Tara Williams (right), the 1980 junior queen. (Courtesy of Tammy Roberts Preusse.)

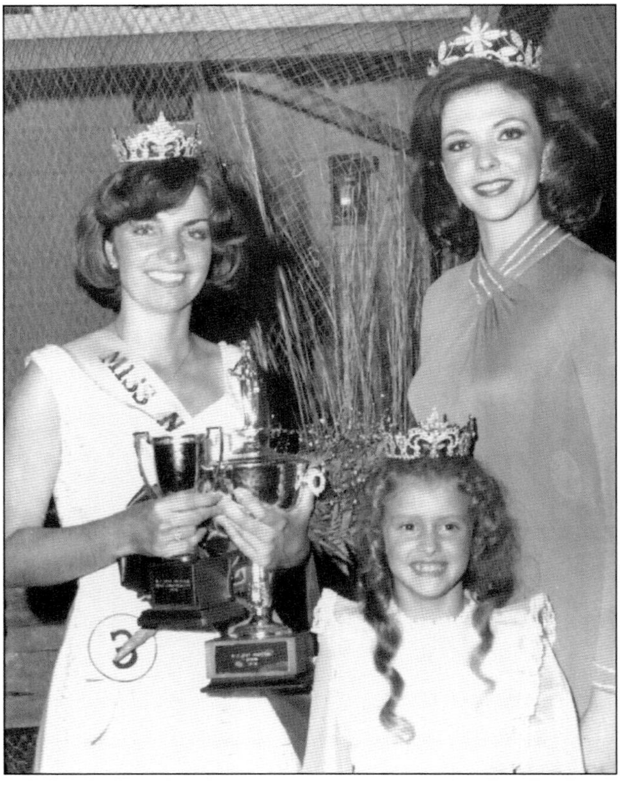

Sharon Manness (back right) and Kristin Carroll (front), the 1978 rhododendron queens, were from neighboring communities. They attended the North Carolina Spot Festival and were on hand to congratulate the new Spot Festival queen, Kathy Britt. (Courtesy of the Wilson Collection.)

The 2003 rhododendron queens, Stephanie Chang (right) and Brittany Buchanan, were both local residents. Chang was from Bakersville, and Buchanan lived in Spruce Pine. The festival that year took place just a few short weeks after a devastating jail fire in Bakersville that claimed the lives of eight individuals. The decision was made to have the street dance at another location, away from the scene of the tragedy. That night, at the street dance, Chang made a very kind and symbolic gesture that is remembered today; she presented her bouquet of rhododendron blossoms to members of the Bakersville Fire Department. (Courtesy of Bob Hensley.)

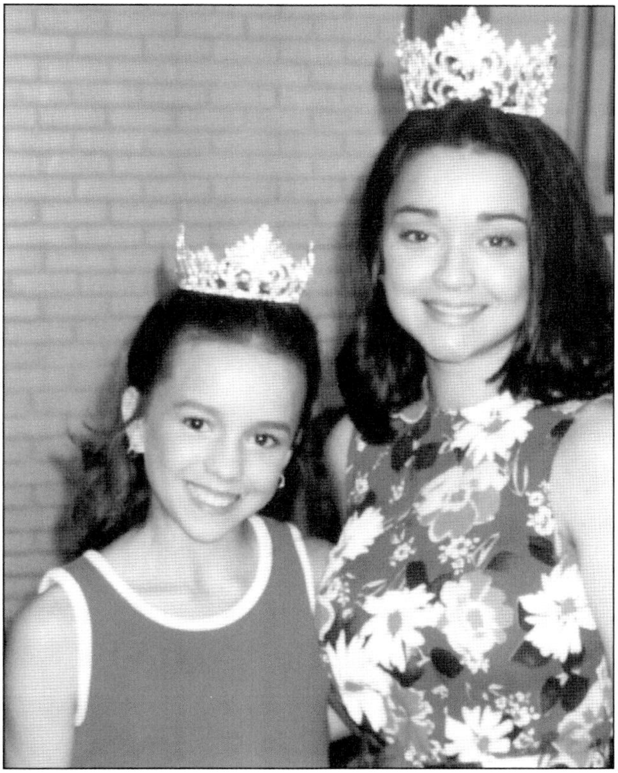

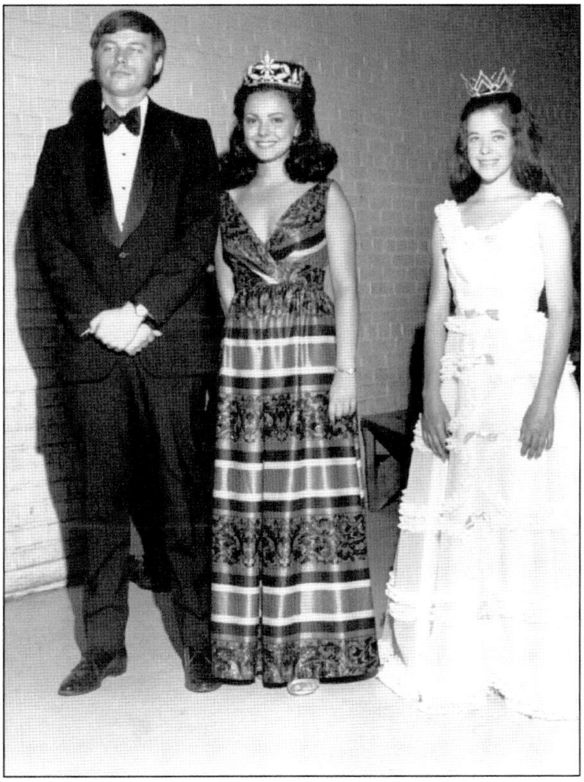

Carol Ann Bass (center), the 1971 rhododendron queen, attended the Rhododendron Ball, an event that was discontinued in the early 1970s. She is pictured here with her escort for the evening and with the 1972 junior queen, Kathy Memory. (Courtesy of the Wilson Collection.)

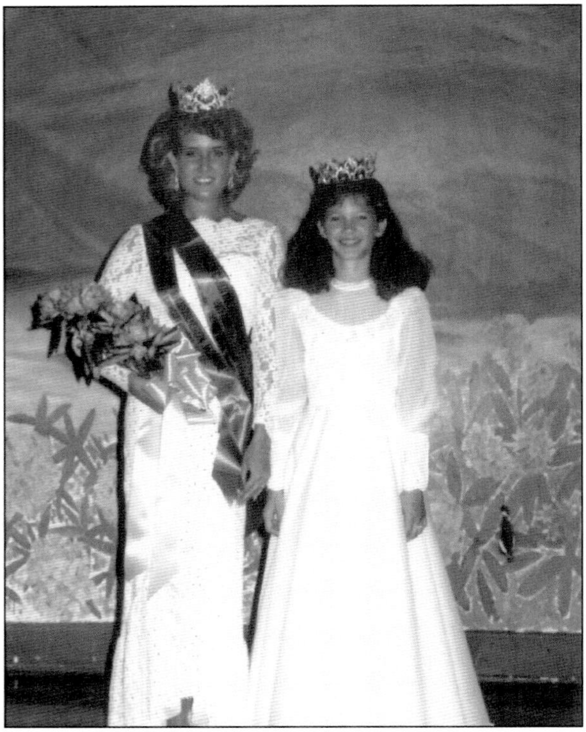

Tracey Russell (left) and Jessica McClellan pose on stage for an official photograph just before embarking on their year together as the 1988 North Carolina rhododendron queens. (Courtesy of Bob Hensley.)

Alette Peake (right) and Heather Boone sign contracts shortly after being selected to represent Bakersville, Mitchell County, and Roan Mountain as the 1991 North Carolina rhododendron queens. Heather's younger sister Ciji would win the junior title six years later. (Courtesy of Bob Hensley.)

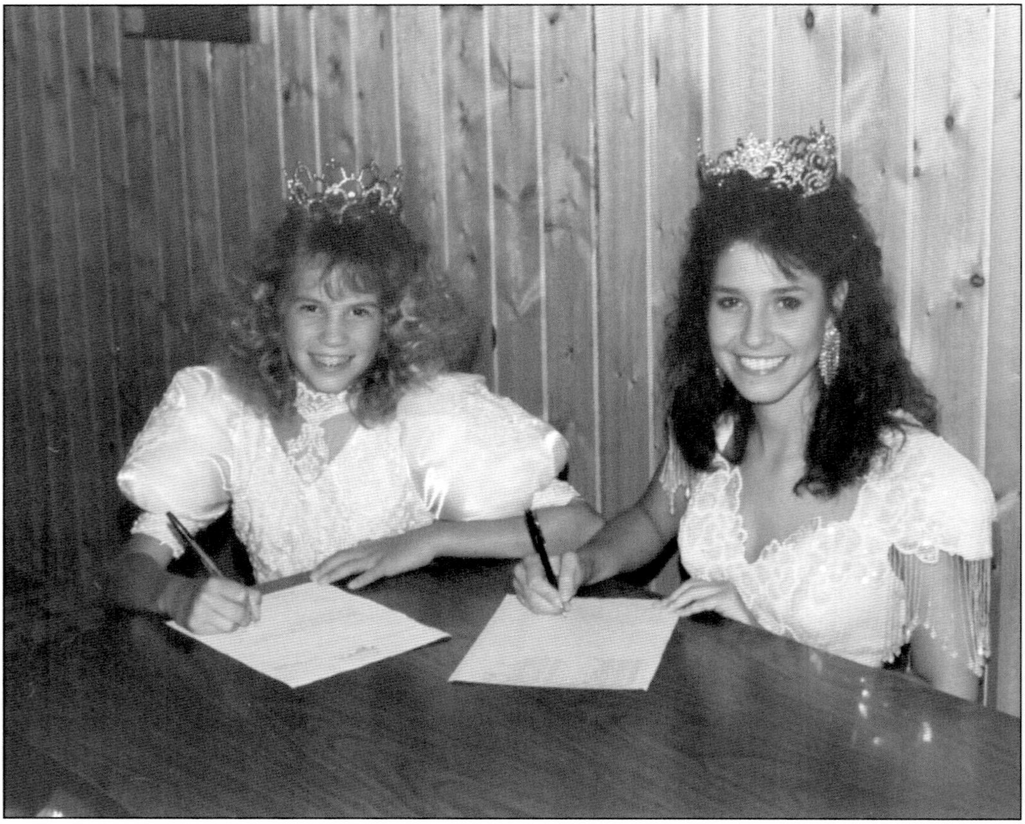

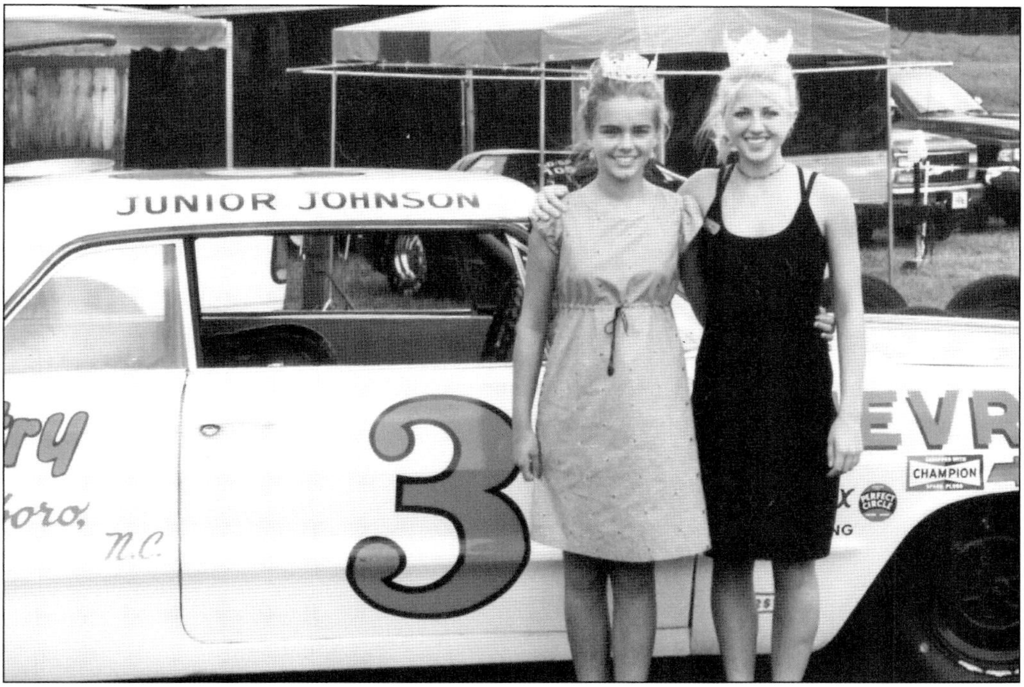

While on a round of personal appearances, Hayley Johnson (right) and Whitney Ray attend a charity benefit car show, Rods in the Park, at McCrae Meadows, the site of the Grandfather Mountain Highland games. The 2001 queens paused for a photo opportunity with Junior Johnson's No. 3 car. (Courtesy of Bob Hensley.)

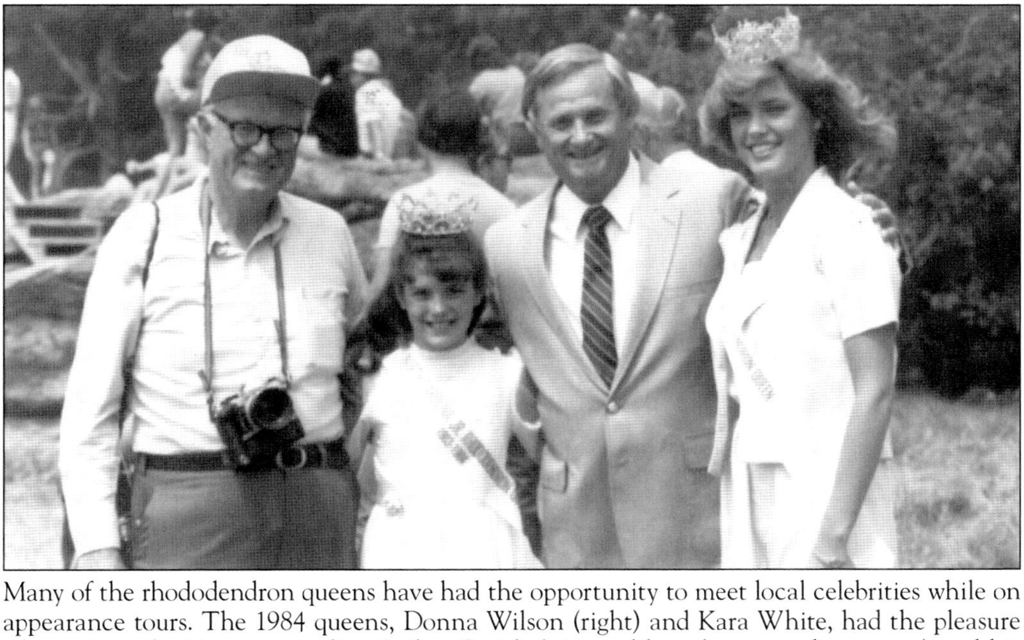

Many of the rhododendron queens have had the opportunity to meet local celebrities while on appearance tours. The 1984 queens, Donna Wilson (right) and Kara White, had the pleasure of meeting television personality Arthur Smith (pictured here between the queens) and his brother Ralph. The *Arthur Smith Show* was the first nationally syndicated country music show on television. Smith lived in Charlotte and ran the first commercial recording studio in the Southeast. (Courtesy of Bob Hensley.)

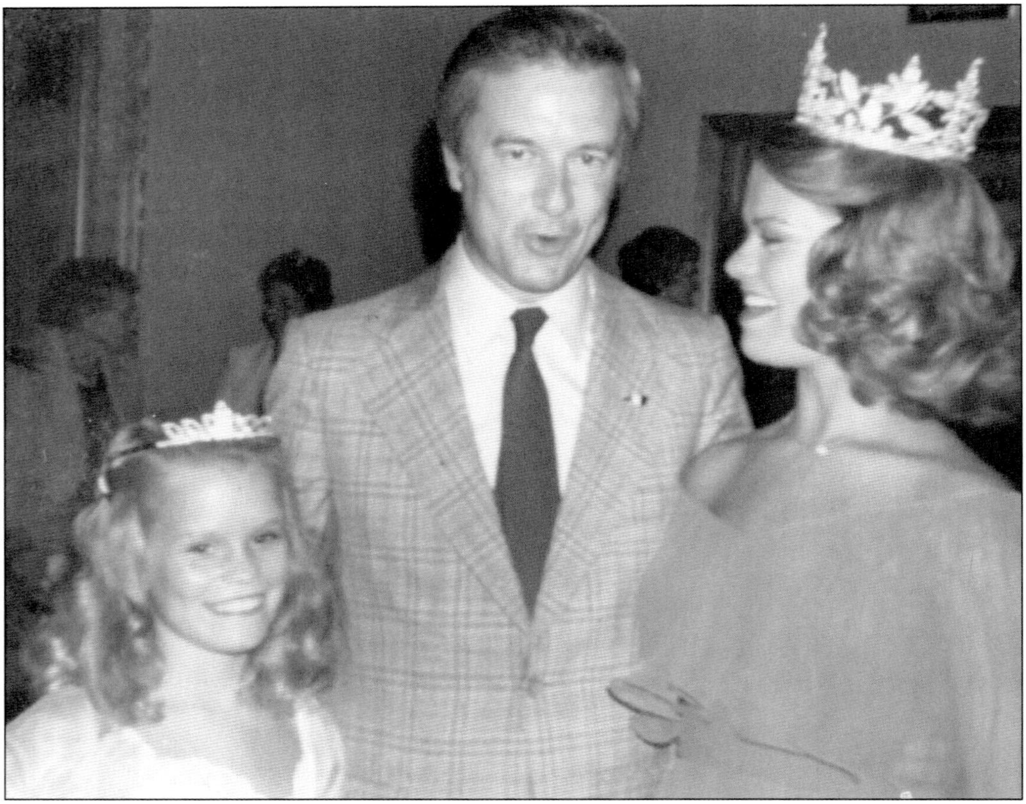

Teresa Strawser, the 1981 rhododendron queen, and her younger sister, Kim, were honored to meet North Carolina governor Jim Hunt. (Courtesy of Bob Hensley.)

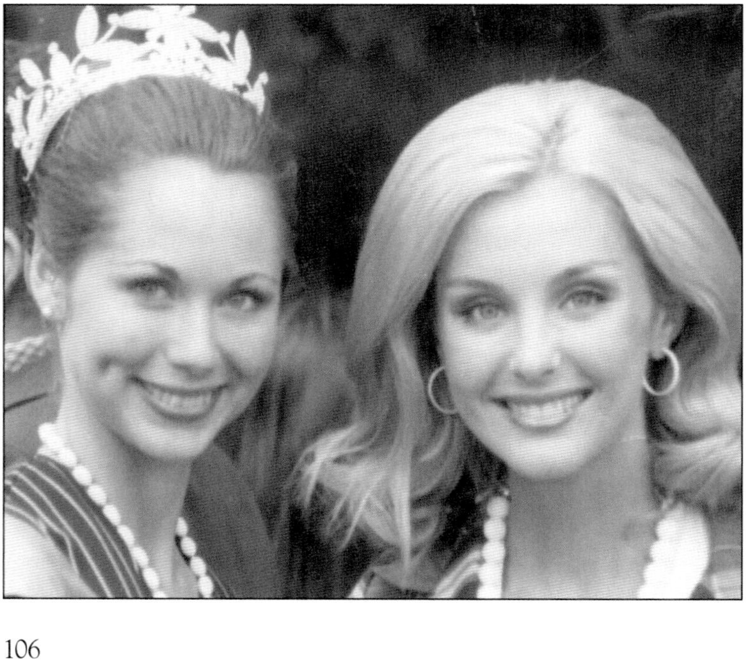

Betsy Jo McDonald (left), the 1975 queen, is pictured here with former queen Marcia Burton, who held the title in 1973. (Courtesy of the Wilson Collection.)

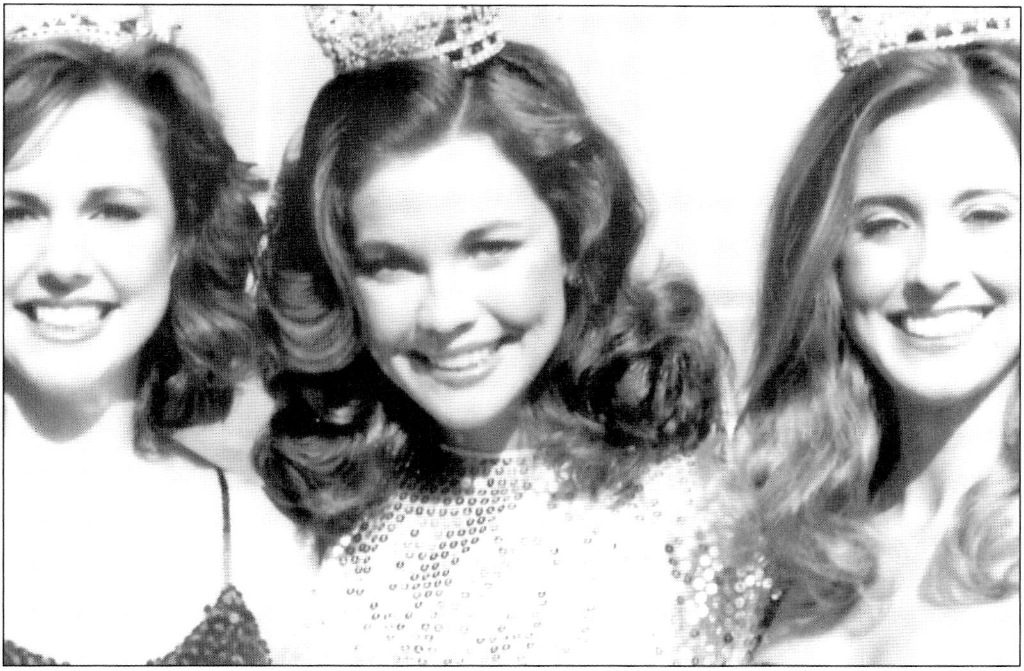

While on a round of personal appearances, 1980 North Carolina rhododendron queen Tammy Roberts (left) had the opportunity to mingle with good friends Jane Perkins (Miss South Carolina) and Monta Maki (Miss North Carolina). (Courtesy of Tammy Roberts Preusse.)

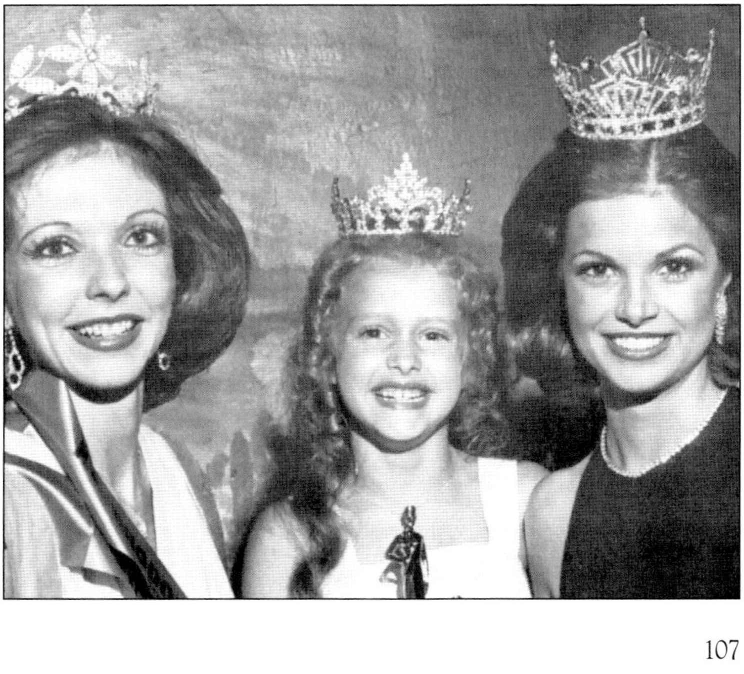

Sharon Manness (left) and Kristin Carroll (center), the 1978 rhododendron queens, appeared with Miss North Carolina, Kathy Fleming. Kristin's younger sister Jennifer would win the title of 1982 North Carolina junior rhododendron queen. (Courtesy of the Wilson Collection.)

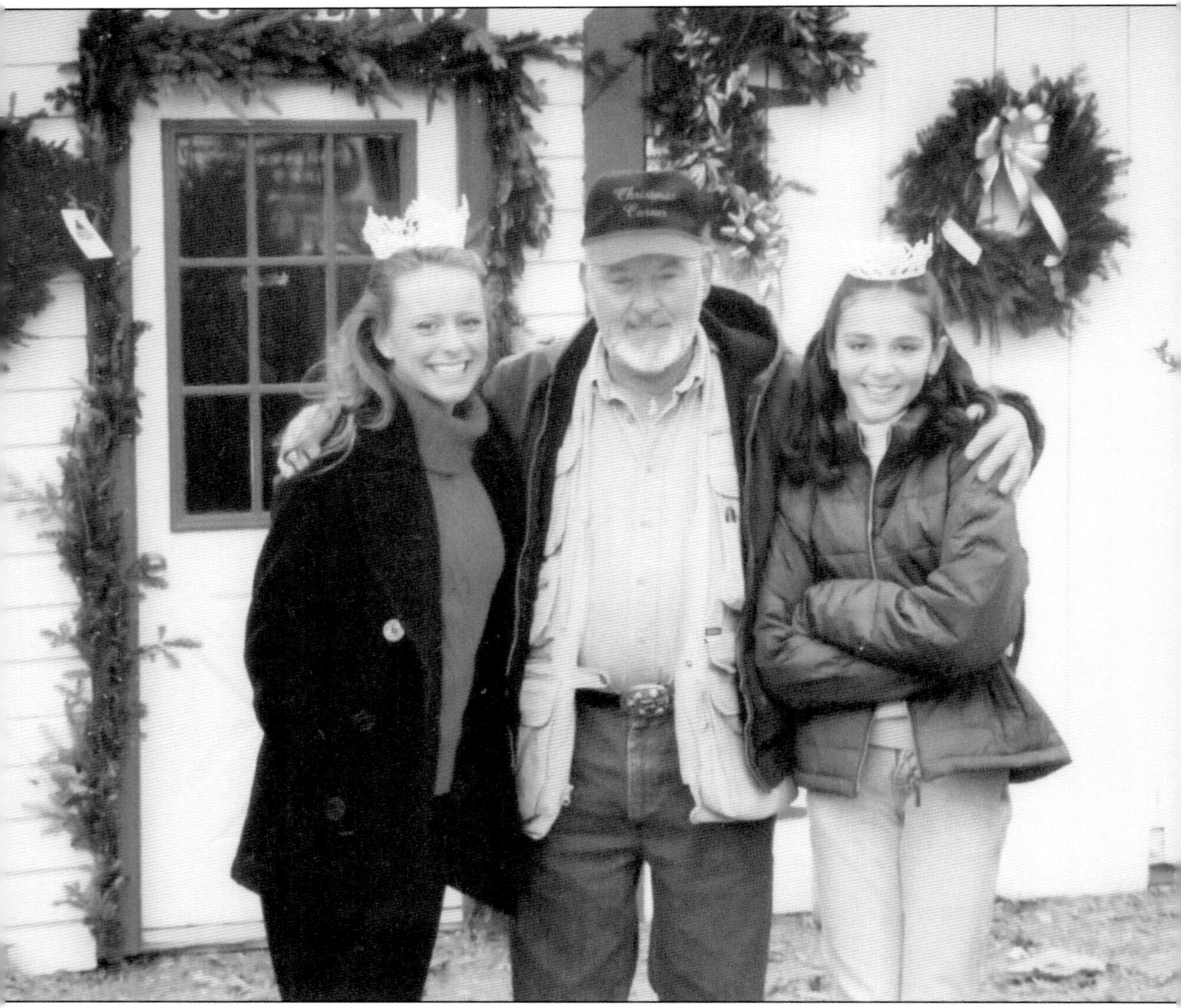

Every year, Doug Clark of the Christmas Corner in neighboring Avery County graciously provides the queens with a freshly cut Christmas tree from his farm. Jennifer Aldridge (left) and Carly Calhoun (right), the 2006 rhododendron queens, visit with Clark. Savannah Spencer, the 2013 junior rhododendron queen shared memories of the day she and Lindsey Robinson selected their trees. Spencer said that climbing the hills and roaming the tree farm took her out of her comfort zone, but that the memory of Bob Hensley and Lindsey carrying her over the rough spots would be something she would cherish forever. (Courtesy of Bob Hensley.)

Ed Wilson also served as business manager for Betsy Jo McDonald (left). He is pictured here with her on stage during the 1975 North Carolina Rhododendron Festival pageant along with junior queen Tina Banks and performers. (Courtesy of the Wilson Collection.)

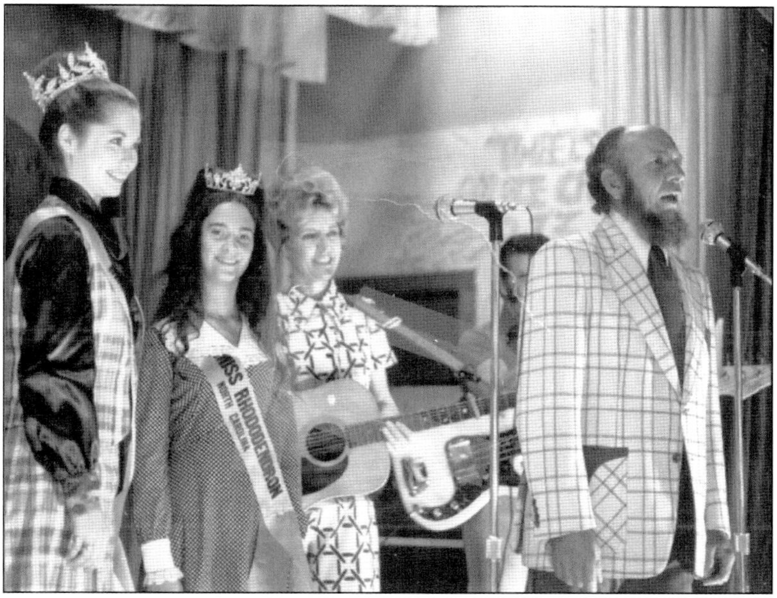

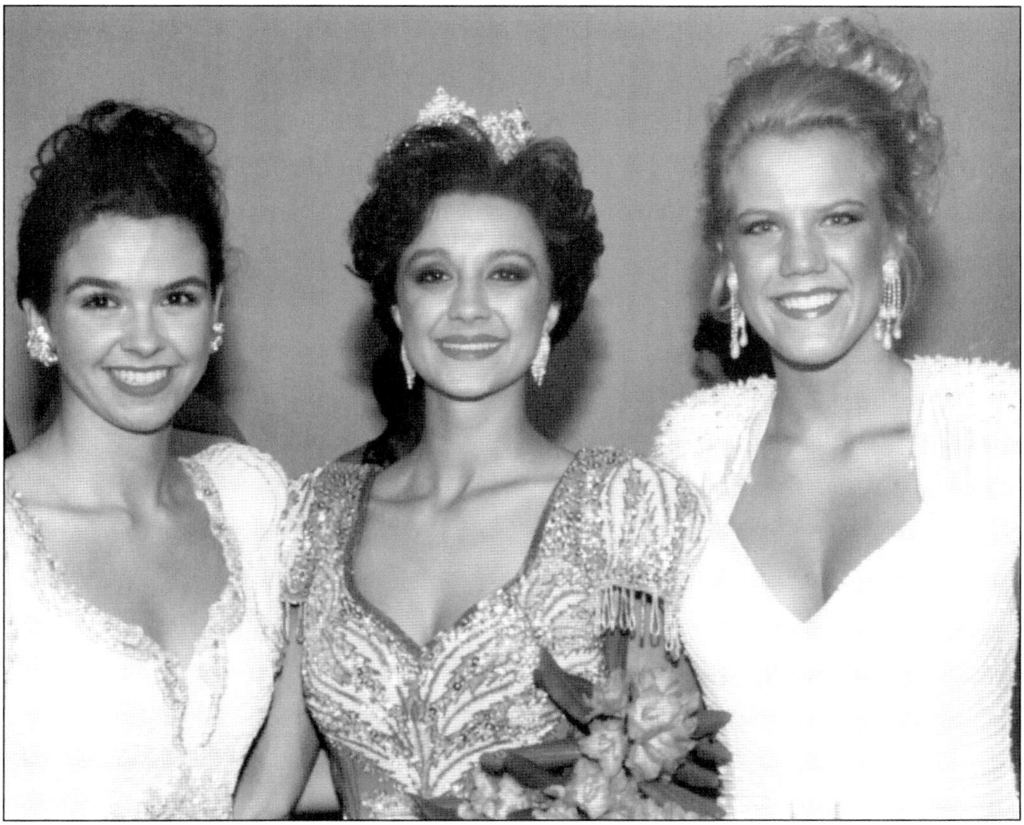

Sheri Benge (center), the 1994 North Carolina rhododendron queen, is pictured here with her runners-up. (Courtesy of Sheri Benge Maxwell.)

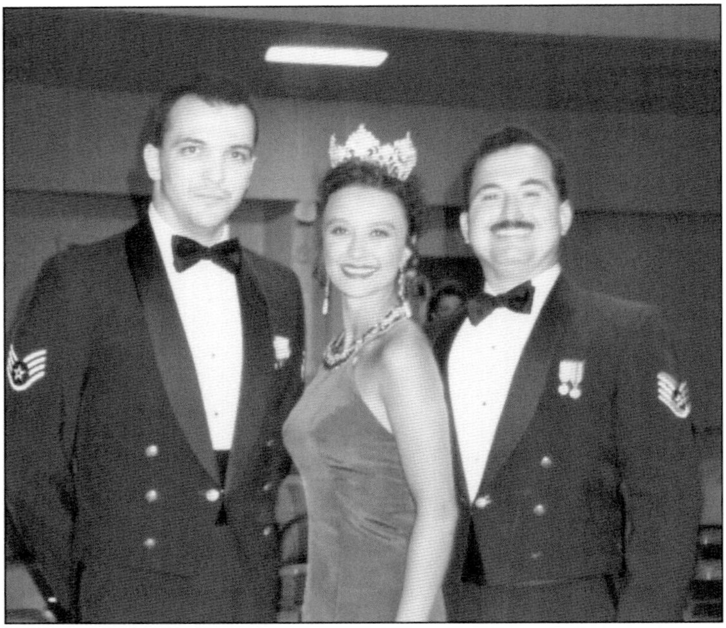

Sheri Benge, the 1994 North Carolina rhododendron queen, made an appearance in Myrtle Beach, South Carolina, at the 1994 Sun Fun Festival. The crowd was unusually large that year, prompting Sun Fun Festival officials to provide visiting queens with military escorts. (Courtesy of Sheri Benge Maxwell.)

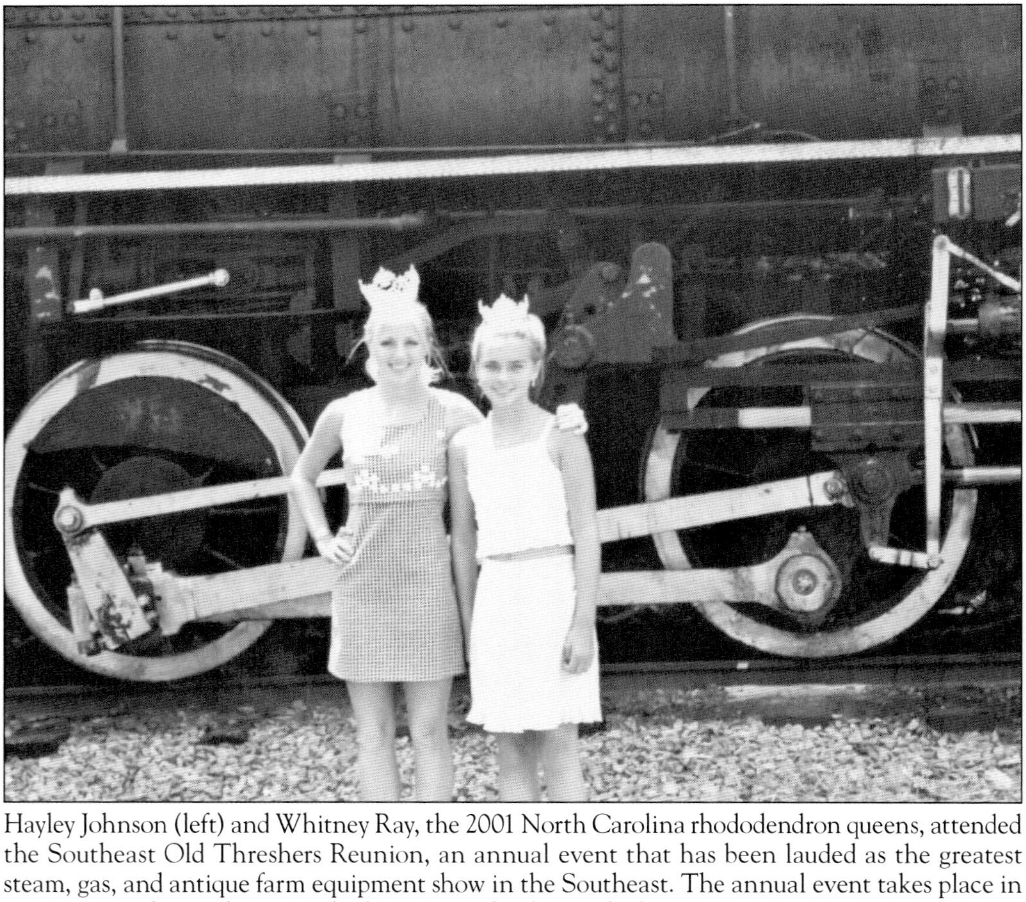

Hayley Johnson (left) and Whitney Ray, the 2001 North Carolina rhododendron queens, attended the Southeast Old Threshers Reunion, an annual event that has been lauded as the greatest steam, gas, and antique farm equipment show in the Southeast. The annual event takes place in Denton, North Carolina, in July. (Courtesy of Bob Hensley.)

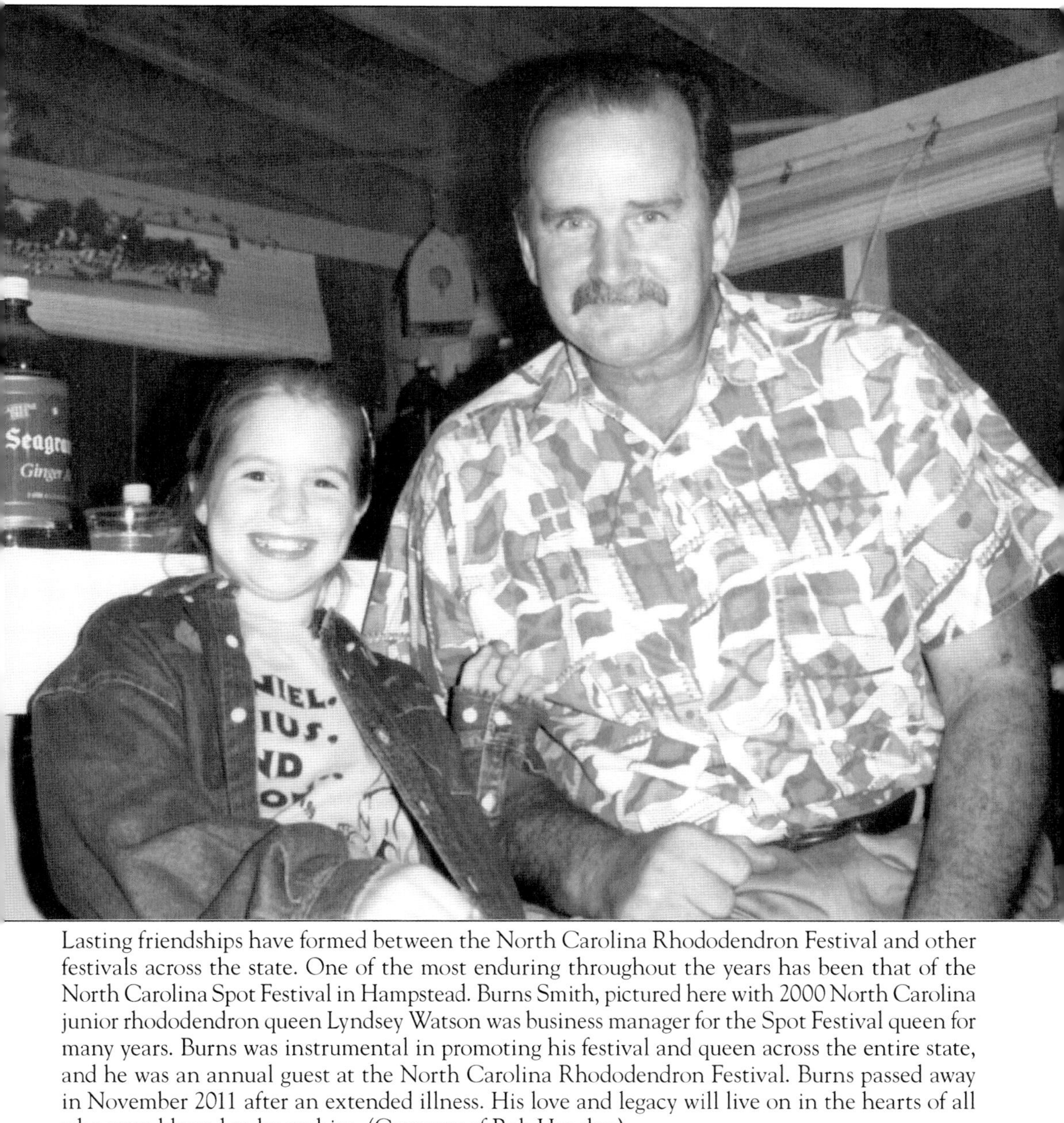

Lasting friendships have formed between the North Carolina Rhododendron Festival and other festivals across the state. One of the most enduring throughout the years has been that of the North Carolina Spot Festival in Hampstead. Burns Smith, pictured here with 2000 North Carolina junior rhododendron queen Lyndsey Watson was business manager for the Spot Festival queen for many years. Burns was instrumental in promoting his festival and queen across the entire state, and he was an annual guest at the North Carolina Rhododendron Festival. Burns passed away in November 2011 after an extended illness. His love and legacy will live on in the hearts of all who were blessed to know him. (Courtesy of Bob Hensley.)

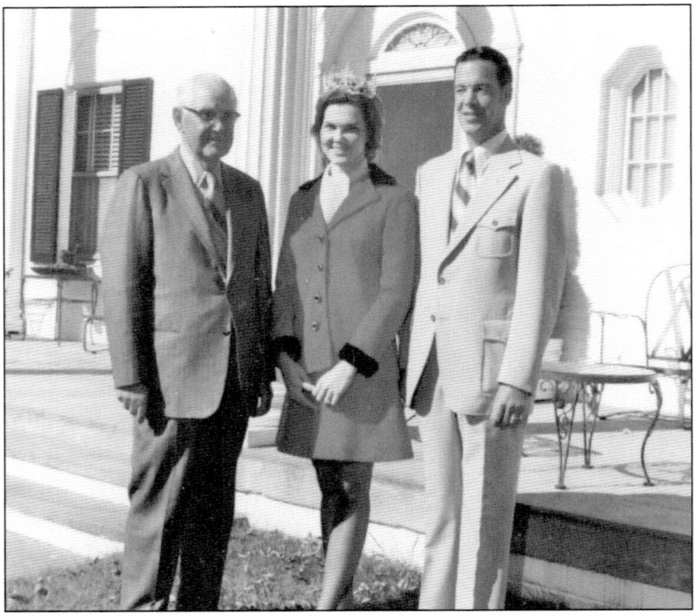

The festival family has expanded over the years to include scholarship donors and devoted volunteers who give freely of their time to make the rhododendron festival the respected and elite festival that it is today. In the 1970s, Don Brewer (right) was a dedicated volunteer, serving for a period of time as business manager. He is pictured here with scholarship donor J.E. Broyhill (left) and the 1974 North Carolina rhododendron queen, Andrea Mull. (Courtesy of Geneva Brewer.)

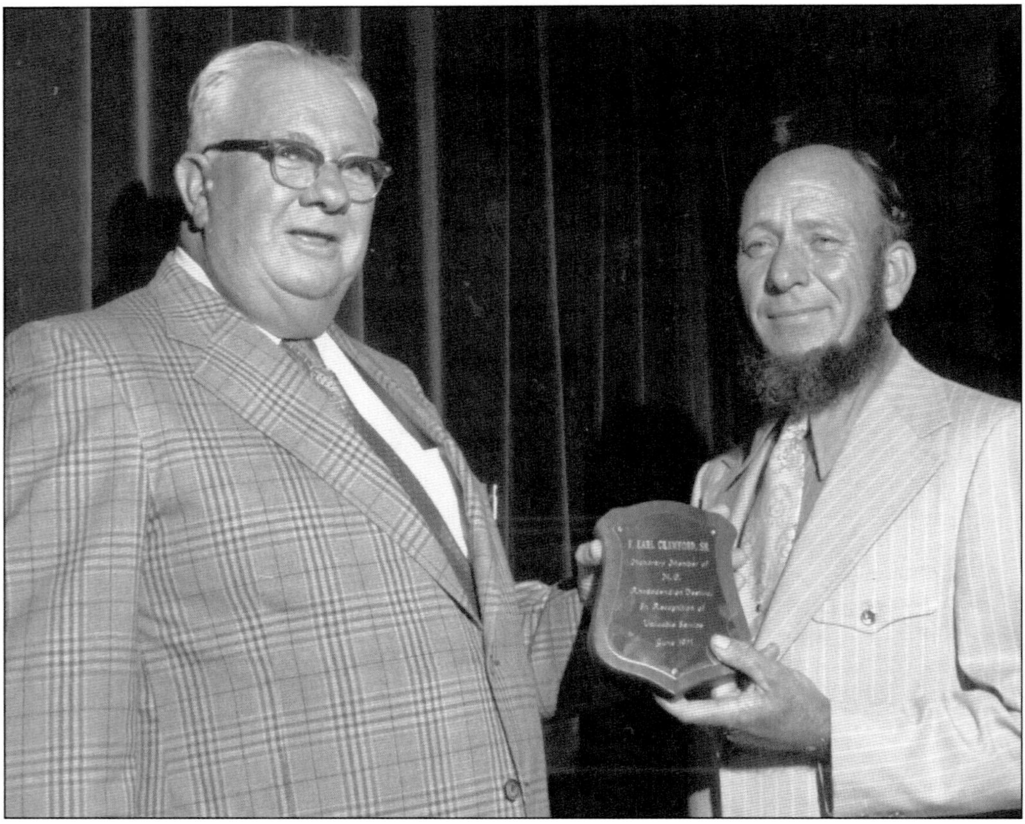

Earl Crawford (left) first attended the North Carolina Rhododendron Festival as a judge, in the 1950s. Crawford was vice president of the Carolinas Carrousel Organization. In 1971, he was honored by Ed Wilson and given an official plaque recognizing him as a friend of the rhododendron festival. (Courtesy of the Wilson Collection.)

The success of the North Carolina Rhododendron Festival is due solely to the contributions and efforts of a staff made up entirely of volunteers. During the 1960s, 1970s, and 1980s, Bob and Mary Lee Barron were active on the festival committee. For many years, they opened their home—which soon became affectionately known as "The Barron Hilton"—to the rhododendron queens. In 2012, the 1983 North Carolina rhododendron queen, Betsy Jones Gillespie, and her mother, Wanda Jones, returned to Bakersville to serve as pageant judges. They generously offered to add to the North Carolina Rhododendron Festival scholarship fund, to be made in honor and memory of Bob and Mary Lee Barron. The Barron family graciously matched their gift, and in June 2013 the Barron Memorial Scholarship was created. (Courtesy of the Barron Collection.)

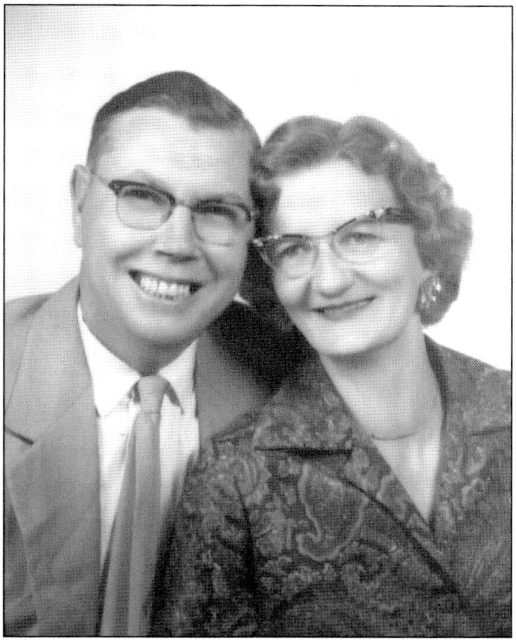

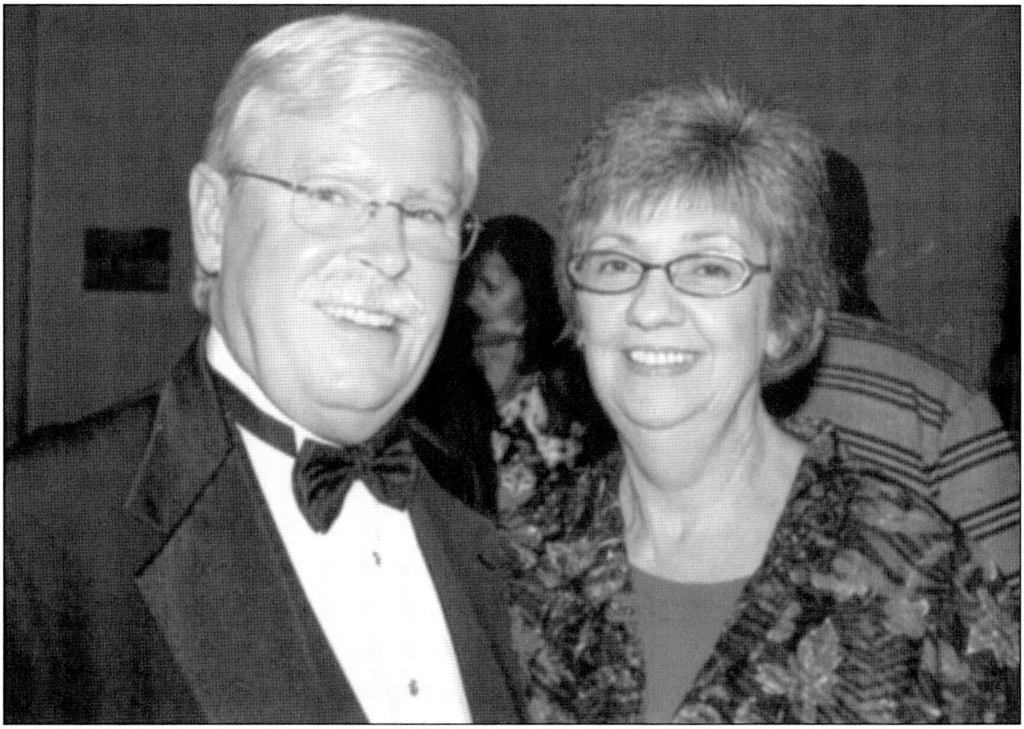

Bob and Janie Hensley have volunteered their time and services to the North Carolina Rhododendron Festival since the late 1970s. Bob currently serves as business manager for the rhododendron queen as well as master of ceremonies for the festival pageant. Bob and Janie head up a crew of volunteers who work tirelessly throughout the year to ensure that the festival and pageant remain among the most elite and respected throughout the state. They also spend much of the year traveling with the rhododendron queens on appearance tours. (Courtesy of Bob Hensley.)

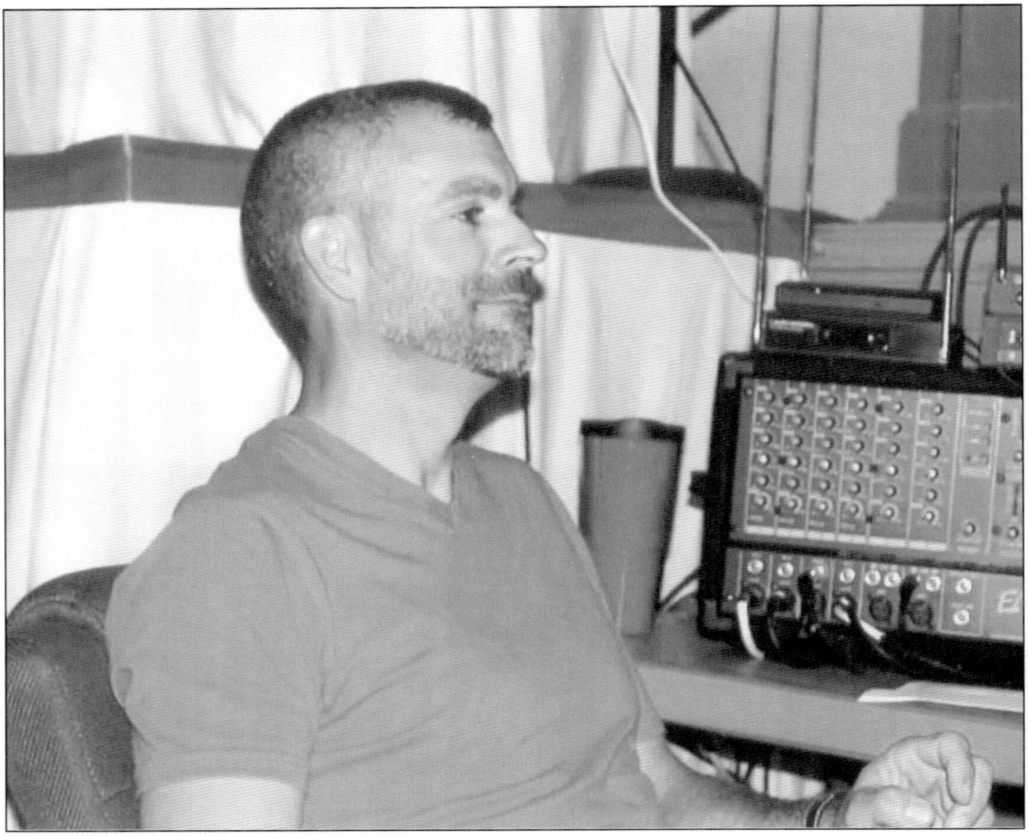

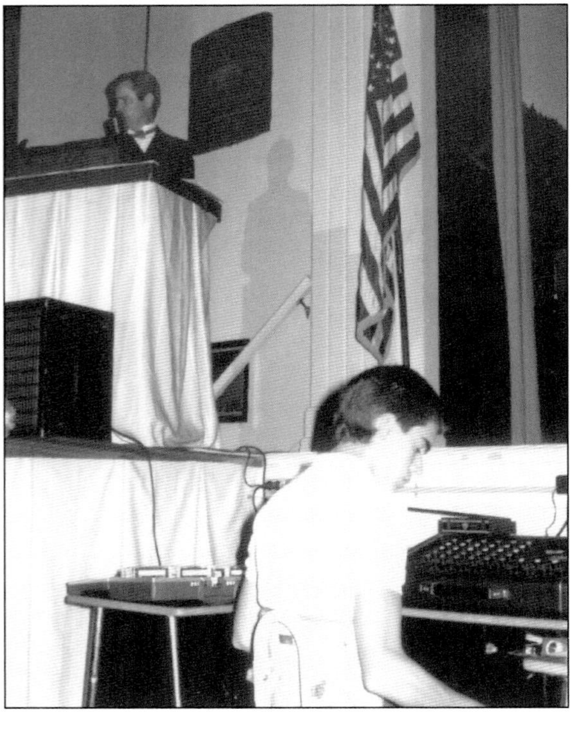

The festival is indeed a family affair. Rob Hensley, son of Bob and Janie Hensley, has served in the role of sound technician since he was a teenager. He and his family return to his hometown of Bakersville every June to participate and lend a hand in the production of the North Carolina Rhododendron Festival and pageant. (Both, courtesy of Bob Hensley.)

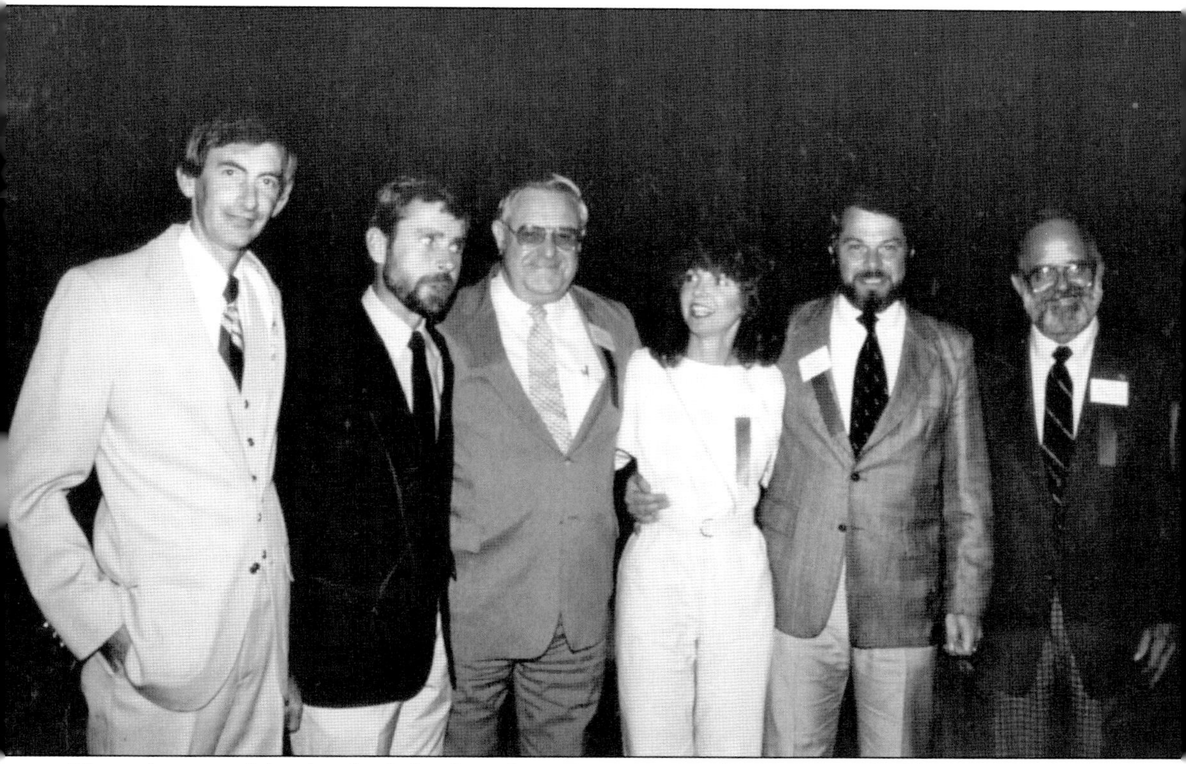

The judges panel for the rhododendron festival pageant is often comprised of local celebrities. In the early 1980s, Bob Taylor (second from right) and Jim Patterson (far right) from Charlotte's WBTV were guest judges. They are pictured here with, from left to right, Alfred Blanton, Bob Hensley, Henry Bernhardt, and Lou Altman. In 2011, the festival welcomed Shane Mason from the hit TLC show *King of the Crown*. His mother, Nancy Maltby, also served as a judge. (Courtesy of the Barron Collection.)

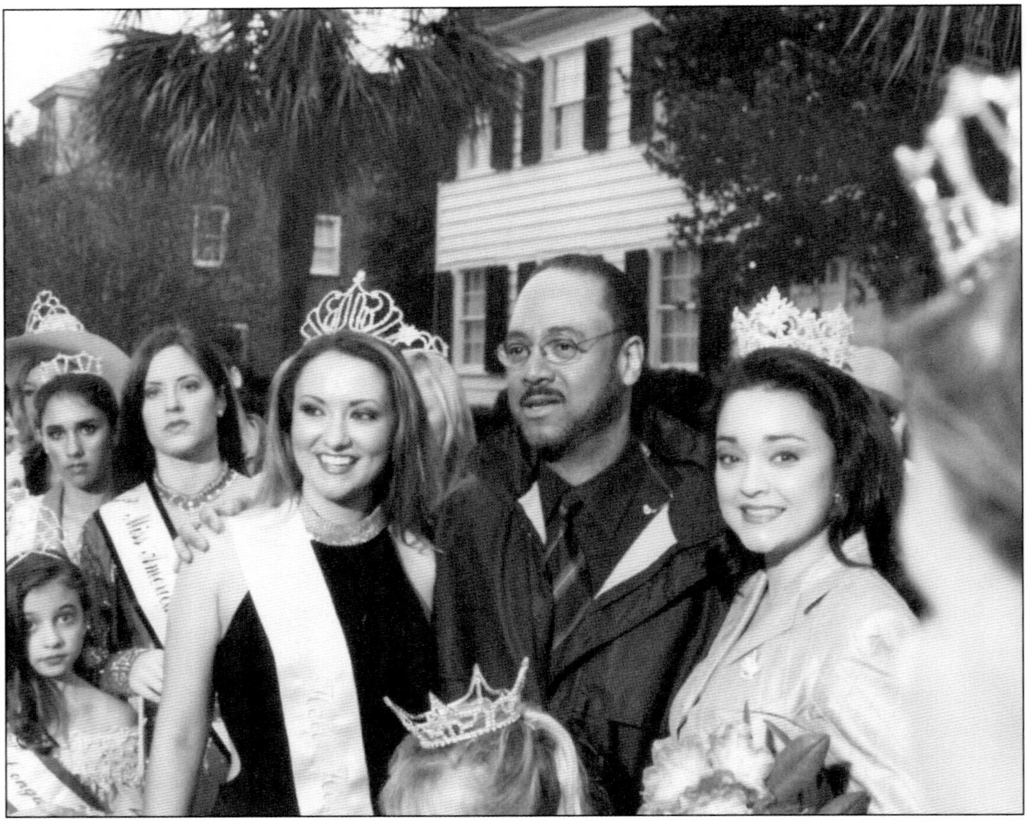

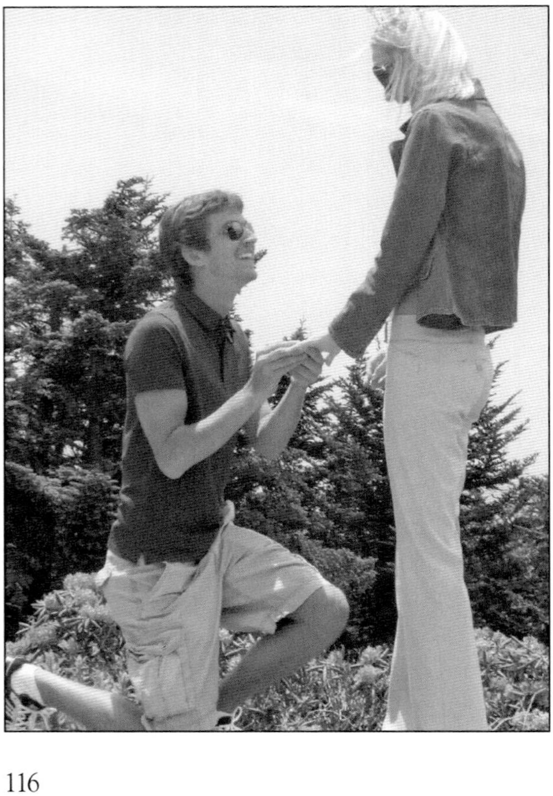

In 2003, North Carolina rhododendron queen Stephanie Chang was invited to appear as a guest on the set of *Good Morning America*. She traveled to Mount Pleasant, South Carolina, for the show's taping. She is pictured here on the right with another invited queen and ABC weather anchorman Tony Perkins. (Courtesy of Bob Hensley.)

Each year, visiting queens from across the state of North Carolina, along with contestants vying for the title of rhododendron queen, are treated to a tour of Roan Mountain and the world-renowned Rhododendron Gardens. In 2011, in the midst of the tour, Rosa Creech, the reigning North Carolina rhododendron queen, was delightfully surprised when David Marsh chose the setting of beautiful Roan Mountain to offer his proposal of marriage. (Courtesy of Bob Hensley.)

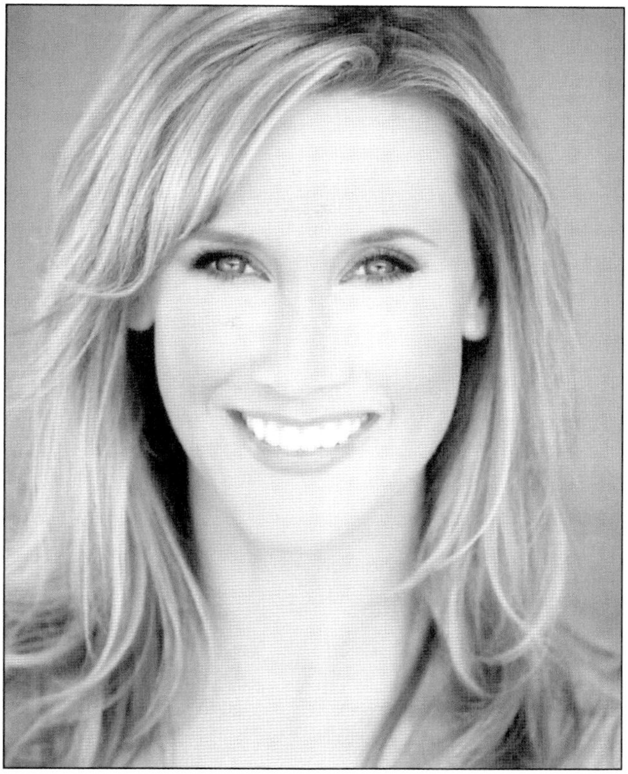

A number of rhododendron queens have gone on to have successful careers in the entertainment industry. Beth Troutman (right), the 1987 junior queen, is one of the stars of the syndicated show *Right This Minute*. Donna Wilson (below), the 1984 queen, had roles in several noteworthy movies, including *Get Shorty* and *Enemy of the State*. She met her late husband, director Tony Scott, while filming the blockbuster *Days of Thunder*, in 1990. (Both, courtesy of the Barron Collection.)

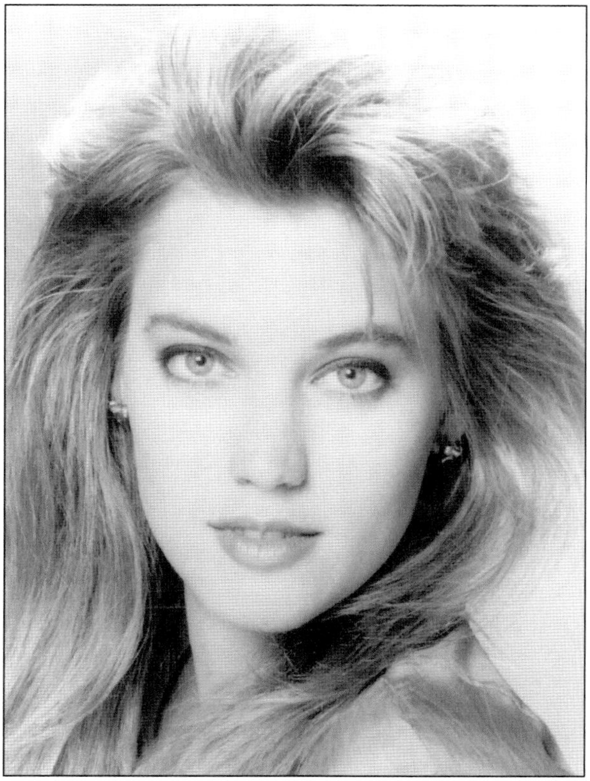

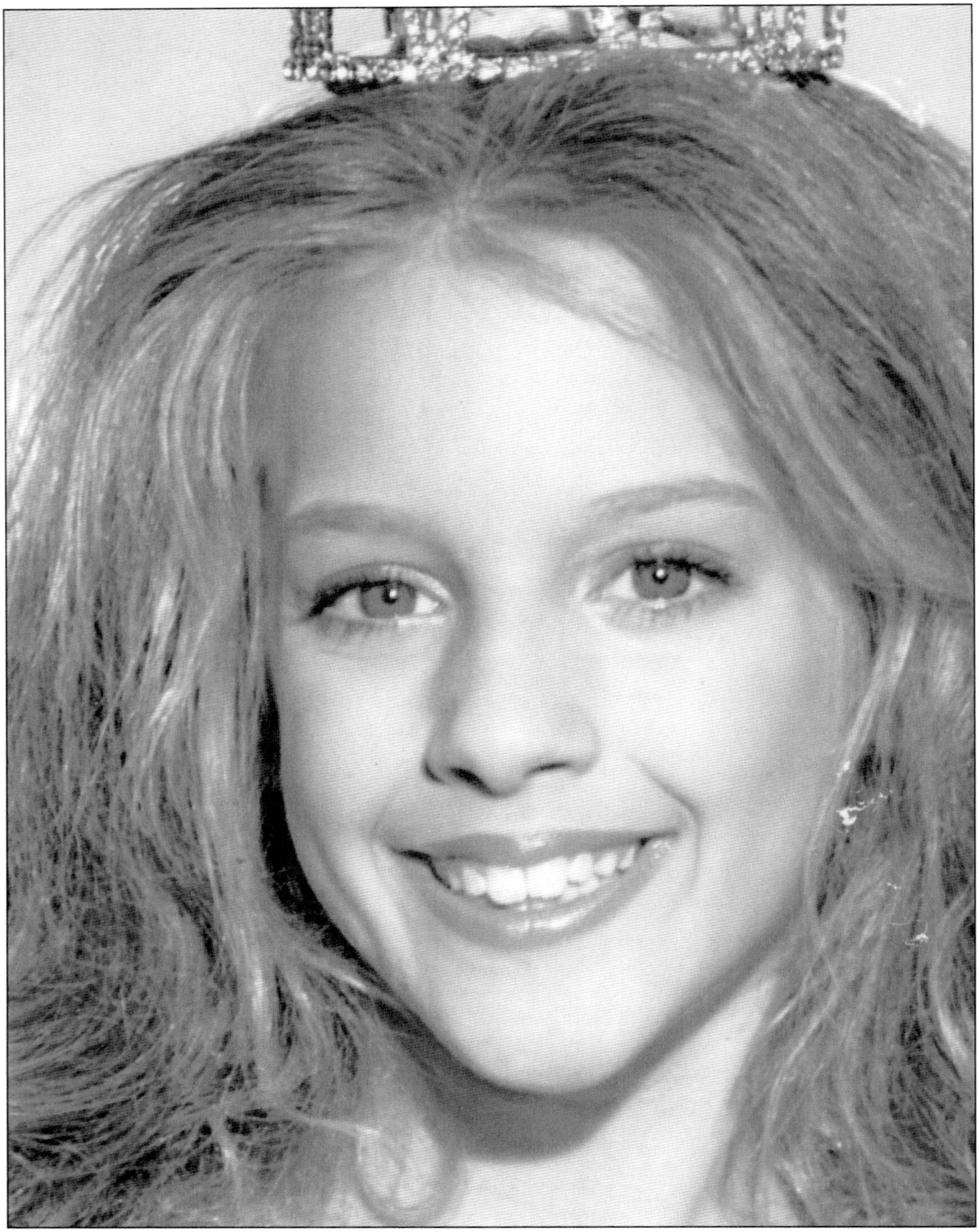

Tara Tucker, the 1989 North Carolina junior rhododendron queen, appears on the cover of her first album, produced when she was only eight years old. (Courtesy of the Barron Collection.)

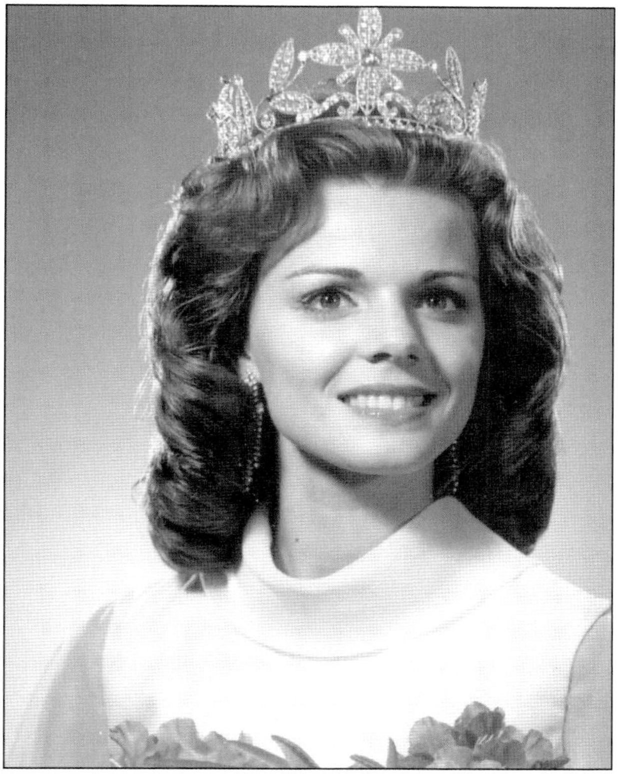

Only four young ladies who served in the capacity of North Carolina junior rhododendron queen have returned to vie for and capture the title of rhododendron queen. Debbie Shook (right) was junior queen in 1967, and she was crowned rhododendron queen 10 years later. Laura Curtis (below) was junior queen in 1999 and queen in 2009. (Right, courtesy of the Wilson Collection; below, courtesy of Susan Curtis.)

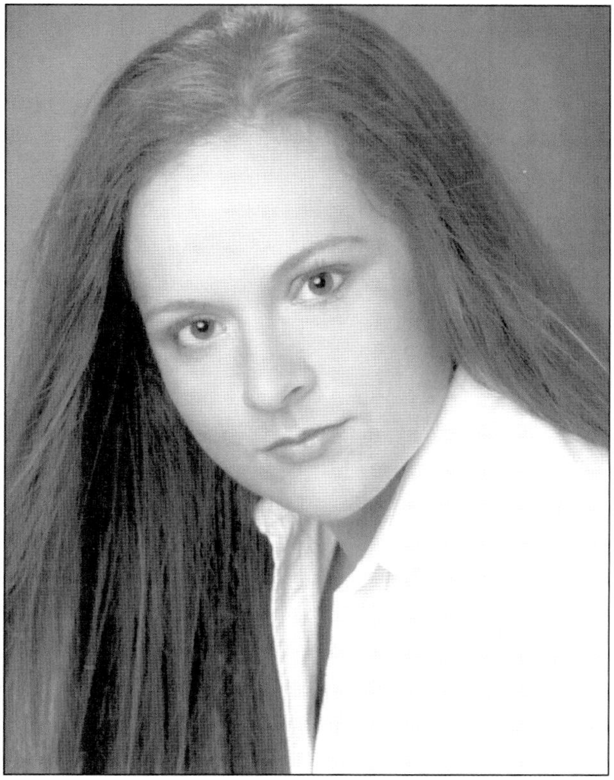

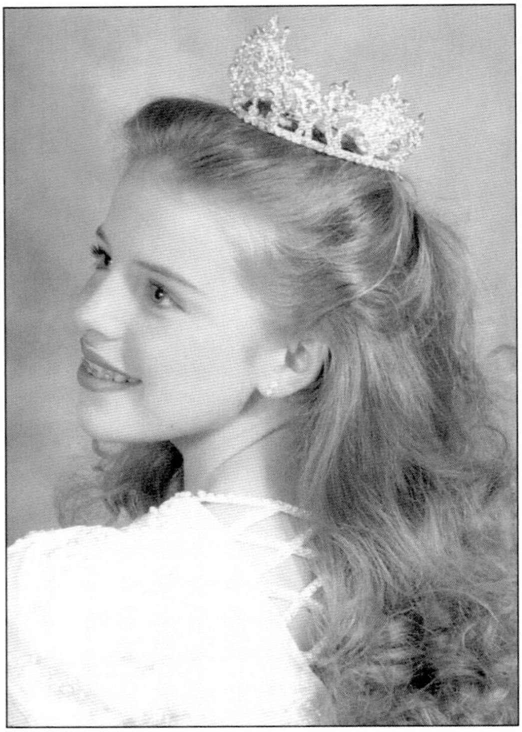

Amelia Wilson (left), who was junior queen in 2005, returned to win the title of queen in 2013. Andrea Hall (below), who held the title of junior queen in 2010, returned in 2014 to capture the title of 2015 North Carolina rhododendron queen. (Left, courtesy of the North Carolina Rhododendron Festival; below, courtesy of Denise Jhant.)

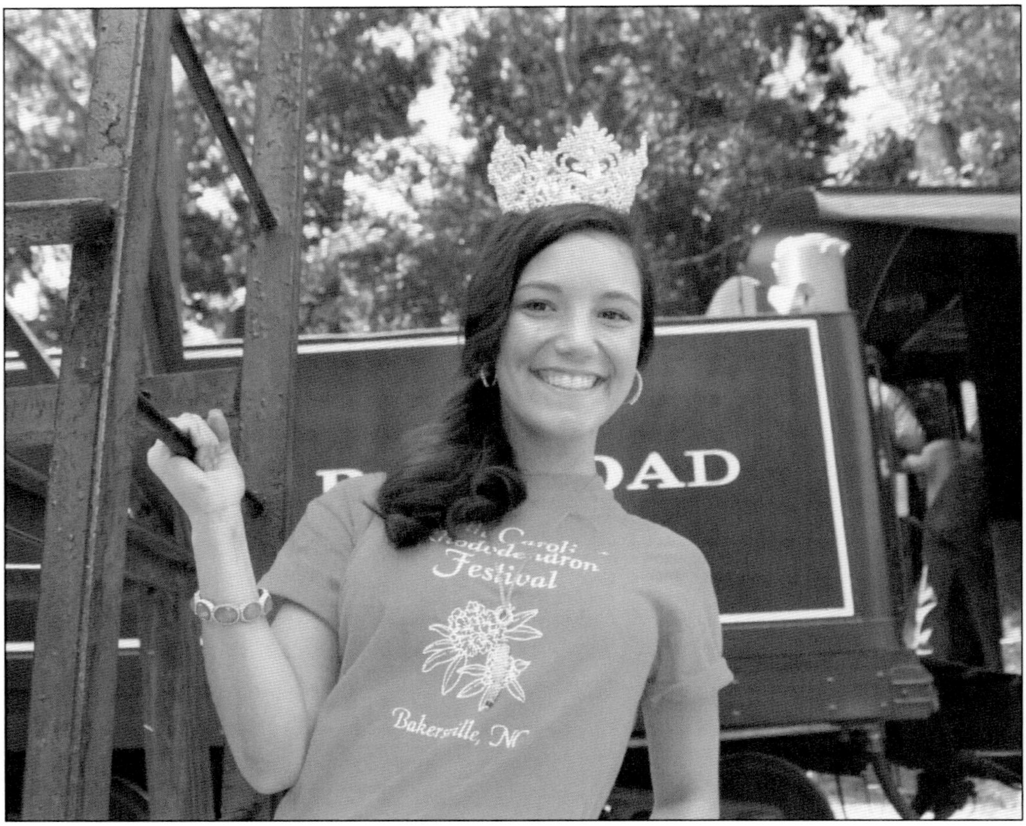

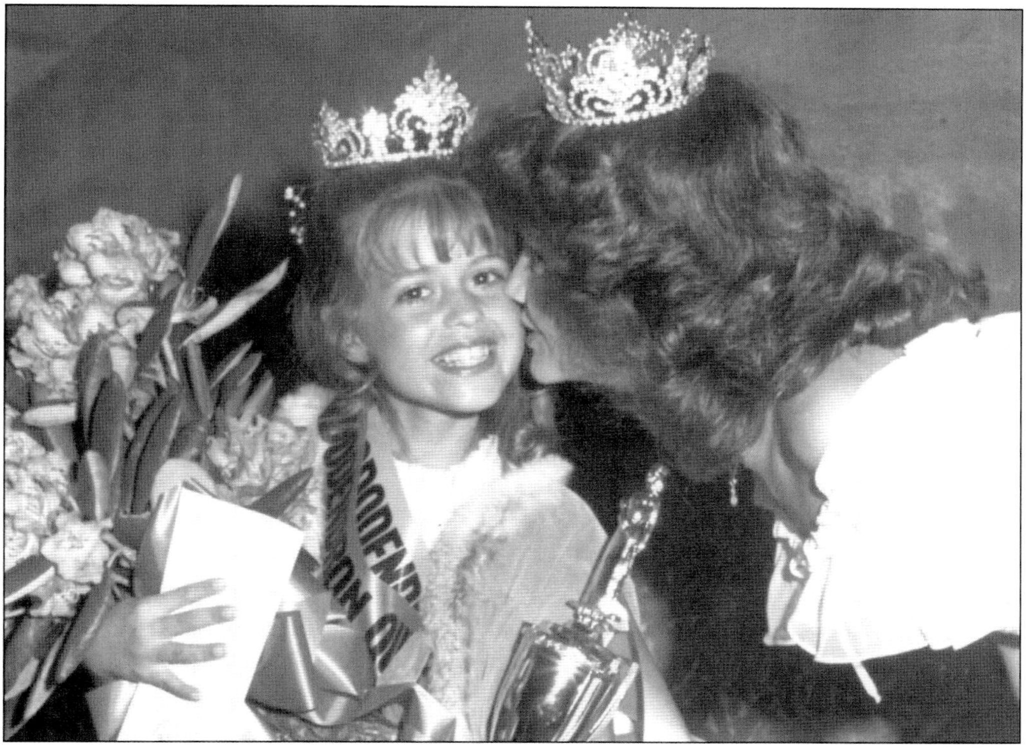

The North Carolina Rhododendron Festival has featured several sister teams over the years. In 1982, Jennifer Carroll followed in her sister Kristen's footsteps when she won the junior crown. Jennifer is pictured here being congratulated by Lori Boggs, the 1982 North Carolina rhododendron queen. Paige Wilson (below) was the 1986 junior queen just two years after her sister Donna won the queen title. (Above, courtesy of Geneva Brewer; below, courtesy of the North Carolina Rhododendron Festival.)

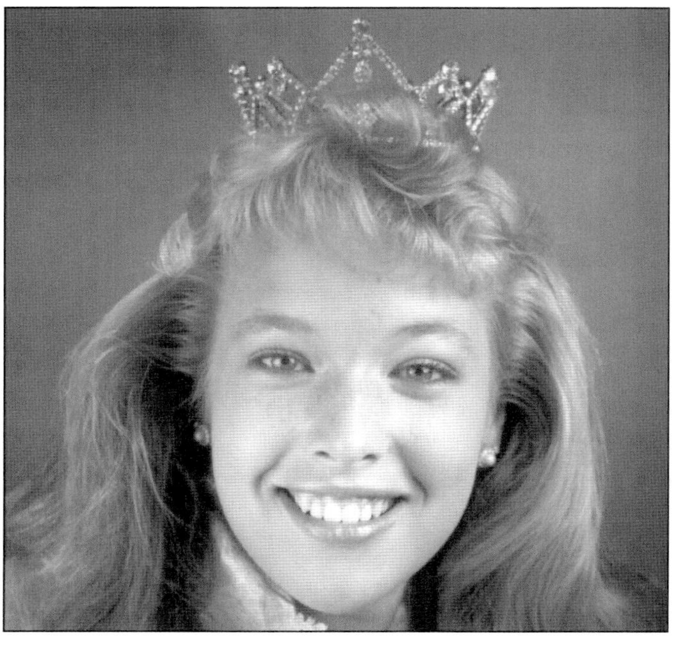

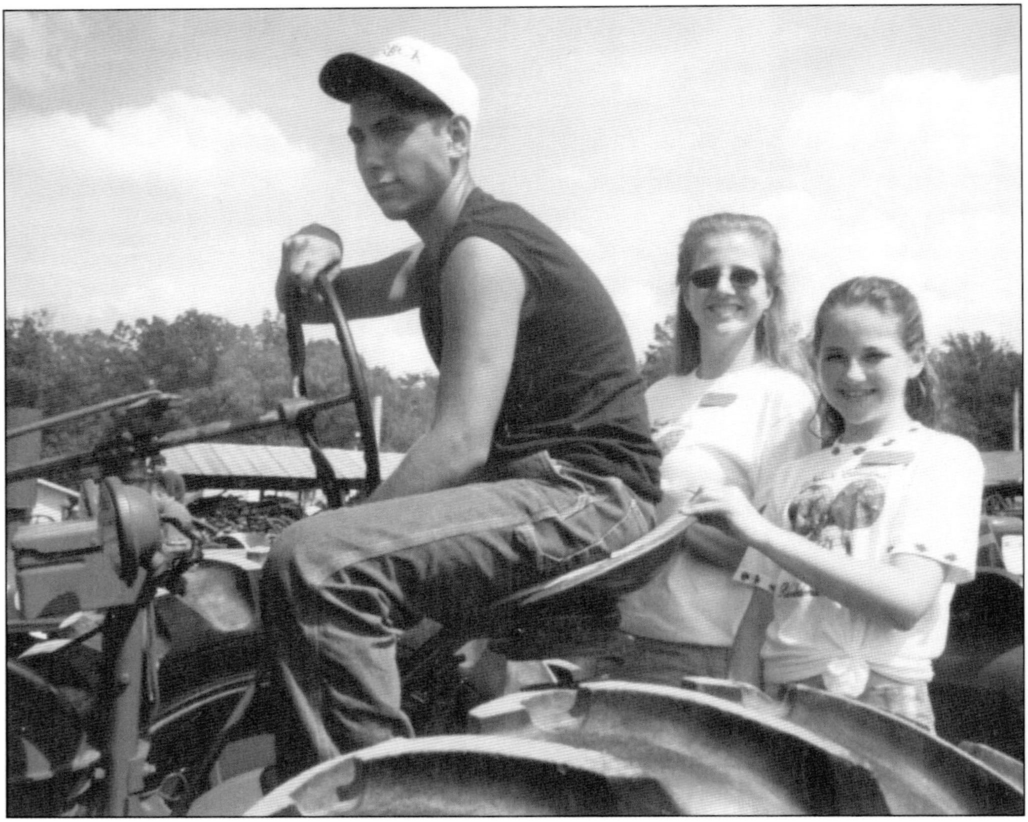

Laura Curtis was junior queen in 1999, and her older sister Alicia (center) held the queen title in 2002. Alicia is pictured here with 2002 North Carolina junior rhododendron queen Courtney Henderson (right) while appearing at the Southeast Old Threshers Reunion in Denton, North Carolina. (Courtesy of Bob Hensley.)

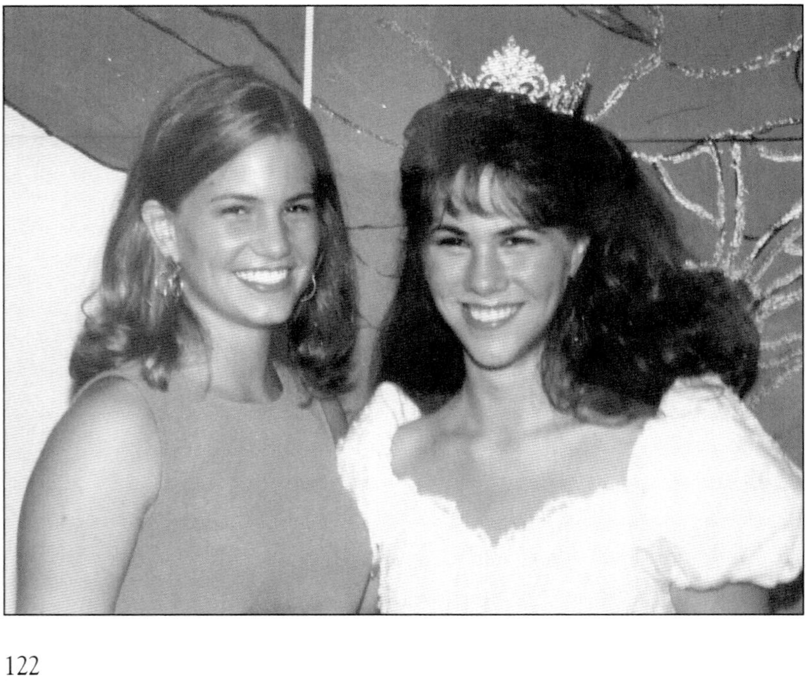

Heather Boone (left) and her younger sister, Ciji (right) both held the title of junior rhododendron queen—Heather in 1991 and Ciji in 1997. (Courtesy of Ciji Boone Dellinger.)

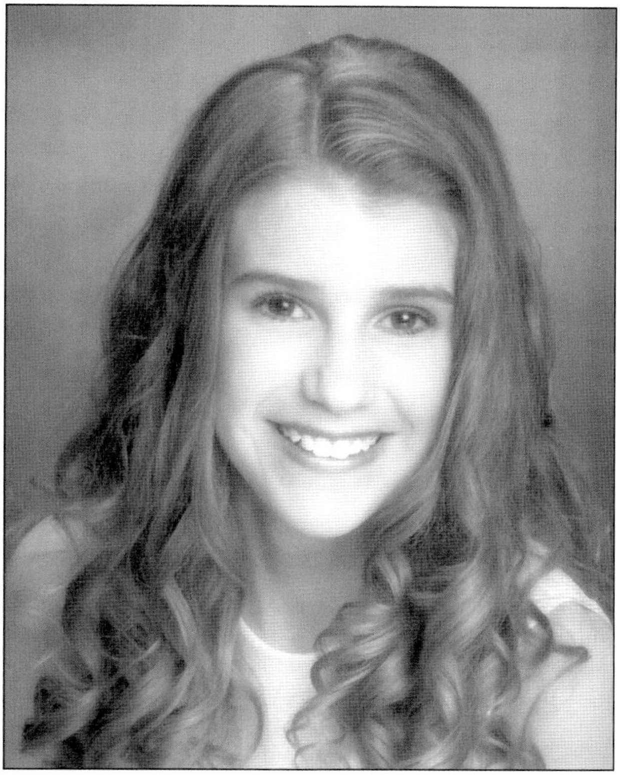

Courtney (right) and Cassidy Greene (below) each held the junior title—Courtney in 2004 and Cassidy in 2007. Courtney and Cassidy are from the neighboring town of Spruce Pine. (Courtesy of the North Carolina Rhododendron Festival.)

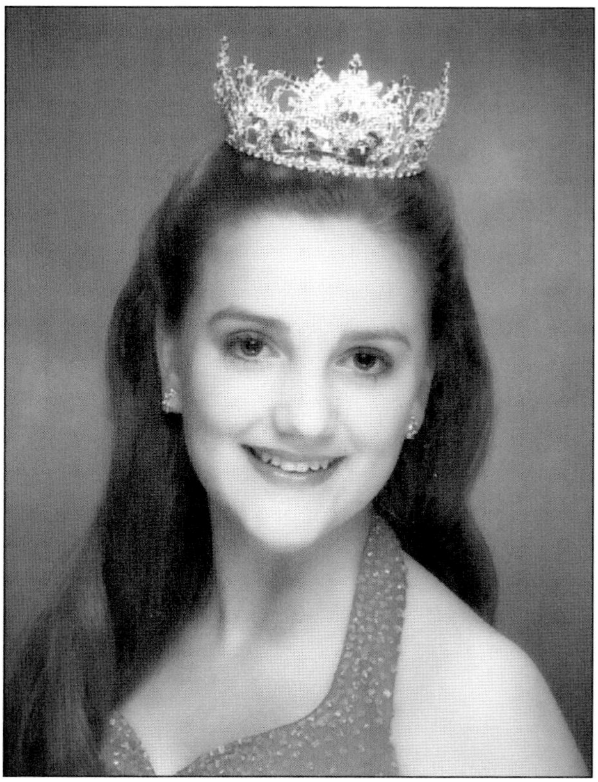

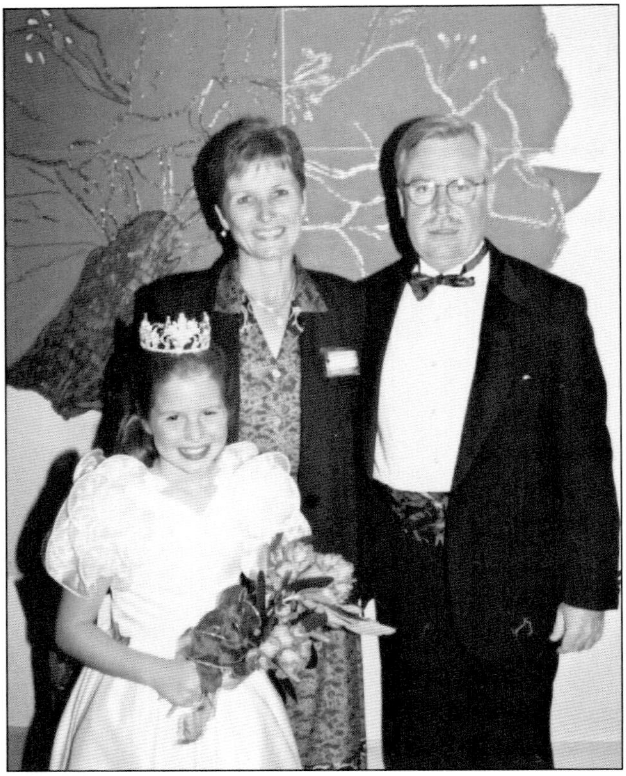

To date, only one mother-daughter team has worn the rhododendron crown. Sherree Banks was the 1965 junior rhododendron queen, and her daughter Lyndsay held the title of 2000 junior rhododendron queen. The Banks family of Burnsville is the donor of a scholarship that is presented each year to the junior rhododendron queen. The scholarship is made in honor of the mother-daughter team and is called the Sherree Lyndsay Scholarship. (Courtesy of Bob Hensley.)

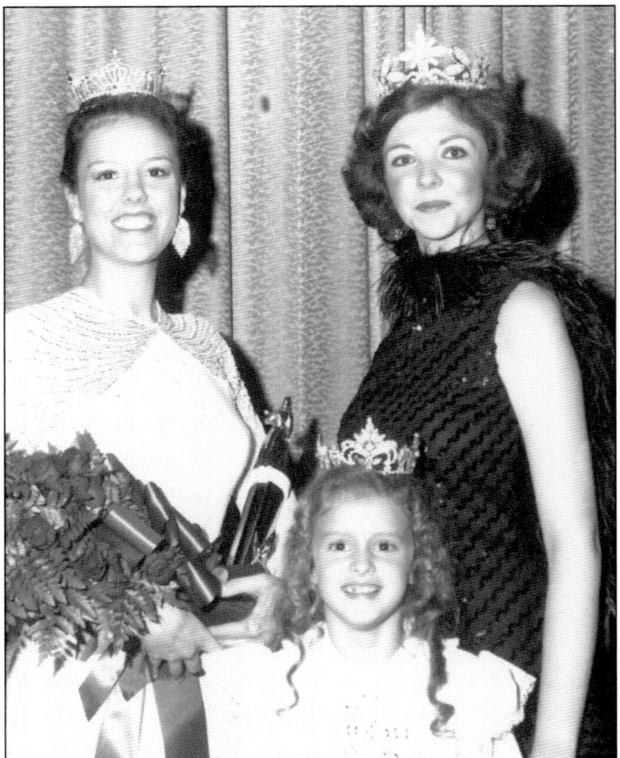

Sharon Manness (on right), the 1978 rhododendron queen, is pictured here with junior queen Kristin Carroll (center) and Lisa Everhart. Both Sharon and Kristin went on to own and operate successful dance studios as adults. In a recent interview, Sharon was asked what part of her life she would like to relive. The answer was easy: her year as rhododendron queen. (Courtesy of the Wilson Collection.)

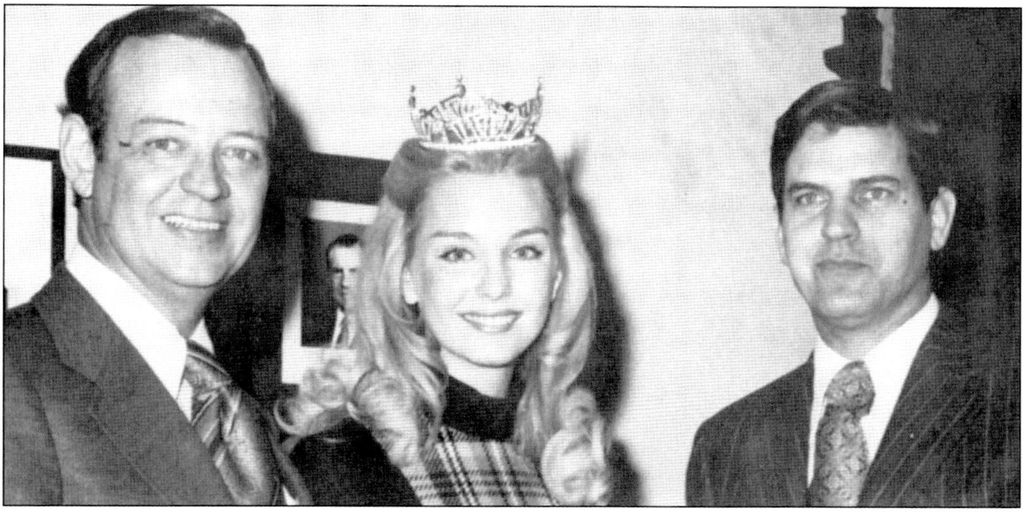

Many rhododendron queens made special and lasting memories. Marcia Burton, the 1973 North Carolina rhododendron queen, had the opportunity to meet with Congressman James T. Broyhill (left) and Congressman James G. Martin at a reception in her honor in Washington, DC, in March 1973. (Courtesy of the Wilson Collection.)

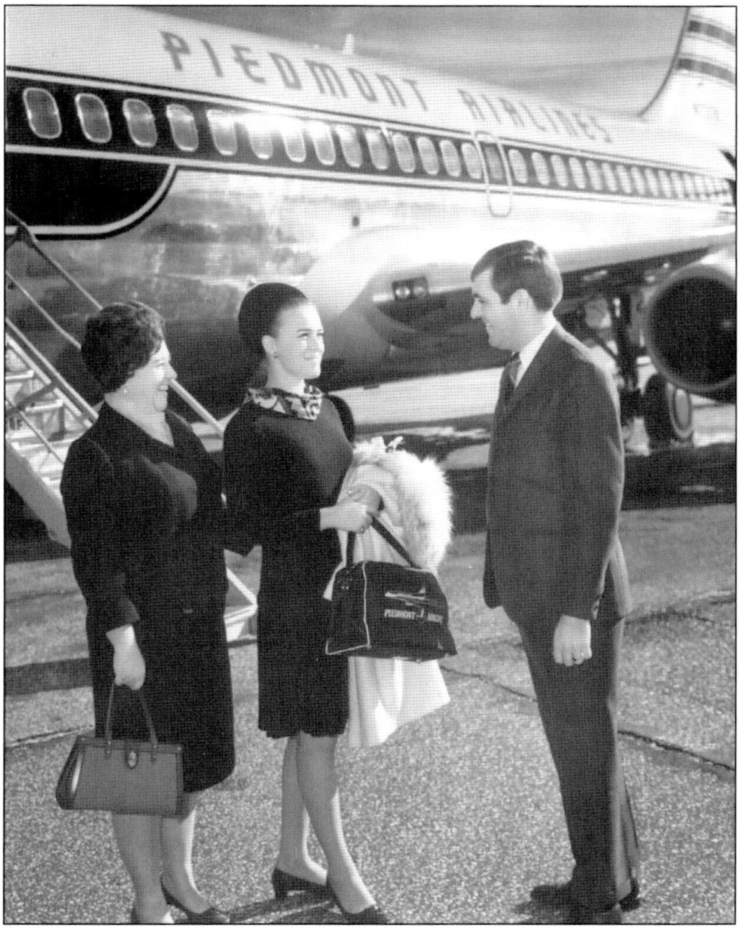

Many of the North Carolina rhododendron queens, when asked about their most memorable experiences representing the festival and state, will respond by relating stories of their travels across the nation and abroad. Brenda Heath (center), the 1969 queen, is pictured here getting ready to board a plane for a round of appearances on the West Coast. (Courtesy of the Barron Collection.)

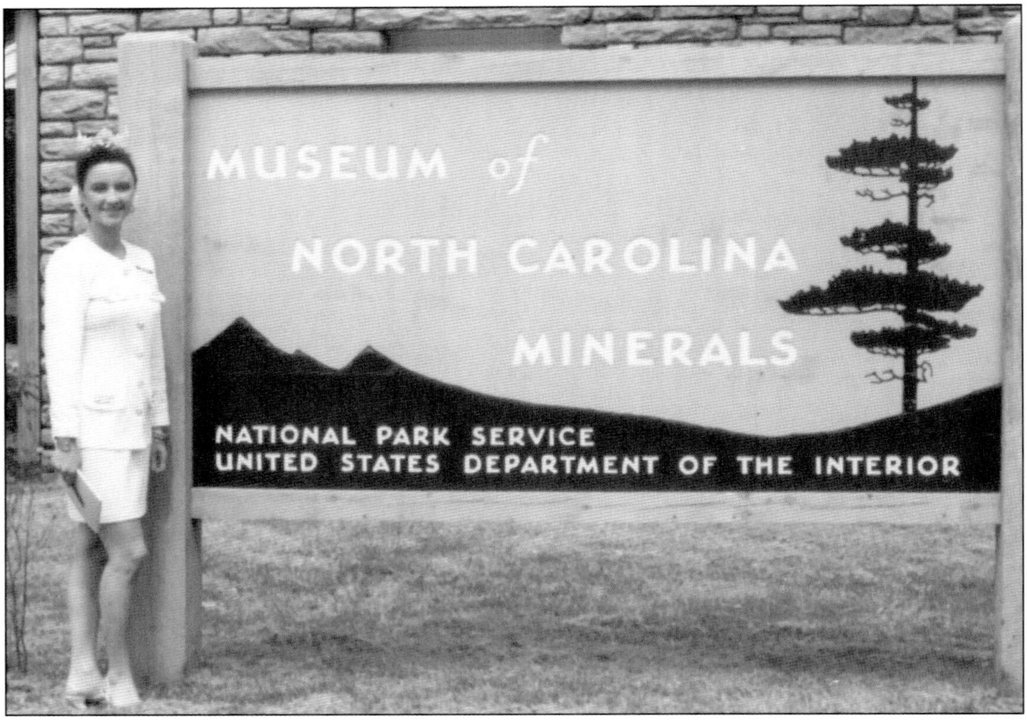

Sheri Benge, the 1994 North Carolina rhododendron queen, has many fond memories of her year. She is pictured here during a tour of the Museum of North Carolina Minerals in nearby Spruce Pine. (Courtesy of Sheri Benge Maxwell.)

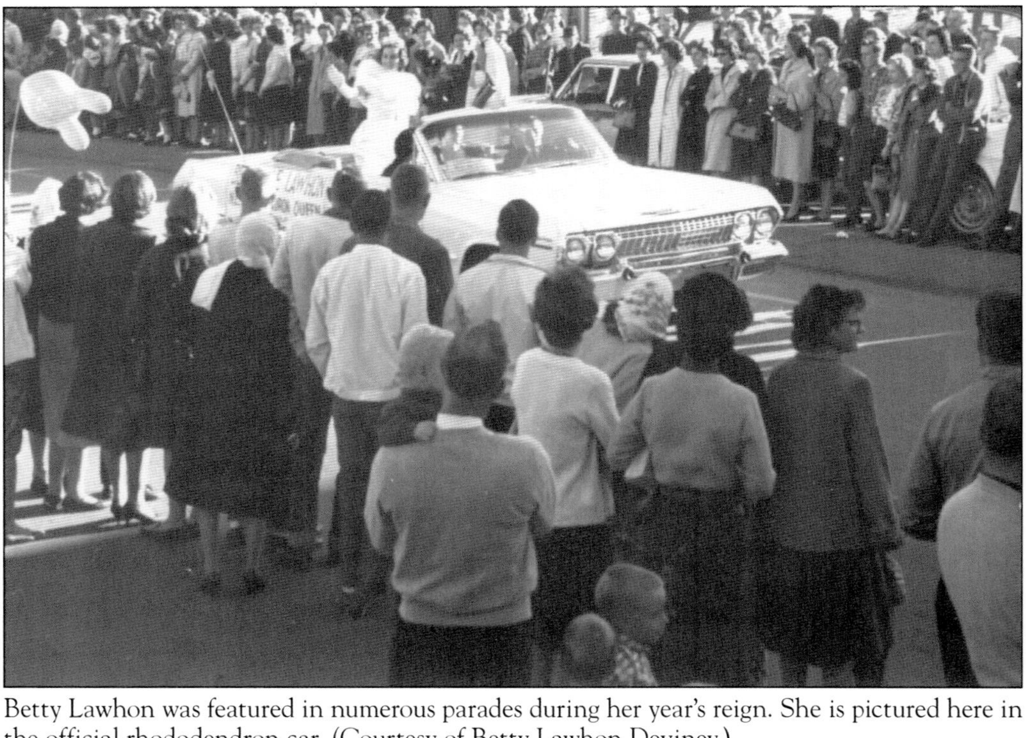

Betty Lawhon was featured in numerous parades during her year's reign. She is pictured here in the official rhododendron car. (Courtesy of Betty Lawhon Deviney.)

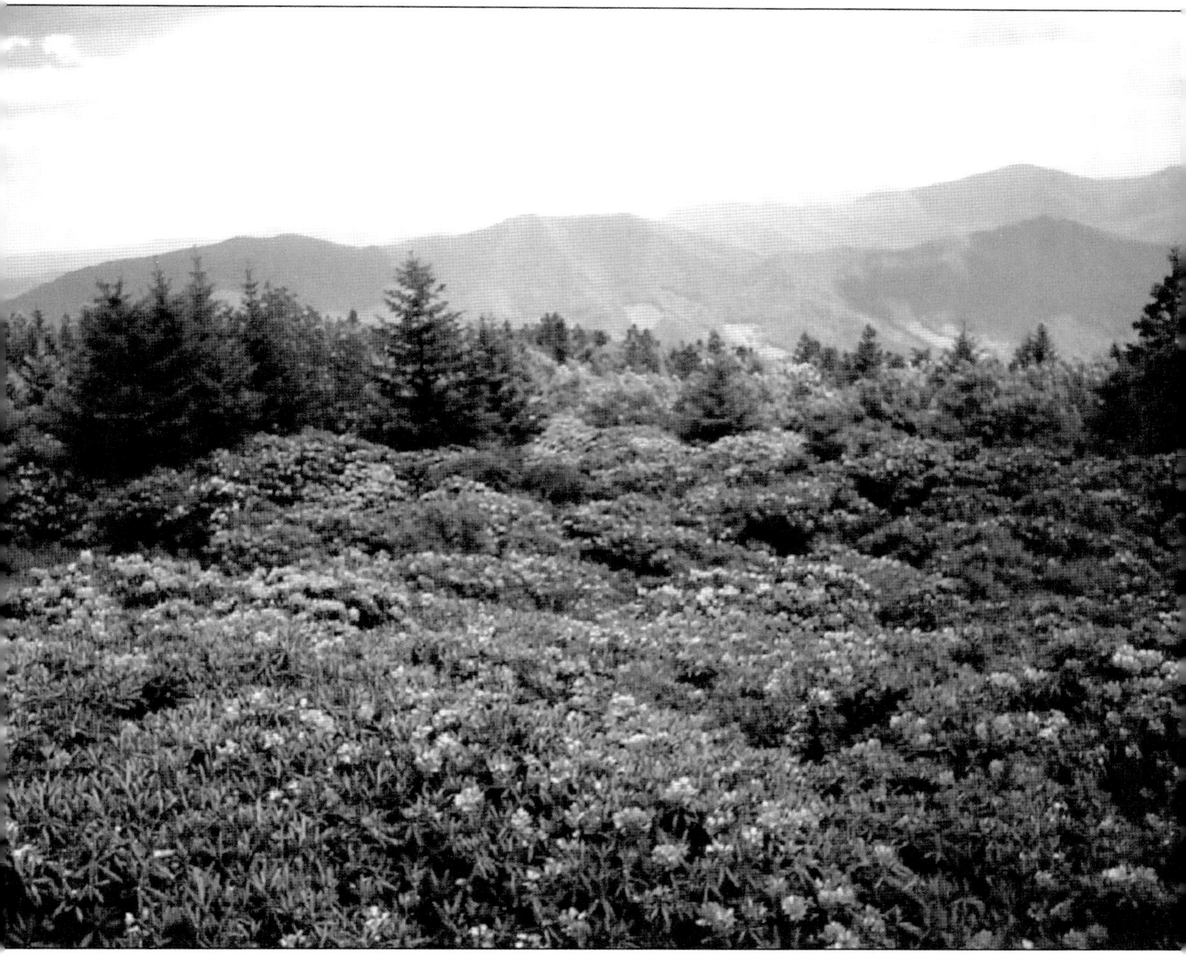

The Roan . . . It is truly mystical, magical, majestic, awe-inspiring, and a constant source of pride for the residents of Bakersville and the surrounding area. The North Carolina Rhododendron Festival is an event steeped in an enduring tradition. In these rugged mountains, there prevails among the people an eternal reverence for tradition and heritage. Ingrained in the souls of the mountain folk is a rare and beautiful respect for nature's majesty. Beauty abounds in each of the changing seasons; the brilliant hues of autumn's splendor stretched across an endless mountain range, the purity of rime on the trees regally standing in the midst of an unmarred, windblown expanse of snow-covered winter terrain, and the newness of spring's freshly budding foliage. But at no time is the area's natural grandeur more manifest than in mid-June, when the Rhododendron Gardens are bursting with full and glorious bloom. Each year, during the celebration of this wonderful event, the pride of the mountain people is displayed in so many ways; from the pageant to the street dance, to the crafts fair to the 5K run. It is the Roan and its incomparable Rhododendron Gardens that we celebrate—our way of paying homage to God's spectacular creation and the understanding that we are blessed to be able to share it. (Photograph by the author.)